Vi

(Graham)

"The Final Chapter"
Vol.3

Stephen Richards

Mirage Publishing

A Mirage Publishing Book

Publishers of Investigative authors
New authors welcome to submit manuscripts

New Paperback

Published in Great Britain
By Mirage Publishing 2001

A CIP catalogue record for this book
is available from the British Library.

ISBN 1 902578 16 3

Mirage Publishing
PO Box 161
Gateshead
NE8 4WW
Great Britain

Printed and bound in Great Britain by

C P Print Ltd, Swalwell, Newcastle upon Tyne, NE16 3DJ, England

© Cover designed by Artistic Director: Sharon Anderson

Contents

Dedicated to Stephen,

Obstacles are doorways to learning
You've learned well my son

Andre Martin

Holder of 16 Black Belts
Professional Close Protection Trainer and Operative

Foreword

When you read the name 'Viv Graham' stop for a few seconds and try to think what you conjure up in your mind's eye exactly what sort of description you would give a man with this name? First of all would you not indeed think of a feminine looking type of man with a small stature that was not capable of opening doors let alone working and running them, I think so. But don't be mistaken I mean hugely mistaken, like I have said the name may conjure up that particular image of a female but it is far from the truth Viv Graham was a formidable looking man, larger than life you may say when you consider that Viv stood with an impressive $17^1/_2$ stone muscular frame along with this he had a hand speed that would put many lightweight boxers to shame once you have taken this into consideration then you might be starting to get the full picture of what he was all about.

Viv was an amateur boxer and like many guys who were involved or training in the fight game he turned his hand to working the doors of both the public houses and night clubs of the North that desperately needed a type of large human silver back to man its doors and ride the place of violent Neanderthals. I can relate to that because I too have worked the doors of Coventry's roughest nightspots and have been brought in to train the special services in fighting techniques.

Viv faced many a drunken lout and large violent gang eruptions just like I have had to over the years but unlike myself Viv turned to the darker side of life and became embroiled in the goings on of the underworld and that was his big mistake. I should know because I've had my life threatened by many well formed and organized gangs wanting to deal drugs in the public houses and nightclubs I've been

Foreword

employed to look after. Viv encountered some of the same problems with drug dealers but he paid a higher price for this than I did.

For any man to die in the gutter like a dog is sad but when you've had three bullets fired at you and two have torn your body and flesh apart and blood is flowing in every direction it adds a sadness that words can't express. That is how Viv died. Like many in the door trade who live by the sword and die by the sword and as another famous and not to be forgotten saying should be listened to in any walk of life and that is if you play with fire you will you certainly get burnt.

I'm 5ft 5ins tall and 8 stones in body weight, which maybe surprises you but with 16 black belts and various other combative arts behind me as well having a streetwise understanding of psychology and the understanding pre cursor signs to an attack it does give me a slight advantage. Regardless of my lack of stature in measuring up to Viv I can understand some of the things he went through in order to get where he did in life and it wasn't without making a few enemies along the way that he and I have achieved recognition let me tell you that. Viv was recognised as the 4th Emergency Service of Tyneside and I became known as 'Little Andre the 5ft 5 and on the Door doorman'. Some of my family still live in the Washington and Whitley Bay areas of Wearside and Tyneside, which helps me write this foreword knowing the character Viv was.

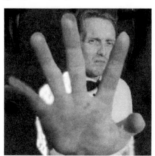

Condolences,
Andre Martin

Hire Andre from www.crimebiz.co.uk

Introduction

Following on from the two Viv books you might have already read this is the final in the trilogy of the Viv series of books. There's been much feedback from my readers and for that I thank them and having digested the suggestions forwarded I've tried to draw a happy medium for you all herein.

In the previous Viv books I've given you enough facts and figures to fill a whorehouse full of university professors so I've done away with as much of that as I can. Many have been happy to read the interviews of the women in Viv's life, but some have commented on too much emphasis being put on these women…mhhhhh, a man's world eh! Those of you against such things can be satisfied to know that there's only one interview in this book from a female relating to the underworld. Many of my readers are female so I can't very well assume it's only men that read such books.

My investigations into Viv's murder led me down many avenues of false hope, many people tried to put me off the scent, many gave me incorrect information in the hope that I'd lay off – not me though. I was carrying the hopes of all of Viv's followers on my shoulders and it was with their encouragement that I pushed on and found out just a little bit more than I bargained for.

Yes, I found out the identities of Viv's killers, the identities of Paul Logan's killers! (Remember the pizza deliveryman from Shotley Bridge, Consett) Disgruntled policemen, pissed off at how the system's corrupt and how informers get away with murder, have helped me, the anti-Masonic movement have helped me, anti-racist people have helped me, registered police informants have helped me, top flight criminals have helped me and liars have not helped me!

Introduction to Viv vol. 3

The verbal support, the many thousands of letters and emails sent from all over the world in the last three years have overwhelmed me. The Viv books have been acclaimed all over the world by professionals and criminals, my writing style was knocked by the spoilers but I've fought through it all and keep with the style I started out with. Not many people know this but I'm a dyslexic, I was born left handed but forced to write with my right hand…this fucked my head up a bit in the sense that I became word blind. Now before any of you start thinking Richards' is off his trolley have no fear I'm of sound mind. Although we've got spell checkers on computer programmes and proof readers I prefer to do away with them and leave it warts and all for you. Many of the fancy book critics knocked Salmon Rushdie's book *Fury* saying it lacked basic grammar, bollocks to them is what I say. I salute Rushdie for standing by his style of writing.

You see when a writer submits a typescript to a publisher it has to be submitted without errors, double-spaced (out), double line width. Fuck ups have to be cleared up and even then the publisher will still tickle about with the typescript in the hope of getting it right. I dispense with all of that because if this book was tinkered about with and one word of it was changed then it wouldn't be my work, would it? So what you see is what you get.

I was encouraged by the way the Americans praise such a puritanical writing style yet the Brits mock it as if though it revealed some shortcomings in the brain department. Every mistake has a subliminal meaning to it, a hidden message. And it is with that in mind that I encourage people to develop their own writing style in their own way. I've been able to use people's low opinions on my writing style to gain information from them. Some professionals equate poor grammar with a lack of brainpower and that's gained me a great advantage over many who believe themselves to be superior in intelligence to me – I love it!

Some people say to me, "Hey, read your book, great stuff," I ask them which of my books they've read and when they give me a particular title name I ask them what they thought of the piece about the dolphins and they reply "Great, loved it," well the thing is I've not ever written anything about dolphins, apart from now. Some people are just full of shit, but best to let them get away with it and let them continue thinking they're clever because that's what will always give you the edge over them and that's one of the tactics I've used over the years to obtain the info I want and as a consequence, you lucky lot, I'm able to get you the best info there is.

You're going to get shaken and stirred throughout this book, you're going to wonder how I obtained my information, I'll tell you how, it's all based on trust. I straddle the white line between those in the underworld and those in another world we call everyday life, I've gained the respect of 99% of those I deal with because of my integrity.

I've obtained information from one off killers, serial killers, hired assassins, muggers, robbers, psychopaths, hard men, blackmailers and ruthless underworld enforcers and they all have one thing in common – they all trust me not to reveal who they are or to spill the beans on them. I am their father confessor, I can't absolve them from their sins but I can take away some of their torment that some of them have carried for many years.

During the course of my investigations many of the characters I've interviewed have been relieved to be able to impart certain information to me, I've listened to their confessions and witnessed the relief they've gained from such an exercise. You'd expect people to be bragging about this and that and claiming to be the biggest gangster since Al Capone – not true. On the other hand I've had people tell me that they know plenty of big time gangsters, but when I've pushed them on who these gangsters are they turn out to be burglars and small time drug dealers.

Everyone's perception about the definition of what a gangster really is varies. I've had people I assumed to be gangsters talk of 'real gangsters' and that in turn has changed my perception of what a gangster really is. The old time gangster image has just about gone, but when it's carried off well it beats modern day cardboard (or as the Italian's say 'Cartoni') versions by a mile, most are men of honour although I've met a couple that stand out head and shoulders above all the rest of them. I've met one 'Cartoni' gangster who tried to blackmail me, but more of that in another book and another Cartoni who tricked me (and he thought without my knowledge) into a meeting with a real gangster, more of that in '*Sex, Drugs and the Stamp Scam*'.

I've managed notorious psychopathic UK prisoner Charles Bronson and that was an experience and a half and it stood me well in the sense that I couldn't take things at face value. The very same hand that feeds such men can be bitten off as equally well as it was respected a short time earlier. But all in all Charlie is in a hellhole and its not all his fault for how he goes on. 27 years of torture and punishment haven't helped him, maybe now he's married to the lovely Saira he will settle down. People's words can turn to mush, promises mean nothing in this game and that's helped me understand what people really mean when they say "Call me in a few days," or "Leave it with me and I'll get back to you, blah, blah." All bullshit and meaningless words, shovelling smoke is what I call it.

I've become familiar with the chaps (gentleman criminals) and learned what the word 'respect' really means and for that I thank them in being able to show me what a better class criminal really is. If they had a ruck with another underworld figure they'd try to resolve it, if it couldn't be resolved then one of them might mediate and that's how it went, killing was very rare, but how things have changed from the days of these wonderful characters. I've learned how to discern between a top class act and a slummer and for that I'd like to thank Joe Pyle, Freddie Foreman, Charlie Richardson, Dave Ford, Roy Shaw, Tony and Chris Lambrianou, Howard Marks, Dave Courtney, Johnny Nash, James Crosbie and a whole host of other chaps that made it possible for me to see what the word 'understated' really meant.

The killers of Viv had no integrity and are not gangsters in the sense of the way I've described a gangster to be. No understated violence, no respect, no ideals, no mediation, no other way of handling it just plain overstated violence way beyond a normal person's comprehension of how such a killing came about.

Not once have I seen a tear fall for the weight these killers carry on their shoulders, but I've seen many thousands of tears fall in the memory of Viv Graham and Lee Duffy. Lee Duffy has come into this equation in a very odd way and I'd like to thank the people concerned in doing so because Lee Duffy plays an important role in the life of Viv Graham. I'll reveal things you never thought possible for me to find out, you'll wonder how such men as Graham and Duffy are just as alive in the memories of their followers today as when they were alive, I'll show you how in this final chapter.

I don't believe we'll ever see the likes of Graham and Duffy if we all live to be as old as the hills. Two lives that ran parallel, like a pair of railway lines running side by side but never meeting yet so close to doing so. Two kings on a chessboard of life, each meeting an untimely ending and all for what, that's the essence of it all and yet the killings still goes on. No lessons have been learned, people are selfish and only want their own style of retribution at any cost, they don't care about the pain and suffering the families and friends of the deceased go through.

Drugs fuel their courage and gives them a false sense of security making them believe they're untouchable when in reality it's only the protection afforded to them by their informants status that gives them a thin rizla cigarette rolling paper sized piece of protection that can so easily be removed by the very police officers that gave them it in the first place. That veneer of protection afforded to the prized possessions of the police can so easily be stripped away and when all is revealed you'll stand easy knowing the full and true story of it all.

I can tell you categorically that propaganda put out there by certain people has come to an end, the lies and double dealing hasn't stopped and now I must take you to the truth so with that I ask you to stop and think for a few minutes about how this book might change your life because it will and I promise you that your whole thought process will have changed by the end of this book.

Maximum Respect, Stay Strong

Stephen Richards

AN APOLOGY

I apologise on behalf of the people of Tyneside to all of those who were let down by Newcastle upon Tyne city council's inability to organise the planned 'Love Parade' and thereby cancelling it at the very last minute and fucking up a lot of peoples' planned enjoyment when in fact they had six months to plan the safety aspect of car parking and policing.

Radio One worked on the planned event for six months and yet councillor Tony Flynn said: '...*the logistical difficulties in bringing 250,000 people into the city safely in a very concentrated time frame proved insurmountable by the deadline Radio 1 set.*' Ah well maybe Radio 1 will give councillor Flynn six years notice the next time, eh?

I was flabbergasted that Newcastle in a joint bid with Gateshead to win the European City of Culture tag for 2008 has acted in this way. In promoting the twin pact the keyword used in advertising is 'Buzzing', I think the words 'Ballsed Up' sums it up better.

Amazingly Newcastle council blamed Gateshead council for the cancellation by their refusal to help at the last minute by supplying car parking spaces for the 'Park & Ride' system planned. This was a dummy run to see if in fact such a city as Newcastle could cope and sadly they have failed and I defend Gateshead council in their stance not to get involved at the last minute by a cap in hand Newcastle council. Yes Gateshead could have housed the cars, I mean they've go that lovely big Get Carter car park that's standing idle, yes they've got overflow car parks in the Metro Centre and zillions of square feet of spare land but why should they take responsibility at the last minute, if anything had of gone wrong whilst in the care of Gateshead council then who would have got the blame – Gateshead.

I apologise to Dr Robert G Hollands of Newcastle University for turning down his book, which I was going to publish. The book was going to be part of the bid for the European City of Culture. I couldn't support such a bid in the light of the monumental cock-up. I believe Leeds to be most progressive city in the UK at the time of writing and I would ask Newcastle to take a leaf out of Leeds' book in order to see how they can turn their failure around to their advantage. It can be done but it needs someone like Robert Holland to do it. Maybe he should run for cultural leader of the council.

1

Stu Watson

I start off this chapter by reminding those of you who are unfamiliar with the incident that took place inside of Hobos nightclub; Newcastle in September 1989…was it that long ago, it only seems like five minutes. Viv attacked Stuart Watson in a totally unprovoked attack that was caught on CCTV video cameras and was also witnessed by two undercover police officers that did nothing to intervene. (Covered in Viv Vol. 1)

For the first time ever Stuart has spoken of the brutal attack and of the circumstances surrounding the build up to it and why he couldn't retaliate, but even so he still managed to humiliate Viv by taking his best shots without returning any and still not going down. Stu takes up the story prior to the Hobos incident:

"It went back further than that with me and Viv. We had a bit of a do down at Julies nightclub about 18 months before the Hobos incident. He comes in and a few words were exchanged, I didn't know he was in the building. He come across and put his arm across my shoulder in a friendly sort of way and he said, 'You're Jobie's pal?' (John Jobie) I replied, 'Yes,' and he gave me an uppercut on the chin. (Stories are coming out about Viv that confirm what other people have said.) I've still got a scar on my chin even now after all these years. He didn't drop me, I pushed off him and we had a bit argy bargy and Rob Armstrong and a couple of other kids were with him, we burst out on to the street and a few words were exchanged. We were going to have a fight up the back lane but then all the doormen on the quayside were his mates and more or less worked for him down there, the trouble dispersed.

Viv - The Final Chapter

It never stopped at that though and I was supposed to meet him up at the bridle path up at Whickham (An area near to the Metro Centre shopping complex.) the next day on a Sunday. He ended up actually shaking my hand after the set to on the Saturday night and said, 'I'd like you to come in with me,' and as he shook hands with me he said, 'I'd like to get all this sorted out.' I met with a few of the lads down at Dunston and it was me and a lad called Stephen Vaughan, who used to be a good friend of mine, and I went up to Whickham to meet Viv, him and Armstrong (Rob Armstrong was once a close friend of Viv's.) and they never turned up so that was that.

A while after that Cecil and Reg Levy offered me to do the door at Hobos. Cecil said, 'Will you do the door,' and he went on to say that he didn't want the likes of Viv Graham or the Sayers' in the place I said I would keep them out. So the first couple of nights nothing was said but word got back to me that a few of them were running around the town and were coming up to see me. I told the lads on the door at the time, Joe Quince, Stephen 'Flash' Gordon and a few other lads who were working with me. I said, 'Don't let them in the door, if they come to the door give me a shout, I'm inside and I'll come and sort it out.'

One of the doormen come and told me that Viv and his team were at the door. I said, 'At the door,' so when I goes in they said that Viv wasn't at the door but actually in the foyer of the club. I said, 'Who's let the fuckers in?' So I goes straight out to the foyer and I went to the door and they were like standing in the corner and as I went through the door I actually walked past them. Again I said, 'Who's let these in?'

A voice behind me, Viv's, said, 'WATSON.' I turned around and he gave me a left hand straightaway and I went back and the rest of them, five or six of them, stood around me and were saying to Viv: 'Go on Viv do him, kill him, kill him, do him.' I knew two or three of them were blade merchants anyway and I knew they'd be tooled up.

Soon as he hit me I knew he hadn't done anything with me I was going to have a shot, but I could see I was in a no win situation with him especially when the doormen who were supposed to be standing with me fucked off out of the door, I was dropped like a hot pebble. My girlfriend was there and she could be heard squealing in the background when the court played the video footage. One of the doormen had a hold of her, she wanted to intervene herself – I'm married to her now.

Viv is still giving it to me, batting me and at the finish we burst into the club itself and he still couldn't put me on my arse. Viv by this time was running out of puff and he says to me, 'Go down! Go down man!' The others who were with Viv had kicked open the fire exit doors by this time and everybody had made a big space for them and they were saying to him: 'Get him outside, we'll kill him,' so Viv was still shouting at me, 'Go down, go down.'

Viv was more concerned what was going to happen because he didn't have the arse for it because if they had of killed me or stuck me then he was in the shit and he knew it. I didn't go down though, I kept a hold of the spiral staircase, he didn't hurt me but they were like a pack of dogs and jumped in and started punching and kicking me. Viv stopped it he was shouting, 'HE'S HAD ENOUGH. HE'S HAD ENOUGH THAT'S IT!' I was all cut and Viv was looking worried. I said, 'Is that it then, are you finished?'

My wife, Sharon, was crying her eyes out. I said, 'I'm alright, they haven't hurt me, I'm alright.' I went to the toilet to clean my face up and gets in the car and went to hospital to have a few stitches put in. That happened on the Friday or Saturday night and I was back at work on the Monday. Davie Lancaster was there, he was the instigator, he's a little man with a big mouth and he likes to throw fuel on the fire. I've never professed to be anybody; I'm just a man off the streets.

I was a one who wouldn't bow down to them, if I was given a job to do and they asked me to do a job and I was being paid to do that job then I did the job and if they didn't want them in the club then I'd keep them out. If you're getting paid to do the job then you do the job, if you cannot then they'll just get somebody else to do it.

After that I was arrested three times for perverting the course of justice because I had a meeting with John Sayers, which the police knew about. And he started out by telling me that I should do this and do that, he didn't ask me at first. I said, 'You don't tell me to do nothing, ask me and then we might get somewhere, but don't tell me,' Dodgy Ray Hewitson was there at the meeting.

What happened on the night of the fight was there were three or four undercover police in Hobos and when Viv and the others were up in court the police were asked about when they were supposed to intervene in any sort of violence? They said that they had orders from the top saying that they didn't have to intervene at all; they had to let it go to see what happened. That's why you get people turning against the police full stop because they were using me. They were hoping I was going to get killed or if I was stabbed up then they had to do nothing! Their orders were not to intervene at any time.

I said to the police that I threw the first punch but of course it was on video and they weren't having any of it. I made an affidavit (A sworn statement usually made thorough a solicitor and sworn to be a true and accurate statement.) saying I'd started the fight. The police asked me if they owed me anything? I said, 'You owe me fuck all, I owe you nothing and you owe me fuck all, I want nothing off you.' (Stu Watson refused to allow his medical records to be used in court and did not give evidence at the court hearing when Viv and his team faced charges for assault. It can also be said that the police brought the action without consulting Stuart Watson.)

When Viv comes home on a home leave from his three-year sentence he had a big party. I went down, the whole lot of them were there and I went down and showed my face. Dodgy Ray said, 'He's out, do you want to break the ice,' I replied, 'I'm not bothered about going down, I'll go down.' They were all in Maceys and I went down, as soon as I walked in the front doors you could have heard a pin drop. The whole place went dead quiet.

After that Viv and me were working together at Rockshots nightclub, Dodgy Ray was the go between for Viv and me. Every time Viv and me were there you could cut the atmosphere with a knife. I could tell that Viv was dubious of me and wasn't sure if he could take my shots or not and it was always the case where he was always doubtful and you could feel the atmosphere there all the time and I knew from day one that it wasn't going to work me and him working together because he just couldn't let things go at that and he wasn't sure what would've happened if we did have proper fight.

So when we're working Rockshots together he was getting X amount of pounds and I'm getting X amount of pounds and he was coming in once every two weeks, three weeks and I was there like a mug standing on the door and he's getting the same money as me. So they say they want the west end lot kept out because they were making a nuisance of themselves and some of them were doing what they wanted.

So I said on the Thursday, 'Right, no more west end in,' to the lads at the door and I said if any names come then I'm inside and they should come and tell me and then I would tell them that they cannot come in. I said, 'You lads on the doors don't get paid enough for that, that's my job.' They were kept out good style and not one of them got in. Viv was half paly with the west end lot at the time but he said 'alright.' It was getting to the point that I was fighting nearly every other day on the door and I was getting threats to kill, 'You're going to get shot,' and all the usual shite. Then Viv was away for six weeks and I still had his money and then Dodgy Ray said: 'Viv wants his money!' I replied, 'Tell Viv he's not getting his fucking money!' He says, 'He's not going to be happy,' my reply was, 'Tell him I'm not happy, me doing his fucking work and he's getting the same money. Tell him he's not getting it!' So he says: 'You know what he'll be like,' I replied, 'I don't give a fuck, he's not getting it, I'm not going to do his job on top of mine, I couldn't give a fuck what he says.' Dodgy Ray went to see Viv and he half accepted it and told Dodgy Ray, 'Tell him he can keep the cunt for his fucking self.'

So I pulled a few more lads in rather than me keep his money so I felt a little bit more secure and I had some decent lads with me. Viv was up at Madison's, say, three or four times a year or so and he'd phone Rockshots up and he'd say to me, 'Peoples' telling me I can't fucking do you,' I said, 'Who's telling you this? He'd reply, 'Peoples' told me that,' 'Well who the fuck is it?' I'd reply. He's giving it the big one on the phone so I said, 'Who's saying this?' It turned out it was Mackem Tommy who used to work for me then he went to work for Viv up at Madisons.

Viv - The Final Chapter

Viv was still on the phone saying, 'He told me I didn't drop you,' I said to him, 'Well you didn't fucking drop me!' 'I'll tell you what, I'm going to come down,' was what he said so I told him to come down but 'there's just going to be trouble, but I'll tell you what I'll do I'm going to come to your house tomorrow.'

I went to his house with Geoff Brown because Geoff knew where he lived. I went there, knocked on the door, he answered all apologetic and shaking my hand and that. I said, 'What the fucks a matter with you. If you're going to listen to people then we're going to be at each other's throats all the time,' and he'd say, 'Aye, I know, I know.' Three or four months would pass and there'd he'd be on the phone again, the same fucking scenario! Obviously it was eating him away that he couldn't put me down."

Just then Terry Mitchell who had just joined our meeting a short while earlier interjects: "Viv could have a fight but at the end of the day just say a big kid come in here he'd have to go over and knock him out for no reason at all just because he'd be feeling that little bit insecure in himself in thinking this kid was bigger than him."

Stu continues: "We were once in Rockshots when we used to work together and Dodgy Ray come across and he says, 'Stu, Viv wants you to go over and knock that kid out.' I said, 'Viv wants me to go and do what?' I wasn't doing Viv's dirty work so I said, 'Tell fucking Viv to do it himself. I'm not his fucking monkey, tell him to fucking do it!' He must have thought I was going to work for him, I didn't work for anyone, I worked with them."

Terry Mitchell sums it all up: "It's not just because he's my pal, anybody can tell you that he…" as he looks in Stu's direction, "…. can have a fight and so could Viv but one goes round throwing his weight about like that and one's just a normal friend and a gentleman who can sit in the company of his friends and his friends can take the piss if they want. I mean I should be booted all over the car park the way I talk to him," and again Terry nods in the direction of Stu.

Stu goes on to tell me of a further confrontation he had with Viv: "I was at the gym with a friend of mine called Todd and Viv come in and he said that he wanted to see me outside. So we're standing at the front of the gym and he says to me, 'I want £15,000 off you or

Adrian.' He wanted this for his part in keeping trouble out of Rockshots. I said, 'You're getting nothing out of me!' This was two years after he had left Rockshots, he was short of money and he was a gambler.

He sees that you're doing half alright and wants some of it. Todd comes out of the gym and Viv said to him, 'What are you fucking coming out for?' Viv went to throw a punch at Todd and I grabbed a hold of Viv when he went forward to punch him and pulled him back and he said to me, 'Don't you fucking jump on my back!' I said, 'Jump on your back! I haven't jumped on your fucking back, it's got fuck all to do with him, it's between me and you.' Viv then says, 'Get round the fucking back with me,' I told him, 'Anything you've got to do with me you can do round the front, I'm going round no back I don't know who the fucks round there.' 'I want fifteen grand off you,' Viv said and my reply was, 'You're getting fuck all off me. I'll ask Adrian about it and if Adrian doesn't know anything about it then you're getting fuck all.'

I saw Adrian and said to him, 'Tell Viv he's getting fuck all and that I'm standing by you.' At the time the club was in trouble anyway, it had lost its drinks licence and he wanted fifteen grand out of a club that wasn't making anything.

Then it was a couple of nights after that we went down to The Lion (A frequent haunt of the hard man fraternity based in Felling, Gateshead – now closed down.) and it was a Bank Holiday Monday, he was coming out of The Lion as we were going in and there was a little bit of animosity you could feel and we were having a bit eye to eye. He said, 'Are you alright,' and I went, 'Aye, I'm alright.' He left a message that he was coming back on the night time and he was going to come up to The Malting House pub.

So we're sitting up at The Malting House and I said to the Hammer (Stephen Eastland), Geoff (Brown) and Terry, 'If he comes in then let me and him fucking get it on and see what the fucking outcome is, I'm sick of all this shite.' And he, Viv, was in a bar (The Lion) about fifty yards away and he never come up. He was threatening he was going to come up but he never. It was a stand off all the time, I wish it had of getting off the ground but it didn't."

Viv - The Final Chapter

I put it to Stu that now he's considered to be a businessman then the transition from what he was to what he has become must have been difficult? "I think it's hard for the community around me especially the council and the police. I took the kids from the school across the road to see a pantomime because they couldn't raise the money. They can't understand how a man can change but give a dog a bad name. I've got two pubs and none of them have a drugs problem, no one is allowed to smoke joints in them and that was made clear from day one. I'm not going to give the police that chance to come down on me.

When I first took this pub over I got a visit from the police, they used to come in here fifteen and twenty handed on a Friday night, a Saturday night and even when the place was being done out ten or fifteen armed police would be running around the front. Then they'd be coming in and pushing and shoving people about saying, 'It's twenty past eleven and people are still sitting in here!'

They'd come in numerous times but now they know I run a clean place they don't bother. They used to come around smelling and looking in all the ashtrays looking for joints, but I wouldn't let it happen. The police kept it up for nine or ten months and they would send two vanloads, but it must have been costing them money to do that."

(It is to the credit of the police that they didn't get people to plant drugs in the place, as this is a ploy some bent coppers get their informants to do before such raids. In theory the police were trying to make it a no go area, but since then the pub has flourished and the police realise it's not the 'den of inequity' they first thought it to be – a credit to Watson.)

During the interview Stu tells me he's looking for sponsors for his junior football team and I think to myself that this man really has changed, I mean I've even heard reports that he's chased people off the local football field when youngsters have been caught riding motorcycles across it. If that's not a community spirit then I don't know what is, who knows maybe we'll be seeing a sign above his office door in years to come saying 'Councillor Stuart Watson cares for his community.'

2

Gunfight at the OK Corral

Anyone recall a great western film called 'Gunfight at the OK Corral', okay I'm showing my age and a misspent youth of watching hours and hours of cowboy shootout films, well here we've got our very own gunfight where bullets worth £50,000 are used...no kidding.

Operation Domino carried out by Northumbria Police Force was a two-year investigation into gangland violence, intimidation and racketeering and it concentrated heavily on two of the north's big league players in the crime world – Paul Ashton and Robert Webber. The result of the operation led to Ashton receiving sentences totalling 31 years and his lieutenant Webber receiving 18 years. A known associate of Ashton's, Paul 'Monkey' Lyons, received $19^{1/2}$ years for his part in the activities of Ashton and Webber. This stemmed from a gunfight that took place outside the home of Stu Watson on 12th January 1996 when gun tottin' Ashton and trigger happy Webber lay in wait for Watson to return home. An attempted murder on Terry Mitchell by Paul Lyons that took place in 1995 was also part of the sentencing strategy.

On 12th January 1996 shots were fired from within Ashton's parked Jaguar in the direction of Stu Watson and his friend Terry Mitchell as they pulled up in a van outside of Watson's home. For ease of identification I'll call it 'Gunfight at the OK Corral'. Gunfire was returned in Ashton's direction and soon after that Ashton was seen to be driven away at speed. Bearing in mind that the gunfight at the OK Corral took place in a private residential estate in

Gateshead it did attract a little bit of attention and it wasn't long before the police were called by concerned members of the public or as is rumoured by Ashton himself as he was driven away by his accomplice Robert Webber.

During the time it took the police to arrive five men, including Watson, returned fire and stormed Ashton. Stu Watson tells of the build up to the incident. "The first time I ever saw Paul Ashton was after I'd met Terry (Mitchell) a few times up at Foleys and at a pub called The Winchester (Gateshead) and at that time Paul Ashton was in prison. I was in a barbershop and Terry come in with Ashton out of the blue. Ashton was an ugly thing; once you've seen him you couldn't forget him.

It was an incident after that when Ashton had a run in with Stephen Eastland (Stevie the Hammer) at the After Dark club when they were chasing about after each other with knives and they were supposed to meet up the next day at The Malting House pub and have a fight this is, allegedly, what Paul Ashton said to the police. We've just been chucked for that, me the Hammer, Geoff (Brown) and Terry had charges against us dropped this year." (2001)

(Unbelievable that a set of events that allegedly took place over ten years ago should be pursued against these men given that Ashton is trying to maximise his case for appeal it would be better that such sleeping dogs were to left lying in peace. The CPS sat on it for two years waiting for Watson and others to be released from prison for which they were serving time for the gunfight at the OK Coral, perhaps the CPS were hoping to have them banged up again?)

Stu continues, "Ashton said that we run outside and that I chased him up the street, this was said in a statement that we haven's seen, him and Webber were there.

He allegedly said that Terry had chopped Ashton with a sword across the back and that I got Webber out the car with a shotgun and splattered the car full of lead shot. Then Ashton further alleged, if we were there that is, that he ran into Felling police station at the top of the street.

After that Ashton went to jail for four years for the burglary of a cash & carry warehouse. When Ashton got out he and the Hammer had a further run in but the Hammer had some steroids in his pocket and he went and put them under a brick because he didn't want the police coming along and nicking him for them (possession of steroids, at the time of writing, for your own use in the UK is legal).

The Hammer said, 'I'm not running away, I'm just putting these away in case the busies come.' So the two of them gets the blades out and start having a ding-dong and the busies come along in a car and just sit there watching, the Hammer gets rid of his blade and soon after that they arrested him. Ashton didn't get arrested though?

I've got the statement where Ashton met Stuart Hay; he was a sergeant then, and Ashton showed him where the tablets were. They were swapped over by the police for paracetamol tablets and then put back where they were originally hidden. (A common safeguard in such events.)

The Hammer was locked up over the weekend for the knife incident, he was at court on the Monday morning, I went to pick him up from court. The Hammer asked me to take him home, he jumps out of the car, goes and picks up what he wanted and then the police are there waiting for him…he got set up off Paul Ashton.

Somehow the steroids had changed into headache tablets. When the Hammer bought the tablets they were supposed to be steroids. (Which in all probability they were, as you'll find out later on.)

When Ashton and the Hammer were jumping about with their knives a busy was sitting watching them from his car. I've got the transcripts from the Hammer's trial and the judge says that Ashton informed on this case. Sergeant Hayes was asked a number of times in court if Ashton was his informer and he said he couldn't answer that question."

At Eastland's trial Judge Vos told the jury:

"If the Crown satisfies you that the Defendant is guilty, on the whole of the evidence so that you are sure he is guilty, you are bound by law to return a verdict of "guilty". It is no use saying, "Well, what a dirty trick, that fellow Ashton got away with all kinds of things and he doesn't appear before us so, although we are sure the defendant is guilty, we'll say "not guilty." You can't do that. If you are sure he is guilty, you are bound by law to say

he is "guilty."

Judge Vos went on to say: **"The defence is that a malicious person disposed to the defendant, had taken away the steroids and substituted £750-worth of street value Ecstasy, and told the police that it was there to get the defendant into the serious trouble that he stands in now. ...Police have to rely, if they are to do there job properly, on what is known as intelligence, and all too often intelligence is an informant, and it happens again, and all too often that the informant, the informer, or the 'coppers nark' as they used to be called, is a criminal and quite often a serious criminal himself, and he is playing one off against the other. He may be hoping for a bit of good treatment from the police, bail when perhaps he should not have it, and all that sort of thing. But the one essential prerequisite is that his name should never be disclosed. There is a kind of tacit understanding between police and criminal informants that the names should not be disclosed, and you can see the reason why. Once he is known as a "grass", as I say, he is finished with the criminal fraternity and he is of no more use to the police. So that is the basis."**

As a consequence of the jury finding Eastland guilty of intending to supply Ecstasy he was given a five-year prison sentence and for the knife fight with Ashton he entered a plea of guilty and was given a further six months for affray. Counsel for the defence, Mr Duffield submitted an appeal against severity of sentence on behalf of Stephen Eastland and in his application to have the five-year prison sentence reduced amongst his many submissions he added the following:

'There is only one possible ground of appeal in that the trial judge refused my application to cross-examine the investigating police officer as to the name of the admitted police informer. The identity of the informer was crucial in that the defence of Mr Eastland rested upon the informer having himself substituted Ecstasy for other uncontrolled drugs in an attempt wrongly to secure the prosecution of Mr Eastland.

Although I was not permitted to ask the direct question whether Ashton was the informer, I was permitted to ask a series

of questions which were answered and which established without any real possibility of doubt that Ashton was in fact the informer. Indeed, in his summing up, the trial judge made plain that the evidence pointed only in the direction of Ashton. In these circumstances, I do not consider that my inability to ask the direct question gives rise to any realistic ground of appeal against conviction. Accordingly it is unnecessary to review the authorities which the judge considered before ruling that I could not ask the direct question.'

Most top-flight criminals, not all though, have a policeman in their pocket or if the worst comes to the worst they do something what the criminal fraternity frowns upon…they inform their way out of trouble. In the case of Ashton he did a little more than inform his way out of trouble, he designed a situation in which Stephen Eastland was to be arrested and taken out of circulation for a long, long time and in doing so it gave him that little bit more time to work on other matters. Did he swap the steroids for the Ecstasy tablets knowing that Eastland would go back for his stash and in so doing he would fall right in to the Venus flay trap…what do you think, let's find out. Judge Vos:

"He (Detective Constable Heywood) had a discussion with Acting Detective Sergeant Hay. Before this he had received certain information as to the background of the fracas, and the fracas was the fight, so that immediately links it up, does it not, with Ashton. But when Acting Detective Sergeant Hay was cross-examined about this, he threw even more light on it, in answers to questions that I did permit Mr Duffield to put. He said he had been face to face with the informant, who told him: "If I went to the old people's home, at the corner, I would find something that had been hidden."

He had seen somebody (the defendant Eastland) go there. The information was received some time between the end of the interview of the defendant, which was about 8 o'clock or so, it is recorded at 8 o'clock or so, and 9.15 pm. when the Ecstasy was found.

'During that time I did speak to Mr Ashton. He would not

come to court as a witness under any circumstances. He would not make a statement. I would have been surprised if he had been willing to. The meeting at which the information was given was by chance. During the course of seeing the informant, as a result of enquiries into the fracas, I was given this information...'

That is what I mean when I say by chance. Now, if you knit those pieces of evidence together with the fact that, whatever the basis of the trouble between Ashton and the defendant was, and the fact that the defendant in cross-examination said that Ashton could have seen him go...."

When the fight between Ashton and Eastland took place it was in fact, as Stu Watson said, witnessed by a police officer, Detective Constable Heywood and something very important is said that everyone including the defence barrister seems to have missed out on and in order that I can point this out to you we have to hear what Judge Vos says of that:

"Well, Detective Constable Heywood; 5 o'clock or so on Saturday, 1st May of last year, came upon this scene. What did he see? He said the only person he saw with a knife in his hand was the defendant. Ashton was on the retreat, as it were, throwing bricks. Then he said that seemed to fizzle out. The defendant went to that lane which gave access to the Hillside Grange Retirement Home.

'He came back to the corner of Coxon Terrace by The Duke public house and went over to Ashton's car, and then Ashton drove away and the defendant went into Hedley Gardens where he left the knife.'

He gets the information later that night. He has arrested the defendant. Discussion with the Acting Detective Sergeant Hay, which I have mentioned to you, and they go and find Exhibit No. 2.

Can I just remind you, be careful about Exhibit No. 2 as you see it. When the police found Exhibit No.2, both tablets and capsules were in one cellophane packet, but then, when they were sent for forensic examination — and you remember the scientist's evidence being read out — all the capsules were put

into the separate little packets and a new cellophane packet was put in for capsules and tablets, so it had a slightly different appearance when the police found it, but that is what they found, members of the Jury...."

Remember what time Detective Constable Heywood reported the fight between Ashton and Eastland taking place, 5 o'clock! Now let's look at the time the information was passed on to the police regarding the steroid stash, which had miraculously turned into Ecstasy and then into paracetamol. The court heard the information was received some time between the end of the interview of the defendant, which was about 8 o'clock or so, it is recorded at 8 o'clock or so, and it was 9.15 pm when the Ecstasy was found.

Doesn't that seem very strange, over fours hours for the police to discover the stash, why did Ashton need this sort of time, why wasn't Ashton charged with affray, obviously Ashton wasn't an agent provocateur but there are cases when the police have got informers to do things that help convict the innocent, I am not suggesting that this happened here, but what I am suggesting is that Ashton used this ploy to secure his own conviction against Eastland and it took a little while to organize.

I have been told that the police use informants to visit people in prison in order to secure their services as witnesses in high profile criminal trials.

A well known Newcastle underworld figure was allegedly used in this way after being caught with a drugs and weapons stash in his house, can't say much more here because I await the final piece of the jig-saw so maybe it will squeeze into the book or maybe it will have to go up on a particular web site in time. (**www.johnsayers.com**)

Back to Stu Watson: "Ashton was in prison doing his four stretch and he'd just got the Hammer his big sentence. I had a pal doing six months so I visited him. Ashton was also being visited by someone at the same time and when he seen me he started grinning so him and me had a bit of a set to.

He was sitting at a table about twenty feet away in front of me, I stood up and walked towards him, he knew what was going to happen. Because he was in a prison visits room he thought he'd goad me so I just give him it and then the screws threw me into a cell and they said, 'What wing are you from?' I replied, 'I'm not off a wing I'm visiting someone,' they let me out straight away.

Ashton got out of jail and he turned against Terry (Mitchell) because Terry was speaking to Geoff Brown and he hated Geoff Brown (Over an alleged domestic matter.) so he now hated Terry. Ashton and Geoff were going to have a go with each other.

Ashton used to bully all of his palls because he knew them from being a kid and he used to take liberties with them so Geoff was a bit dubious of him so I said I would stand with Geoff while he had a fight with Ashton and Webber (Andy) could stand with Ashton.

One morning Kevin Brown, Geoff's brother, knocks on my door and says, 'Paul Ashton's at the bottom of the street and he wants to see you.' So I throws my top on and went out, 'What do you want,' I said to Ashton. 'I wanna get it on with Brownie, Brownie's a grass,' was his reply. 'I'll tell you what, Paul,' I said, '…you go and get it on with Geoff and I'll search you and Webber can search Geoff and we search each other and just you and him have a fair paggor, we'll end it at that,' Ashton replied, 'Right, up at the back of Fiddlers (pub in Felling, Gateshead.) on the field up there.'

This was supposed to happen at twelve o'clock on a Monday, he didn't turn up so I'm phoning him on this number I've got for him I said, 'Where is he, we're sitting up here waiting for him,' their reply was, 'We're going to phone him, they're coming, they're coming.' It got a little bit late and I was getting a little bit worried thinking that it was going to a be a set up. So now I find out afterwards that he was asking Davie Glover (More on David Glover Jnr in another chapter.) to sit there with a rifle and pop Geoff Brown off!

So Ashton wasn't even willing to have a straightner with Geoff. This is why he ended up hating Terry for speaking to Geoff Brown and I was just vacuumed into all of this, I wouldn't let my pal down. I never carry a grudge, why back track, my life's going forwards not backwards.

From then on Ashton had sent someone to shoot Terry, Geoff was there with Terry as well. They tried to shoot Terry at his front door with a pump action shotgun that blasted its way through a fence first and from then on everybody went around tooled up."

Terry Mitchell explains what went on after this: "One morning I came out of the house, I'm always alert to what's going on around me and I was looking at the woman at the bus stop opposite and she was looking at the side of my house. I was coming down the stairs and as I hit the path I veered off and jumped down off the wall with the bairn and I looked to the side and there was Lyons (Paul 'Monkey' Lyons) standing there pushed back into the bushes.

I bowled straight up to him and said, 'What are you doing standing there like that?,' and he went, 'I'm not doing nowt mate, nowt.' He nashed up the road as fast as he could, he flew up the road and I'm not saying that to make myself look big. I never thought anything about it and usually I'm really alert.

I walks over to the garage to get the car out to take the bairn to school and as I'm driving up towards the school, bearing in mind it's about ten past eight, here's fat bags (Ashton) and Webber come past me. Now usually when we seen each other, whoever had the most in with them chases the other. If I was by myself and he was by himself we just used to pass, but if he was with Webber or somebody else he'd give chase if I was on my own, it was just hatred. I looked at Ashton and Webber and they pretended they hadn't seen me and I still hadn't clicked on, I'm dead sharp usually.

I come back home for the gym and I was rushing to get in, I grabbed my towel and went to the car, it had blacked out windows and a fancy jack plug immobiliser fitted, which was under the dash. I was bent over to push the jack plug in and Lyons come along with a big bayonet and stabbed me in the shoulder as I sat fiddling about under the dash, as he stabbed me in the shoulder I was half sat on the seat and he was trying to push the blade right in but it was stuck in my shoulder blade so it couldn't go through it, he was trying to kill me!

The initial shock had gone then and I said, 'When I get out of here I'm going to fucking kill you.' I was trying to get out by now and he was just stabbing at me and the blade was going straight through the seat, BOOSH, BOOSH. I was kicking at his legs, I put my hand up and he stabbed me in the wrist and the blade came out my forearm, I was out of the car by then.

I got a hold of him by the throat and threw him over the wall and started giving him it but my damaged arm meant my hand was losing its grip. By then I could see he was starting to shite himself and was ready to run away, I literally threw him over the top of the Sierra. When I had him over the wall he was still stabbing at me. One stab went straight through my ear and out of the side of my cheek, as I had a hold of him I could see six inches of the blade out of the side of my face and he was riving at it and my head was moving with it like a lollipop on a stick.

As Lyons was running away down the grassy bank I looked over the wall and there was fatty (Ashton) and Webber leaning on their car. Ashton was jumping up and down shouting, 'You've fucking killed him, you've killed him, you've killed him.' He was a bit excited."

Subsequently when this case went to court Lyons defence called a female witness who was allowed to give evidence in disguise and to use a nom de plum (to us what can't speak French it means a false name). This female witness said that the attacker was wearing a mask. Of course the reason for this was to discredit the evidence of the prosecution, if Lyons was wearing a mask then of course how could Mitchell have picked him out of an I.D. parade. This ploy was thought by the police to be a strategy to discredit prosecution evidence. Now don't all go running off shouting that Mitchell is a grass because you haven't heard half nor quarter of it, read on please.

When I went to interview Stu Watson I had no idea Terry Mitchell would be joining us to give comment, which I'm now pleased he did as it gives a clearer picture for you. But like anything every coin has two sides and in my possession is a letter from Paul 'Monkey' Lyons, which he'd written to me in March 2001 some many months before Terry Mitchell very kindly gave comment on the attack. I'd like to throw in a few snatches of comments from Paul Lyons' letter, which was mainly about claims of corruption within Northumbria Police Force. I am not the judge or the jury in what is written here and I can only put peoples sides of events so as to show you that I am being fair to all in allowing some sort of right to reply but in this instance Lyons had already written what follows before Terry Mitchell gave his side of the story. Paul Lyons:

'I am expecting to go the appeal courts this year. I don't know how much you've heard, Steve, about it, but I can guess with the contacts you have and the people you know you will be well aware we fell victim to a major police fabrication from the beginning. Steve, it was a farce basically they wanted Ashton I only had a minor part of the case, one alleged stabbing of a self confessed member of a gang, Terry Mitchell was the victim. He made no complaint to the police until he was in serious trouble himself, some sixteen months after he was stabbed.'

(For the readers thinking that Mitchell was an informer I will explain the situation. Ashton was prepared to swear the lives of Watson and co away in order to get them locked up for a long, long time because they weren't prepared to buy a bullet from him for £50,000. This bullet was supposedly the one fired at him when he was a passenger in Robert Webber's Mercedes car on 11th January 1996. (See statement of Linda Simpson, common law wife of Paul Ashton, further on.) This offer to buy the bullet was made whilst Watson and his associates were on remand for the OK Corral gunfight.

Ashton was in a difficult position because it didn't look like Watson and co would be facing long jail terms if indeed any jail terms at all for the OK Corral gunfight, his plan was starting to backfire on him and he was preparing to produce even more secreted evidence in order to bang his rivals up for even longer. Ashton had more tricks up his sleeves than Paul Daniels and more white rabbits in his hat than David Copperfield.

Ashton was pulling out all the stops, he produced to the police a Mercedes car, which had a bullet hole in the front windscreen Ashton felt that if he introduced the £50,000 bullet into the equation then Watson and co would be eager to purchase the incriminating evidence, but this was the start of the end for Ashton...Watson and co told him to stick it and decided to play Ashton at his own game. By Ashton introducing such evidence via his common law wife's statement to the police it immediately brought the limelight onto him and his fellow associates in crime.

For Stu Watson and co it looked decidedly like a slippery slope, what could they do, it was either shut up and accept twenty year prison sentences based on Ashton's trickery or turn the tables on him and that way they would only have to face what they had coming for the gunfight at the OK Corral incident, what would you do? Lyons continues his letter to me:

'**The prosecution's case was that I carried out the attack on Mitchell on behalf of Ashton and Webber for money. I don't know if you know either Ashton or Webber but if you do, Steve, I'm sure you would agree they are more than capable of carrying it out themselves. Mitchell implicated me 'cos he knew at the time he was assaulted I was friendly with Ashton & Webber. Me and Mitchell had a run in at Durham unit in 1996, only four weeks after that he picked me out on an I.D. parade. I'm as innocent as the day is light everyone knows it. Everyone tells me I will win my appeal including my legal team.**

There's been a few times I've wanted to write to you. I think to myself "This fellahs not afraid to say it as he sees it," I respect that in a man. The tactics of Northumbria police/prosecution/solicitors the lot would make a good book. The police have finally admitted they breached the Codes of Practice and illegally searched my room. The judge allowed the jury to hear evidence obtained from that illegal search. The appeal courts have said it was wrong.'

Terry Mitchell goes on to say: "After the attack I was at work the next day and I was in the town by the Friday because I signed myself out of hospital. I didn't know Lyons was knocking about with Ashton, I never ever forget a face."

Back to Stu Watson: "The main incident that happened in the Hobos incident with Viv involved Rob Armstrong, now I don't hold a grudge so when he wanted to be in Rockshots after that incident I let him back in. When Viv got killed Armstrong got Viv's job down at The Venue (Spennymoor, County Durham. No longer there – caught fire.), him and Joe Hunt were working the doors.

Gunfight at the OK Corral

Armstrong stopped coming into Rockshots for some reason but I didn't realise why until I went down there, it was me, Terry and Malcolm Faith went for a night out at the Venue. When I got there one of the lads was standing with his arm across the door and I said, 'Watch your arm,' and I felt there was a bit of animosity there, a little bit of tension and I thought 'What the fucks a matter with these?' I knew some of the lads there because some of them worked for me at Rockshots at the time.

I had a canny night in there and the following morning about eleven o'clock I had a phone call from one of my friends and he said, 'After you left last night down at Spennymoor Armstrong come in and they told me that you were barred and not to let you in.' I replied, 'BARRED, not let me in, why?' I was told that he didn't know why and my friend went on to say that Armstrong was told, 'If you want him kept out then you tell him he cannot get in, that's not our job, we don't get paid to tell him he cannot get in.'

But I'm the kind of lad that if I knew I was barred I wouldn't have went because there was people there that worked for me so I wouldn't have put them in a position that they needn't be in. After they finished at Rockshots my lads would go on to work at The Venue and I said to them that I didn't want to see them lose their jobs over me. Armstrong was supposed to have sacked them all that night after he found out I'd been in. Joe Hunt was supposed to have come in at about 3am or 4am and supposedly he spotted me, went upstairs to talk to the owner and then he left, I wasn't aware of what was going on in the background.

So the next thing I know is I'm back at loggerheads with Rob Armstrong and I'm wanting to know why I'm barred.

There's a pal of mine Davie Zivvers who was working around at Buzz on a Saturday night and it used to get full of shite and he also worked at Rockshots.

Davie tells me that this lad had pulled a knife on him and he said he'd be back on the Saturday night with a couple of lads. I said I'd come around with a couple of lads on the night, it got to about 1.30am and the kid never showed so I said I'd have to go back round to check on the club to make sure everything was all right. I was just leaving Buzz and Armstrong come in and he tried to acknowledge me and I thought to myself, 'What a cheeky bastard after trying to bar me.'

So when I left Buzz, Armstrong comes over to Davie Zivvers and says, 'What's fucking Watson doing in here? It's not his club, that fucker tried to set me up in Cramlington.' (Place in Northumberland)

So there was kids standing there listening to what Armstrong had said and they couldn't wait to come and tell me, they set their necks to tell me what he'd just said about me saying I'd set him up.

But they didn't realise what he was set up with. I said, 'I saved his fucking neck up in Cramlington because Geoff Brown was going to kick the shite out of him at a boxing event held there.' But he was with an ex pal of mine, Steven Vaughan who's a big man with a big mouth who can't back it up.

Steven Vaughan, who was my pal at the time, was running about with Armstrong and Geoff was going to chin Armstrong but I knew if Geoff had of chinned Armstrong then Steven would get wrong as well so I stopped Geoff from setting about Armstrong.

So Steven was full of drink and drugs and he goes and tells Armstrong that he was getting set up at the boxing do and throwed the shite in with it. Vaughan then started talking and telling tales out of school but if the truth was known I saved Armstrong's neck.

So on the Sunday after doing the Saturday night stint at Buzz I went around the town (Newcastle) looking for Armstrong and during this time we've still got the flack going on with Terry and Ashton and now the flack starts with Armstrong. I seen one of Armstrong's pals on the door and said to him, 'Get that fucking Armstrong on the phone and get him down here now, I'll fucking set him up. He got a by the last time but he's not getting a by this time, get him fucking here and we'll get it sorted out.'

So after Armstrong was phoned I was told, 'He's not coming down, he won't come down.' I replied, 'That's because he's a big useless cunt that's why, he couldn't fuck off.'

He wouldn't come down to have a do with me and it was getting near to the Christmas so we had a few drinks by the Sunday night. So on the Monday we went off down to Sunderland to get the kids' rings for Christmas and I must have had a guardian angel looking over me because usually we were religiously at the gym for twelve o'clock dinner time every day.

There was twenty of them with blades and knives and guns come into the gym looking for three of us but we weren't in because we were visiting Sunderland due to having hangovers from the drink.

What had happened was Armstrong had phoned Ashton up and said, 'We've got a rick on with Watson and Mitchell and them,' so they joined together and come team handed. Among them were Lyons, Ashton, Webber, Armstrong and some other doormen.

So when I found out about this I phoned Armstrong up from my house and there was me, Kezza, Alan, Graham, Terry and Todd in my house then. I said over the phone to Armstrong, 'Where are you?' His reply came, 'Who's that?' I said, 'You know who it is you fucking puke, where are you now, I'll come and fucking see you now and me and you get it sorted before it gets out of fucking hand,' and he says, 'I'm not going to fucking fight you, but Ashton will.' I said, 'Well you come along with him and after I've fucked Ashton I'll fucking do you you fat mug.' He would not come and have a fight because he knew he couldn't do it.

He's never had a fight with anybody who can have a fight. Steven Vaughan was there with Armstrong and I said over the phone, 'Tell Armstrong to come on and we'll get it on now,' and Steven says, 'It's gone too far now, he's not going to come.' I said, 'That's because he cannot come and have a proper fight, he's a proper mug.' He couldn't run a nursery, he's a proper puke, he goes to places he can handle that's all.'

Terry Mitchell takes up the story: "Armstrong was on remand for allegedly demanding money from Gosforth High Street and he come in through the prison reception, we had the kids squared in reception and they told us everything, and he started squealing on because he knew he'd have to come on B-wing with us where we were all remanded and the busies, the CID, took him back out of Durham and back to the police station and when he come back he said he'd be out in 28 days."

Stu Watson: "He come back on remand and Stephen Sayers and

Michael Sayers was in and Nigel Abadom was in. Armstrong went to see Abadom and asked him to sort it out for him so he could come on to the yard at exercise time. He wouldn't come out on the yard because I was there. I was shouting up at his cell all the time: 'GET ON THE YARD THEN ARMSRONG, GET ON THE YARD AND GET IT SORTED OUT.'

He wouldn't come onto the exercise yard at all and he wouldn't even go in the showers. He stayed up on the fours (fourth floor landing) and he would not come out the cell when we were on exercise or on a visit. If Armstrong was on a visit the same time as us they (prison officers) had to ask me not to do anything while in the visits room saying they'd put him at the top end. Coincidently Vaughany (Steven Vaughan) was visiting someone and they were up at the top end and I got restrained on the visit because I was going to do Vaughany.

I knew I was in there as a direct result because he (Armstrong) wouldn't have a fight with me and he got Paul Ashton involved and that's when it all escalated to the gunfight. One of the charges we were acquitted of was supposedly shooting Ashton on the Redheugh Bridge which we were charged with that at the same time we were charged with The Malting House pub incident that according to Ashton's claims happened in 1991.

The shooting on the bridge incident was supposed to have taken place on Thursday, 11th January '96, the day before the shoot out. (Gunfight at the OK Corral) Ashton had a bullet, which he did actually hand in to the police through his wife who made a statement about it. Linda Simpson, Ashton's common law wife, made the statement on 20th January 1996 saying I had £10,000 on Paul Ashton's head and that we'd shot him on the Redheugh bridge and that luckily Paul had a bullet proof vest on and that she had the bullet to hand in to the police."

Proof of this claim is supplied in part of the copy statement of Linda Simpson, common law wife of Paul Ashton, made on 20th January 1996 – something important to remember is it was made only eight days after the gunfight between Ashton and Watson, which took place in Gateshead on 12th January 1996 which supports the claim that Ashton tried to sell the bullet to Watson and co for £50,000 = £10,000 per man facing the gunfight at the OK Corral charges. Linda Simpson's statement to the police reads as follows:

'I live with my boyfriend Paul Ashton. We've been together for about four and a half years. For a good number of years I have been aware of a dispute between Paul and a number of other lads, they include Terry Mitchell and Stuart Watson (Watson just recently). I have no idea what the trouble is between them but it has gone on for years.

On Thursday, 11th January 1996 I went out for the day with my friend Marie Mason. A couple of days before this Paul had heard rumours that Watson and his friends had put up £10,000 for someone to kill Paul. I don't know much about this however; Paul I would say didn't take this seriously. I did take this seriously and tried to persuade him to change his attitude.

Paul owns a bulletproof vest which he has had for about two months or so, he bought this because of the trouble with Mitchell and his friends, he bought it from a shop in South Shields and actually had to have it made to measure. Because of the rumours about this £ 10,000 contract I had to persuade Paul to wear his bulletproof vest that day.

Paul went out before me sometime in the morning however I cannot remember what time it was. He left the house with Robert Webber who is Paul's best friend. Robert also was wearing his bulletproof vest, which is the same as Paul's but a bit smaller. They both decided, I think to start wearing their vests all the time.

I spent the day in Newcastle with Marie and got home at 4pm. I had been in the house only about a minute when I received a phone call from my brother in law David. I don't wish to tell you David's details I wouldn't want him involved.

David told me that Paul had been shot at but that he hadn't been hurt. David told me that Paul was at his mother's house. I then went, collected David and travelled down to Paul's mam's. When we got to his mam's I saw Paul, Robert and Paul's mam were there. We sat in the kitchen talking and I was very upset at

what had happened. Paul told me details of what had happened.

He told me that he had been in Robert's Mercedes, Robert was driving and Paul was in the passenger seat. They were driving down Bensham Bank when they saw Terry Mitchell. It wasn't Bensham Bank it was actually the road that comes from the dual carriageway (Askew Road) up to the little mini roundabout beside the old peoples home.

Robert and Paul were driving down the bank and Terry Mitchell was coming in the opposite direction up towards the roundabout. Mitchell was driving what I would describe as an old jeep which is blue with a white roof, I've seen him driving it quite a few times.

Paul said that there was quite a few lads in the jeep but he only recognised Mitchell. The jeep must have turned around because he said it came up behind them. Robert obviously panicked and didn't' know what to do, he was going to pull into a garage that is down there but Paul told him to keep on driving and not to stop. Apparently Mitchell was able to get in front of Robert and actually blocked them in so that they couldn't go anywhere.

Paul said that someone in the jeep actually shot through the jeep window, the bullet then went through one of the Mercedes windows and hit Paul in the chest. The bullet hit Paul's bulletproof vest and fell somewhere in the car. Paul said that he was lucky because his vest was open at the time. He said he could even see the smoke come out of the end of the gun.

He described the lad with the gun as being stocky with fair hair, he said that he didn't recognise the lad. Robert then reversed apparently and was able to drive away, they went across the Redheugh Bridge and Mitchell followed Robert and Paul across the bridge and there was another five or so shots fired at the Mercedes but I don't know whether they hit the car or not. They lost Mitchell somewhere after that.

I looked at Paul's vest but there wasn't any marks or anything on it. Paul had found the bullet in the car and he gave it to me. I have kept this. It's about 1/2 an inch in length and is what I would describe as flat on the bottom. It appears to have what I

**would describe as black metal inside. The end of it looks to be
jagged as if it had been hit with a hammer. I still have the bullet
however I do not want to hand it over until I have sought advice.'**

What advice was Linda Simpson waiting for, was it instructions
from her common law husband, Paul Ashton, who was, it is claimed,
negotiating to sell the bullet, who can say?

What would you do if, say, you were a member of the underworld
and as a consequence of a shootout you looked likely to be going
away for a 5+ stretch and then the person you had the shootout
against tells you via his cronies that unless you pay £50,000 for a
bullet he's got that will help add even more years on top of that
expected time would you stay mute and take it like a man on the chin
and serve your time and come out after twenty years smiling, of
course you fucking wouldn't. What if you could, say, fight fire with
fire, would you retaliate the same way? Ashton could have remained
silent and watched as Watson and co were led off but he wanted them
banged up for even longer and was prepared to play dirty.

Stu Watson: "He (Ashton) had come along and let about six or
seven shots off and before he got to the end of the street he had
phoned the busies. We were on remand for nine months, first we
were on B-wing in Durham prison for three months and then we got
cat A'd (high risk of escape) through somebody writing an
anonymous letter and sending it to the prison saying we planned an
armed escape.

Nigel Abadom comes up to me in the yard and he said that Ashton
wanted £50,000 for him to withdraw his wife's statement (as
previously seen), ten grand a man. So I said, 'Tell him to keep his
big fat mouth shut, he's not out of the water yet.' We'd said fuck all
for nine or ten months, we were getting interviewed all of the time.
When we were on cat 'A' we were locked up for 23 hours a day and
all privileges are taken away and there's only your wife can come in
and see you and if anyone else wants to see you they've got to be
vetted, it took my brother six months to get in to see me! So there
we were banged up in there and when we were continuously being
taken to court the evidence against us was getting less and less.

We were originally charged with conspiracy to murder first and then it was dropped down to attempted murder and then down to conspiracy to murder and then dropped to possession of firearms with intent and Paul Ashton was hating this because he knew we weren't going down for life because the other charges carry life sentences so from looking at life we were looking at three or four years.

So we were pulled out for conspiracy to murder again because Paul Ashton gave the police a Mercedes car which he had locked up in a garage for nine months. He gave the police this Mercedes with a bullet hole through the windscreen so as to try and get us charged again with attempted murder all because we wouldn't give him £50,000. Now if he hadn't of planned to use this Mercedes then he would have had a windscreen put in it but he didn't and he gave it to the police to get us banged up forever.

At the finish we sat down and said, 'Right, are we going to be kicked in the teeth off this cunt all the time? He's going to try and get us lifed off here.'

And that's when we turned it against him. Eventually when we were let out from the seven-year sentences we got we were charged again with The Malting house incident that took place in 1991, Ashton and Webber made another four statements, but all charges are out of the window now.

They had just made it up and because they are cat A's it meant they couldn't sit down together to collude with each other and because of this their statements were full of holes.

The police let us be free for over twelve months before they sprung these new charges on us that Ashton had made some three years earlier. The same police officer who was Ashton's handler, Stuart Hay, was in charge of the case against us for this new conspiracy to murder charge when we got out of jail and he turned around and said to me, 'You're fucked this time there's statements against you's, you's are fucked.' So when CID's are interviewing me and he wanted to come in and sit on my interview I said, 'He's not sitting in on my fucking interview.' Ashton was saying the police were bent and he had caused an inquiry." With that I leave the interview…heavy!

Gunfight at the OK Corral

It would seem that there was paranoia on both sides from Ashton and Watson, which is understandable given the severity of charges faced and perhaps the previous dealings the police had with Ashton giving rise to the fact that Ashton was the informant of Stuart Hay. I believe that if a criminal is or has been an informant of a police officer then a conflict of interest could arise and therefore any police officer should declare such an interest and refrain from entering into such investigations in order to remain and to be seen as impartial. The 'without fear or favour' motto used by judges and myself is sometimes difficult to apply in such circumstances.

Given what Watson and co faced I believe that there is not one man alive who would not have given Paul Ashton a taste of his own medicine. If Ashton had of allowed the gunfight at the OK Corral case to run its own course then I believe he would still be a free man today but given the hatred within him for his fellow man it consumed him in a battle of wits in which he was out pointed when his adversaries decided they'd had enough of his continued quest to have them locked up and have the key thrown away.

When Stuart Watson and his co-accused retaliated against Ashton with statements relating to Ashton and Webber conspiring to murder Terry Mitchell none of them were given immunity from prosecution and each had to sign such a declaration. The now famous police HOLMES computer software was brought into play to help analyse information secured such was the size of the operation (Operation Domino). Some 1,600 witness statements were taken during the investigation.

Five civilian witnesses not connected with Ashton's fraternity of associates have been given new identities after they gave evidence and as a consequence have lost touch with their families. The police also concentrated on an alleged serious assault by Ashton on a man called Colin Cable a victim of mistaken identity. Ashton was intimidating Cable into giving false evidence in order to discredit the police but he was found out.

Cleveland Police Force was also investigating drug-dealing allegations against Ashton when he had been working as a doorman at the Coliseum Club in Stockton. Ashton pleaded guilty to a charge of conspiracy to supply drugs and was sentenced to eight years in prison by Teesside Crown Court in October 1997.

March 1998 saw Ashton and Webber in the dock of Newcastle Crown Court facing charges of conspiracy to murder and possessing firearms with intent to endanger life. Ashton and Webber received 18 years for the conspiracy charges and 11 years concurrent (to run alongside) for the firearms offences. Ashton's time was to run consecutive to his eight years he had earlier received from Teesside Crown Court.

December 1999 Ashton was back in the dock and this time he was facing charges of violent disorder and attempting to pervert the course of justice in relation to Colin Cable. Ashton received a further five years, which was to run concurrent to the 26 years he was already serving, making a total of 31 years imprisonment!

Paul Lyons received 14 years for his attempted murder of Terry Mitchell and a further 4½ years for other offences was added on to run consecutively, 19½ years for following orders, was it worth it all?

The message was that no one was untouchable, which I do not believe to be true since police informers are getting away with murder right now in Newcastle and I do not mean the Sayers brothers so relax lads. Why is it when I say the words 'informer' and 'murder' that people assume I'm talking/writing about the Sayers'. Informers do not get to be banged up for as long as the Sayers' have.

The final word in this chapter goes to Stu: "I am a forgiving man and as time goes on you start to reflect on things that have happened in your life. I've never held a grudge so when twenty-five of my mates and me were sitting having a meal in an Italian restaurant in the Haymarket area of Newcastle and Rob Armstrong walks in (September 2001) we just talked, one of Rob's two friends who were with him said they didn't want any trouble and I said it was all in the past. I suppose, as you get wiser with age you can reflect, look back and even have a laugh at how mad it all was. Rob's got a life to lead and so have I and we've both said some terrible things about each other but all of that has melted away. I think Rob knows that too and maybe we'll end up sending each other Christmas cards wishing each other all the best."

3

Bent Coppers and Supergrasses

I mentioned Phil Berriman in one of the past Viv books and referred to his 'handler', this indicated that he was an informant working for the police/customs and it wasn't without fuel being added to this assumption via the media, namely newspapers and TV. For anyone involved in the criminal underworld to be called an informant/grass is a dangerous thing because repercussions from the criminal underworld can mean punishment beatings and even gangland slayings for those they believe have grassed them up.

Such a punishment beating was dished out to Phil Berriman by the underworld and that was as a direct consequence of media propaganda delivered to them by the authorities concerned. Now I know a lot of good honest citizens just wouldn't believe that the police or customs would lie to get someone into serious trouble, I know many people who believe the police to be whiter than white and above board and if anyone was to say that a copper is bent then eyebrows would be quickly raised in dismay and total disbelief at such a suggestion. Please, though, don't think that I'm anti-police because I'm not, I'm just anti-bent copper that's all.

As a build up to Phil Berriman's story I want to prove to the doubting Thomas's amongst you that bent coppers do exist and are rather more prevalent than you'd think and of course with 'Operation Lancet' (Police investigating police over allegations of corruption within Cleveland Police Force.) running into millions of pounds (£7m) without any real prospect of securing convictions other than a police officer being suspended over a boiler that was taken from police storage it would certainly indicate to the public that nothing untoward was carried out by serving police officers in the Cleveland Police Force, which if you consider the following items it may seem a little far fetched that ALL police officers in the Cleveland Police Force are straight as a Roman mile.

I work without fear or favour and for that reason I've got the respect from all sides of the fence, including serving police officers pissed off at how their bent colleagues go about things.

November 1999: West Midland's Police Force was one officer short when WPC Michelle Begley, 29, was jailed for three months for harassing a love rival. Dumped by her boyfriend she tried every trick in the book including illegal use of police computers to try and track down her boyfriend's new lover, Karen Noble. (See previous Viv book relating to abuse of power by civilian worker to breach the Data Protection Act by illegal use of police computers.)

Eventually when Begley and her lover, Lee, got back together she obtained Karen Noble's address and a court heard that Begley savagely attacked her and threatened to plant drugs in her home as well as stab her.

November 1999: PC Iain Myers, 28, head butted company director John Greaves outside of top-notch Merchant Taylors' School, in Crosby, Liverpool after he was belittled for his lack of academic qualifications. Ironically Myers mother worked in the school as a teacher and he was there helping as a volunteer (head-butter) at a wine tasting evening, Myers admitted being a little 'Merry'.

December 1999: When £100,000 ends up in a police officer's pocket questions are asked and that's exactly what happened when Detective Sergeant Trevor Howlett, 44, was found with his fingers jammed firmly in the till. Bogus expense claims were made and Howlett forged his commander's signature in connection with expense claims linked to a Scotland Yard operation to smash car crime gangs. A two-year prison sentence and his pension being confiscated was the end result for this bent cop, never pinch off your own is the keyword here.

March 2000: Fake charge cops get sacked. Three police officers have been sacked because they faked charges against an unnamed man. The man witnessed an incident between a pedestrian and the three cops and as a consequence he offered to be a witness against the police, he was so angered at the way the police had went on that he stuck two fingers up at them in a V-sign gesture, which is not unlawful.

The three cops designed charges against the man so as to get revenge and when the time came for them to attend court as witnesses to support the fake charges they bottled it. As a consequence PCs Matt Percival; 26, John Davies; 26 and Paul Preston, 23, were each fined £100 by the Chief Constable of Greater Manchester Police Force, are they still working?

March 2000: Twelve-pint binge cop jailed. What do you do when you've had twelve pints of beer to drink and you've just crashed your car...well if you're Detective Constable Stefan Gdula, 28, you phone your own station up and report your car stolen of course and hope to get off by perverting the course of justice. Gdula received a two-month prison sentence and resigned from the force, the point here is he was prepared to concoct a story to get out of trouble, which must surely bring all of the cases he worked on out of the cabinet to be scrutinised for any possible mismanagement.

March 2000: Let's stick with drunken cops running away from their own crashed cars for a minute. PC Neil Turner, 32, fled from his crashed BMW after a boozy Christmas party in Manchester, of course he claimed the car had been nicked and just like Gdula was enticed to tell the truth so was Turner, by his cop girlfriend who reported him to her colleagues! Hell hath no fury like a woman scorned.

April 2000: Bribe cop jailed. Ex-cop, Robert Harrington, 58, targeted top horse rider Jamie Osbourne during a probe on horse doping. Jamie, cleared of any wrongdoing, was told that £2,000 would buy justice. How much then would it cost to buy justice from an 18-month prison sentence, because that's what Harrington was given?

April 2000: Christmas came early for money find cops. A villain's home was raided by the Flying Squad and when the police found

£14,000 in notes under the bed Detective Constable Terence McGuiness, 42, said to the others, "Christmas has come early lads." Officers then helped themselves to the cash and in its place was put £14,000 in fake notes. Another incident in which McGuiness used his money grabbing skills was when he was on night duty watching a Royal Mint van that had been hijacked and dumped. Within the van was £300,000 in 10p pieces and surprisingly throughout his watch police cars and police officers in their own private cars were ferrying the bags of coins away presumably to give to the tooth fairy.

There were so many incidents of this type that the police anti-corruption unit (CIB2) set a trap and put £200,000 worth of cannabis in a cupboard in an east London house. CCTV cameras showed McGuiness and another officer jemmying the door open and taking the cannabis away. Long story short – McGuiness informs on the cops, some senior officers, 25 get suspended and two get jail and he ends up doing a nine stretch all in protective custody.

May 2000: 17 cops arrest mum and have to pay £15,000 comp. What can I say, what can anyone say when such brute force is applied by so many to arrest pretty mother of three Joanna Laromani, 37, and frog march her Gestapo style past all of her neighbours and lock her up for eight hours in Sheffield police station, remind me to take a wide berth around that area. Oh the crime, hmmmmm, well er, erm threatening police by asking them to call later for her husband's car insurance details because she needed to pick her four year old son up from school. Joanna still awaits a letter of apology from the police after successfully suing Doncaster police when the court acquitted her of the charges. I bet they walk past Joanna's door in riot gear because the petite languages teacher must be so dangerous.

June 2000: Rapist police officer Sergeant Paul Banfield, 33, from Nottingham was jailed for 18 years for a series of sexual attacks on women. Banfield raped a female while she was held in police custody, indecently assaulted two other women in cells, raped a woman while on duty after breaking into her home and attacked a former girlfriend at her home. The attacks were carried out over a three-year period while serving with the Cambridgeshire Police Force who admitted there had been serious lapses in custody procedures, it would seem that a police station isn't the safest place in the world to be, which accounts for the reason Brian Cockerill was driving like a madman to get away from the police because he says he was in fear of his life yet he got 2 $1/2$ imprisonment for his Brands Hatch driving skills. (See his chapter in this book.)

July 2000: Two cops were jailed for viciously beating up a defenceless man that sought help from them. Peter Crane, the victim, was dragged to the floor and then savagely beaten in a terrifying attack. Peter was running scared from a gang of ten after they attacked him and a friend. PCs Steve Watson, 33, and Barry Vardon, 34, continued the beating even while Peter was handcuffed and the proof of it all was caught on video by a CCTV camera. It was after watching the video that the two officers from Bedford were found guilty and given a jail term of three months each.

As Peter lay motionless on the ground, where he was violently flung by PC Vardon, he was kneed in the stomach by Vardon and then Watson run at him kneeing him in the face, this senseless attack goes on and on for some time where Peter is seen to be repeatedly kneed and punched about the body and yet bail was granted to Watson and Vardon pending appeal. Would you believe that the police then held Peter in custody for some 18 hours after he was assaulted and to top it all off Peter was charged with assaulting the police officers?

Peter's father, a retired police officer at first didn't believe the police would have done such a thing, of course they wouldn't have…well not until the video was revealed. The police even suggested that Peter, who suffered multiple injuries, had a knife, yet in the video he doesn't lift a hand in retaliation and no such weapon is spotted, particularly when he's cuffed up and the beating continues.

The police could have killed Peter and it makes you wonder if stopping a policeman for help is the right thing to do, police need a rise in wages and to be more elite with an emphasis on a higher IQ level for entry into the service and need to be vetted for temperament.

August 2000: PC Desmond Pearson, 53, from Doncaster was jailed for six months for stealing a gun that was handed in by man shocked at the Dunblane massacre, the gun was meant to be melted down.

August 2000: Six top cops were caged at the Old Bailey for their part in a drugs racket. **Detective Constable Robert Clark**, 38 - 12 years, **Detective Sergeant Christopher Drury**, 38 – 11 years, **Detective Constables Thomas Kingston**, 42, and **Thomas Reynolds**, 40 – 3½ years each, **Detective Sergeant Terrance O'Connell**, 43 – two years and **Detective Neil Putnam** went QE (Queen's Evidence – Grassing) and was given a soft sentence. The Metropolitan Police Force are planning huge crackdowns on bent coppers that are stealing drugs that they've just seized in raids on drug dealers, they'd then recycle them back into the drug market on London's streets.

This particular scandal is worthy of a book but here we only have a few lines to put it all in, but in a nutshell it turns out that a registered police informer, Evelyn Fleckney, 43, was selling the recycled drugs for the police that they'd seized in raids and she was also made pregnant, twice, by her unnamed police handler. Drug empress Fleckney was given 15 years imprisonment in 1998 for totally unrelated drugs offences and that's when she spilled the beans and as a consequence six police officers were charged but in reality the drug ring was far bigger and clever cops covered their arses and as a consequence have escaped capture.

December 2000: Flasher cop gets court lashing. Met cop Leon Christodoulou, 26, flashed his erect penis at four 16-year-old girls in a park after nipping out of Wanstead police station in east London. Christodoulou was chased and beaten up by two youths as he tried to make his getaway into a car when he had the cheek to produce his warrant card and probably his get out of jail card because he was given a one year conditional discharge. This sort of thing is usually an old man's game caused by hormonal changes but in Christodoulou's case it was because he was dirty pervert. The magistrate said he'd suffered enough, what about the girls then Mr Magistrate?

February 2000: Full Monty flasher PC carpeted. PC Andrew James, 31, dropped his boxer shorts while off duty (although is a policeman ever off duty) as he gyrated to music used in the film while standing on a 3ft high wall at 3am. South Wales Police gave the PC a reprimand even though the CPS decided there should be no charges brought against him.

May 2000: Porn video business cop. PC Rahul Sampla, 31, set up a porn business called Jolly Roger Productions with partner Graham Bulling, 36, and when police raided his home netted some 14 tapes along with a credit card bill confirming an ad had been placed in a men's gay magazine advising, 'Mind Blowing adult videos, satisfaction guaranteed.' PC Sampla was found guilty in Winchester Crown Court.

January 2001: Lawyer disciplined by cop. When a solicitor goes to a police station to represent his client he doesn't expect to be physically intimidated by a disgruntled cop, but that's what happened to Lee Goodchild of Watson Woodhouse Solicitors when he went to represent his 16-year-old client at Middlesbrough's South Bank police station.

A complaint was lodged with the Police Complaints Authority and it was upheld and found against Detective Constable Ian Martin when a complaint of false imprisonment and technical assault was placed before them. A written warning was given to Martin but Watson Woodhouse who believes the written warning wasn't enough particularly as the boy's mother was present when it happened has appealed against such a cop out.

Such legal representation is sacrosanct and when someone intervenes in such a manner then it has to be said that a written warning may not be a deterrent to stop such intimidation happening to others in such a position.

April 2001: Cop hires his wife as £300 a time porn movie star. PC John Murray, 27, of Willesden Green police station in north west London, sets up deals for his pretty wife Linda, 22, who is Czech born. A national newspaper investigated Murray for his inappropriate behaviour.

July 2001: Detective Inspector Trevor Martin, in his 40s, has been suspended pending an investigation into the claim that he used a tax disc from a police van on his own car. Inside sources said that if he's convicted of this offence then he risks going to prison and losing his pension. Out of all the many hundreds of bent coppers' info I have this has to be the biggest waste of public money I've read about. Inspector Martin helped nail a good few heavy criminals in his time, give it a rest please and concentrate on the real bent coppers, leave him alone.

August 2001: PCs Marc Watson, 27, and Michael Hendy, 23, both of Durham Police Force had two disciplinary charges against each of them proven after a six-month inquiry into allegations of misuse of police transport and inappropriate behaviour. Although no member of the public made complaints it was discovered via the website of www.Teesdale2000 that a sixth former was picked up by a police van from Barnard Castle, in County Durham at 3am on New Year's Eve 2000 and she was driven to a sewage works. Both officers were asked to resign from the force and although they could appeal it has been suggested by a police source that this is highly unlikely.

September 2001: Bum pinch cop gets £1,000 battering. Sergeant Nicholas Banks, 49, was found guilty of indecent assault after a week long trial. Banks ran his hand over a female officer's buxom buttocks and said to her, "You've got a lovely bum." He was ordered to pay the female officer £1,000 compensation and he was also fined £1,000 and had to pay court costs of over £1,000 as well as losing part of his police pension Sergeant Banks resigned from the force.

And on a lighter note on the bent cops side of things, boozy bobbies caused so much damage to a statue of police founder Sir Robert Peel that it will take thousands of pounds to repair. (Police used to be called 'peelers'…no not because thy worked in an onion factory but in honour of their first boss Sir Robert Peel and then they became known as 'bobbies' after his first name (Robert = Bob) - end of history lesson.)

Rookie cops training at the Met's school in Hendon, North London damaged the brass statue by placing an ornamental heron, nicked from a nearby ornamental lake, and placed it on his shoulder so as to make him look like the pirate Long John Silver famed for having a parrot on his shoulder, police are investigating!

I think you're starting to get the picture, I could write a book just on bent coppers because I've got so much material on hundreds of them. Of the examples given I deliberately picked a cross section to show the variance in what makes a bent copper do what he/she does. You'll notice it's the same set of items as in most other peoples' lives that go wrong: Money, Sex and Booze but not necessarily in that order.

In a turnaround to bent cops there is a serving top cop, Inspector Andy Catlin, 39, he's set up a website called www.policecorruption.co.uk, which senior officers were accused of using an 'iron fist' to crush any criticism against them when they had his previous website closed down, but this one's here to stay. The website encourages the public and police officers to come forward and bring things out into the open. Andy has martyred himself because he admits that he will not ever get promotion because of what he's done, I think he should get a knighthood.

Using informers to help secure convictions has always been an easy way for police to secure a result when the case reaches trial. The 'supergrass' system of the 70s has changed dramatically because of the disgust some judges had for the system. Just for one moment looking at how Liverpool's John Haase and Paul Bennett managed to secure a Queen's Pardon in 1996 via Michael Howard for a £15m heroin smuggling conviction we will see how the system once worked and how it works now and that way we will be better able to understand what follows.

The Home Secretary is the man that helped secure the Queen's Pardon for two of Liverpool's (barring Curtis Warren) most well known drug dealers, how it came about has been suggested to me directly by John in a communication we had a short while back. I was certainly surprised at his suggestion, but because Michael Howard is a rich man I can't risk disclosing what's been revealed to me, whether this allegation is true or not I dare not comment on but maybe in time all will come out, as the truth does.

Haase, 50, and Bennett, 37, were each sentenced to 18 years imprisonment for masterminding one of Merseyside's biggest drug rings. Two Turks Yilmaz Kaya and Suleyman Ergun regularly travelled from London to Liverpool to collect huge bagfuls of money to take back to Turkey to buy drugs and as a consequence all were arrested and some 87k of heroin was seized.

Both Haase and Bennett entered a guilty plea to the Turkish connection £15m drug deal but it was said that after each had struck a deal to turn supergrass that pardons were granted, which went against all the principles of doing away with the supergrass system, which adds some credibility to what John claims really went on.

When you consider that the Home Office in 1996 asked the press not to reveal the release of Haase and Bennett it adds weight to Haase's revelation. Big time criminal gangs are well financed and most deals are done on 'trust', buy now and if you don't pay later get your legs blown off sort of thing.

Currently John Haase has been convicted on further unconnected charges and entered a guilty plea at his trial in 2001 and is now serving nine years imprisonment.

Past informants have worked on the supergrass system by being groomed by police into spilling the beans on their former colleagues in the crime world in return for lighter sentences usually served in safe houses with the trimmings of every day life.

The supergrass tariff was usually five years while their associates would be looking at 20+ years behind the doors of the slammer. This method worked quite well until the judges got sick of seeing the system being held to ransom by such supergrasses. The straw that broke the camels back was in 1979 when Judge Michael Argyle called two of the Crown Prosecution witnesses as 'two of the most dangerous criminals in British history…and as a matter of policy they have been sentenced to five years each.' The men he was referring to were David Smith and George Williams.

Now at the end of the 70's the 'registered informant' was born and along with the informant came a few added extras particularly demonstrated by the relationship Teesside's Mr Big, David Charrington, had with his handlers and when I say 'handlers' I mean of course that Charrington was an informer.

The new regime meant that when their man in the know had informed them that something 'big' was coming off in the crime world then they had to let it come off even if it meant risking the lives of the public because they wouldn't get a prosecution otherwise so the job has to run. If the informant gives the police the time and date whatever it is it going to happen then they must wait for that to happen and let people commit serious crimes whilst under surveillance.

Along came a dirty word, well two words exactly, and that was *agent provocateur*. Those two words can send shivers up any self-respecting copper's back. The danger was that if the informant was involved with the gang and classed as a 'participating informant' then of course the defence can claim that the informant was an agent provocateur and without his involvement the crime would not have taken place therefore the crime may well have been commissioned by the particular authorities (Police/Customs & Excise) bringing about the charges thereby allowing them to walk free.

Of course an insurance policy in the form of a 'Get out of Jail' card can help the informer tremendously and as touched on earlier the informant builds up their relationship with enthusiastic or bent coppers and this is exactly what Charrington did when he took part in the importation of £200m worth of cocaine inside of metal ingots back in 1993.

Men of the character of Charrington are used frequently in order to secure convictions and bearing in mind all of this I would ask you to then consider what I write about Phil Berriman and what he told me directly when I tell you that he is NOT, as far as I am aware on the basis of what he says, an informant although others are still claiming that he was an informant, I would hope you'd have been given a valuable insight into the murky world of drug smuggling.

I owe this Chapter and the next two to Phil by means of an apology for what the media advised about him being an informant although the Observer newspaper gallantly fought to have reporting restrictions lifted and won and because of that they covered the truth. What I am about to reveal later on goes into the depths of the deepest-seated police corruption that could ever be revealed.

Before we go into Phil's side of things I'd like to show how corrupt police can use informers to their advantage and to do that I've asked London's monarch of the underworld Dave Courtney to be able to tell me how it works. Dave was accused of being an informer by the police in a direct propaganda exercise meant to discredit Dave's image with the public and the underworld and perhaps induce someone to kill him!

Dave is able to reveal the lies told about him in court and just as similarly Phil Berriman suffered in the same way but as equally as Dave proved them all wrong so did Phil in a very remarkable way in which he proved the police were lying, even on oath in the witness box of a Crown Court!

4

Monarch of the Underworld

What follows in this chapter, I believe, is the second most important chapter in this book. For the knowledgeable amongst you then you'll know what I mean, if you don't then by time you finish it you will.

Dave takes up the story, "Strokes were pulled, in the court case I've just been put through. First of all I would like to explain the informant bit. As you know certain people have help from certain corrupt policemen, the 'Fake Informant Relationship' makes all this possible. The police computer is an Aladdin's cave of priceless information and knowledge. But the problem is how does your bent copper justify' using his personal number to enter the computer and retrieve all the required information without alerting suspicion? Easy! If you are down as an informant he can help with 'My informant Mr X thinks he can help with…'

Whatever case you need to know about, and you give me all the information you have on it, and bingo, out it comes. The beauty of this is that you don't actually grass anyone up at all, because you are flagged to that certain policeman, if you are being investigated by any other officer, they would actually contact that officer for help with their enquiries, he would then give you advance warning of who was looking at you, where from and why, he can actually specify what premises the surveillance equipment are in, what department the officers were from and the registration of any cars that would be following you, absolutely invaluable information.

CJB3 knew exactly what my relationship was with the policeman Austin Warnes and he knew he had never given me anything to do for him at all. All of these illegal activities still went on regularly even though I was trying very hard to keep away from him myself, he constantly pestered me to register with him. I thought I'd found a better one but he reported me to CIB3 for trying to bribe him.

If you were ever spotted with your bent copper he can easily justify it by using the informer thing. Now the cloak of secrecy surrounding the informant for his or her protection is the same cloak of secrecy that they use to avoid getting captured for all their illegal activities. It works as a perfect cover for everything, if they slip off for a crafty shag, for a few hours, they just put it down on the sheet as 'went to see an informant.' If they want to have a night out and still get paid for it, as well as providing an excuse for her in doors, they need to just put down they went to see their informant, even if they just want a bit of poxy overtime, they just put it on a poxy docket. They don't have to explain whom because it is a big secret.

The big earner for them is because they can just go in to the bottomless pit of money and take case lump sums to pay their informer, who then signs for it in a moody name in front of the coppers and fucks off with the cash, half an hour later they meet to split the cash 50/50. This is done by all the anonymous calls that came in. There is no informant at all. If the information leads to arrests and convictions the copper just writes out some fake informant sheets saying the information was obtained by him, exactly the same as Austin Warnes did in my case, getting it out of the informant.

He then just puts it down to a couple of fake informants he is already using or just gets a new one to turn up and sign on the dotted line, Mickey Mouse and off walks Mickey with a bag of untaxed, unreported cash. If someone was awaiting trial and a had few months left before court, he could be registered and attributed success cases so that if and when a prison sentence was imposed on him, the fact that he had helped in the other cases will always secure a smaller sentence or a walk out. Another perk for the policeman using the informant system is the ability to re-house acquaintances, mistresses and anyone else that wants to pay.

They also get the information obtained by the bent officer in the car after the arrest on the way to the station, before it is all taped, you know, is there anything you want to tell me about anyone, I might be able to help you out a bit if you do that old chestnut. They also have a network of other bent coppers up and down the entire country that helps each other in many different ways. Such as if they are in the position to know of a pending arrest on someone and have the information on the person and his crime.

They just ring it through to another bent one in the station miles away and they get another one of the fake informants to come in with the info. Another good earner using the fake informant system is the massive amounts the press pay out for information given to them for advanced warnings of things about to happen and for information on very sensitive cases that they don't want getting out, all of these the bent policeman can do, but he needs a middle man to talk to the reporter and collect the money, even if it is Mickey Mouse, so do the press, so they use the fake informant.

Now I have been very aware and instrumental in providing a large number of bent old bill that directly and indirectly came from Austin Warnes and his immediate circle of close friends, with people to use in these ways. Obviously they can't be seen running round looking for them can they? I know this isn't attractive to listen to but you have got to hear the lot, and then you may begin to understand my actions and growing concerns for my family's and my welfare.

You may consider that what I'm doing now is informing on someone but I feel that having been in the position to have learnt all their dirty tricks it is my duty to let everyone out there know of them, and I now make my money touring the country doing 'An Audience With' where I spend all evening telling everyone exactly what happens, I also know that the authorities are well aware of this. (Book Dave through the website: www.crimebizz.com)

It was beneficial for me and mine to being around this fake informant scam in many ways, and because I knew everything that went on, just like the police pretend to be somebody else to get into a group of people just to obtain information for their own gains, I did the same, and they didn't like it and don't want to reveal how easy it is to get into them or how widespread it is.

Viv - The Final Chapter

They had to pretend to like me and vice versa. It was then I became aware of them trying to set me up, and knowing how good at it they were, I tried to scare them off by revealing little things in the newspapers, letting them know that I could if I wanted to, do a lot of damage to them as well. I put in many complaints to the police and Sir Paul Condon, about the harassment I was getting, such as things constantly being confiscated from me and friends constantly being quizzed leaving my home.

I was now aware that the help I was receiving from Austin Warnes was definitely gone, and had been replaced with what seemed like a new zest to catch Dave Courtney at anything. But it had become very awkward because he is now an asset to a lot of my friends, this being the main reason that I decided to renew the association with Warnes as I did when he came to me in a panic and explained why he needed to show his superiors what the relationship was between me and him. He said they suspected him of being on the take and that he was bang in trouble and could I help him out of a spot of bother, he was obviously in blind panic and I took advantage of the situation he was apparently in and got him to agree to do something, which would guarantee he would no longer be a threat to me and cover myself in case the whole thing was a trap, by him and the other lot to entrap me into something that they intended to use against me.

I was wrong, but it was only the fact that I was aware of their tactics that I even thought that way, and done it for my own reasons. I did not accept any reward or accept any favours; I did not want to be part of their scam, whatever it was. I felt I was keeping open a door that everyone I know can benefit from when in trouble, and if the shit ever hit the fan it was purely on my head alone. Because I've been involved for some time that's how I got to know the unsavoury uses they have for some of the people they use. I am pleased to say that I have not, to my knowledge, ever supplied anyone for these dirty deeds, but it has helped explain to me how they actually avoid being caught fitting people up, and how they fool judges, juries, colleagues and worst of all the general public. They use informants as fake witnesses, and pay them out of the informants funds, by just attributing a conviction down to them, and with the help of a couple of fake informant sheets, it's not even so much as queried.

Now personally the use I found most disturbing they have for informants is when in a jury, if their policeman knows any of the officers involved in the case, he will inform them he has someone on the jury if they need him, just to guarantee another guilty vote, once again they would pay him from the informants fund.

They would also be used as a pick-up man in the drugs bust where they leave behind 5k of the 10k of cocaine, and by the time they get to the station and charge the man with 5kilos, no-one in the world would jump up and say, 'No, there was 10,' do they? Austin would always make sure that the fake informants were registered to other bent officers, but would continue to help them by feeding them information that was already known by the police, but would make your reliability look good. Like when he put my friend's kidnapping and robbery charge down to me giving him the information, which was in court proved to be another fake informant sheet.

They also use them when they want to catch someone out on the phone they are bugging in an investigation, and at a designated time they ring the number and leave a very damaging message on the answer phone, cos they had prior knowledge that no-one would be in at the time, and two or three done over the next week or two, when played to the jury in court, would have the desired effect, and no matter how loud he shouts, 'I don't know who that is, or what the fuck they're talking about,' it all adds weight to the prosecutions case of finding 5k of cocaine in the shed, which he also said he knew nothing about, and is even more shocked to find out that a registered informant will be paid if he gets convicted.

With Austin going 'guilty' I was unable to question him or prove him a liar. So not only was it a very good damage limitation exercise, in the fact that it stopped me exposing and embarrassing the police force with another major police corruption case, it also ensured my death. They know I aint gonna run away and it would be such sweet revenge for them to actually get me shot for being a 'grass'. Now I know that's a big accusation, but seeing as I know they knew the whole truth, not only did they fail to enlighten the jury of that fact, but they also seriously embellished on the truth, with claims that I was actually tasked with things to do as an informant.

And references to the length of time I was associated with Austin Warnes, the misplaced letters I had sent to the CIB3 letting them know that I knew exactly what they were up to. But not imagining all this at the time and for purely my own safety reasons, after talking it over with my lady and some friends, I decided to help Austin, and the safe-guards I took was that my lady takes a photo of him talking into a Dictaphone sitting beside me and saying that I am not an informant at all, and that I was just helping him out of a spot of bother with his boss as to why he associated with me and I didn't have any success rate on my informants list.

No convictions were expected out of this, it was just a visual show to his boss that he was in control, and because the people were supposedly fictitious, it didn't matter that I had forgotten most of the facts when I saw his boss. I just made the rest up, I never knew even knew the girl ever existed. That and the fact that they are never checked up on, he could just say it came to nothing. But he could still enter the computer on the strength of your signature.

But the twist in the tail in this little scenario for me was, what I didn't know was that he'd helped set someone up for drugs about a month previous, and it had all gone wrong. He had without my knowledge, put me down as the informant he had used, and was now being pressured to produce that informant, and that was the panic I saw when he came to me. I was looking for something completely different. It never entered my head that the people were real, and that was the scam. I had absolutely fuck all to do with it and had never heard of James, his wife or Reece, and the crime had already happened weeks before I was manipulated into the situation. As the judges stated, '...the conspiracy was already complete before I was brought into it.'

They changed the date of the arrest and left it open until they could get me, then started pressurizing Austin to produce his informant, knowing he didn't have one, and that it had been Reece, who on tape had given him the information. Also in the knowledge that to cover himself, Austin had put in fake informant sheets with my name on them, so they got Austin to deliberately bring me into the trap, that they had planned to eventually get me killed. All had gone according to plan until I produced the Dictaphone tape (See next chapter relating to a similar use of an audio cassette tape.) and photograph. With that and his statement they had no reason to continue taking me to court, and would lose an excellent opportunity to get rid of at best a 'Thorn in their side'. Also the evidence that the CIB had accumulated to convict Warnes and Reece if made public, would be very damaging indeed for the entire police force, and where the Met and CIB fail to communicate, when it was made public, it was a bit late for someone to be told it would be too much bad publicity, just to convict one corrupt policeman.

Also by now, they had done all their investigating and realised that everything I had told them was the truth. Now this was when the normally very independent CIB3 and the Met combined forces and came up with their, 'Lets get Dave Courtney shot' plan, which I must admit, made me look at things a bit different. At first knowing I'd explained completely to the CIB3 exactly who was the handler and who was the informer in this relationship and told them that if they looked they would find all the facts they needed to catch their bent copper they were after and completely prove my innocence, I'd also in my ignorance expected them to make public what they had found out. How wrong I was. Instead, what happened was a friend of mine came and showed me some of the informant dockets concerning Kim James and Ian Tucker that had apparently 'leaked out' onto the street.

Now in my world if someone was to accuse anyone of being a 'grass', they would say: 'Show me the paperwork,' and if they did show the paperwork that would normally be a death certificate for the person involved, and he would also be the last person to know of it's existence. And unless you knew the way in which the police work, you would believe it to be true, but it is a very old, yet effective method the police use for a number of different reasons. It is the easiest thing in the world for them to do just fill out an informant sheet, saying anything they want, about anyone they want, in order to orchestrate death and unrest in the group of people they were concentrating on. Anyway, I was fortunate enough to have them brought to me. I met and informed CIB3 of their existence and demanded an explanation. I was offered the witness protection programme and told that they didn't know how they had got out. I should have known by then what their ultimate goal was, but I didn't as yet. Austin was still lying through his teeth trying to say this was the very first thing he had done illegal concerning me. The CIB chose to publicly believe him, but secretly they knew the truth. It's like saying, that if you stole £5 from your dad's wallet every Friday night when he came home from the pub for the last 15yrs, on the night you got caught, would you say, I've been doing it every Friday night for the last 15yrs, or that it was the first and only time you'd ever done it? EXACTLY.

My solicitor questioned why they were still intending to put me through a very high profile trial that I would be found not guilty in. The explanation was that in case Austin was going to try to say not guilty like his co-defendants, they needed my tape I had of him confessing all, as a part of their evidence. And as it was my evidence against him so they kept me charged just to make sure the tape was played in court, and as soon as the judge heard the tape, I'd be found 'not' guilty and they could then use the tape to crucify' him, and they expected me to be happy about this. To put it mildly, I wasn't, and tried to make what they were doing to me very public, which is what made them try to stop me getting bail.

I had learnt from an experience a few years ago whilst on remand at Belmarsh, of another little ploy they use. They don't mind nicking you for things that they know you're going to get not guilty for, if they can nick a year off you being on remand. This was actually said to me personally by my arresting officer, that, seeing with what you've got away with in the past Courtney, you couldn't moan at us nicking a year off you! In my case they received one of those anonymous phone calls saying that I was going to make an attempt to escape, just like Kenny Noye's anonymous one, (more shit), and I was promptly whisked off to the maximum security unit at Belmarsh, and nobody gets bail from there, reason being, you and the judge are surrounded by machine gun toting policemen while you are pleading your innocence. And once you had been in the unit, you would do your remand, if ever arrested again, at the unit. And knowing that little trick I was ready when they tried it again. Another reason for the anonymous call is, create the excuse first and then do the dirty deed, so if and when it comes on top they've got an almost solid excuse.

The press had printed that I was an informant (as they did with Phil Berriman in the next chapter.) and the fake dockets were out on the street, and if they could lock me up for a year or put me on a witness protection programme, it would be very hard for me to protest my innocence, as it is for Mr Noye.

They put me on fifty grand bail, but I had to leave it (in cash), in their hands the whole time, and they definitely didn't expect me to produce this. I said in a letter to the chief of police and my MP, that I didn't agree with what they were doing to me but I understood why they were doing it as a ploy to ensure the tape be played in court. What I couldn't understand was that if I didn't produce fifty grand, they were going to lock me up for a year knowing I had fuck all to do with it, if you could please would you explain it to me? I also feel that I am singled out and persecuted for things that anyone else in the courtroom can say in their evidence to provide the truth.

I have not changed one word of my original explanation of the whole matter from the very first day, and after thoroughly investigating it all and knowing it all to be true, when I gave them some names of friends of mine that had also received benefits from being able to enter the police computer and didn't mind coming to court to admit this and explain exactly what and when they received help, while being interviewed they were cautioned that if they did admit receiving help gained from the police computer, they would be re-charged for the original crime.

They even got into the maximum security unit in Belmarsh to interview a man who could verify using Austin's help, by gaining entry into the police computer for information on a number of occasions, using my name, but was also given the same caution that he would be re-arrested and charged, so at first it was difficult for me to convince these people to come forward. But after Ian Tucker in the witness box, asked the judge if he'd be arrested if he told the truth on how many times he had used Austin's help, and it was just Austin's cover to get into the computer, (exactly what I had said in the first place), everybody on the list of people that was read to me in court, agreed to come in and give evidence, now knowing that no charges would be brought for doing so.

After Tucker and my lady Jennifer had been in the box and severely damaged their claims that I was actually a real informant, my witnesses were then cut from 19 to 7, because their plan was starting to backfire. They continued to press on to hopelessly try to justify my actually being in the Old Bailey at all. It was plainly obvious to see that if I honestly thought that I was going to be a part of the plot to put two innocent women in prison by planting drugs on them so that the estranged husband could win a custody baffle over the child, which all sounds too unbelievable to actually be true, but it was, I would have gone further than the end of my road to meet him and I doubt very much if I would have brought my wife along to witness this proud event and photograph it while I was taping it, would I? But that is exactly what I did, and the rest of the case is common knowledge, as reported in the papers. But for some reason no reports were printed on the fact that I had in fact taped him saying that I was not an informant or that I had asked to bring to court as my witnesses everyone they said I'd informed on, or the fact that they had actually tried to take my bail away 4 times during the case, or the fact that seeing as they had had every word spoken in my home for the last 4 years, they knew that I had left that life behind, and deliberately dragged me back into it any way they could.

It was obviously more beneficial for them to allow it to be said that I was an informant. Everything I am explaining to you is all on record and will be easily accessible to you. I am aware that by sending you all this information on the court case and their tactics, the CIB3 will be busily cleaning up their act and so will the Met, hopefully well before the investigation gets underway, but I don't mind because I'm not using any other documents than the ones used in the original trials findings and as this case proves the fact that it appears to be an official police document does not necessarily mean that that it's contents are genuine.

I also know that it is only human that when you are admitting something that you are obviously in the wrong for and will be punished in some way, you don't needlessly admit to things that would cause more problems if you don't feel they have to come out. Austin applied this tactic in his statement, the CIB used this tactic when giving their evidence and I used this tactic when explaining to the CIB about the uses of Austin, because it would have meant me giving my friends names as part of my events without asking them, which is in fact exactly what I had said to them on tape. 'If getting myself out of trouble here means putting someone else in it without his knowledge, then I am afraid I am not prepared to do that.'

This was also said in open court, but for some strange reason never made the papers either. Far from being embarrassed of my original police interview, I actually had copies run off and delivered to the people I considered, had the right to be shown the proof immediately and not have to wait to read it in the press a year later. And thank god I did, considering what had been printed. It is far from uncommon for a man in my position at the time to have inside help from corrupt policemen, and over the years, what has turned out to be the biggest bonus to all my friends, is to actually know what dirty tricks they can play in securing fake evidence in a case.

What has got to be the easiest and most common is the simple anonymous, letters, notes and phone calls, one of these can and does cause immense changes in events in whatever case it is used, such as the one to the prison saying you are going to attempt to escape whilst on remand, ensures that when you are actually at trial, both you and the judge will be surrounded by armed officers, and all the jury members will have armed guards sleeping in their homes, how are they honestly expected to maintain an unbiased opinion of the man in the dock? The anonymous phone call to a juror while the trial is in progress is always a good one. The anonymous phone call to the police station saying they have seen drugs entering the premises, the warrant is served on the premises before the caller even gets into the station, and in the following raid finds 5k of cocaine.

As one of the police's educational tips are 'Divide & Conquer', which I must say is so true. On the bits of information he said he'd learnt from colleagues, I had to decipher what was and what wasn't true before acting on it, for instance, he once told me that someone I knew was gonna shoot me because I was being blamed for a murder I hadn't done, he has actually named some of my closest allies as informants.

Also, if anyone is under surveillance they know all the secrets that are kept away from the wife and before the eventual arrest, the anonymous phone call has enlightened her on his other woman, ensuring a break down in the relationship before they eventually arrest him at the spot of their own choice, normally being at the other woman's or man's home as the case may be. Or the anonymous call to a wife whose husband has been served an injunction and on a taped conversation a strange man threatens her life again, it's, 'Go to jail' and forget the £200. Or the anonymous phone call to a gang member informing him of the fact that one of his colleagues is an informant letting him know a fact that only he (and an investigating police officer) would know, if you can catch my drift! And I know of many, many more, but won't bore you with them.

When I first informed CIB that there were fake dockets on the street, which I thought were coming from Austin, who to my complete and utter amazement had been granted bail, they assured me that his home was bugged and that it most certainly wasn't him, and when I asked if my home too was bugged, they took the fifth and couldn't say one way or the other, which didn't surprise me, as I already knew that I was under heavy surveillance and had been for some time now, which was clarified in court, I had been under surveillance for many years.

I suppose I'll have to live with that, but I always thought it was illegal to listen to a man preparing his case, which is why you have legal visits in prison and was exactly what I was doing in my own home. And after showing me a video in court of my house on the morning I met Austin, they would find it very difficult to deny they were doing it. I then learnt weeks after down to someone's big mouth, while out drinking on a boat, that he had a tape of me explaining to my wife exactly what I was going to say in my defence and after learning it off by heart, was completely distraught when he heard that I was not getting in the dock, but he consoled himself in the knowledge that I would soon be shut up for good.

Monarch of the Underworld

I had decided to let everyone else explain their own facts, this accusation I cannot prove (yet) because legal men stick together the same as naughty men do, but I need to let him know that I knew, and that little plan didn't work and nor will this one. I actually do believe that in trying to do what they done to me, that they have shot themselves in the foot because if I was now a real informant out there, looking at this case, I would not feel too safe with my handlers assurance that my identity and information I had given them, would not be made public knowledge, and must also be very worried about what has been put on their informant sheets and about who. And now that I have enlightened you on exactly how the fake informant is used to steal taxpayer's money amongst other things.

It seems far more important for the authorities to make sure that crime is not glamorised and try to brainwash the public into thinking that because you do something naughty as a job that you must be a horrible evil human being and always will be. They will go to great lengths and much expense to drum this fact home at every given opportunity, but I'm afraid they are very wrong. They would even refuse £1m donated to help a London child, from the sale of a record made by the icons in the crime world, rather than have everybody say that they are nice fellahs and it's a work of art, the way they cause unrest and ill feeling in a camp with the seed planting and using the criminal grape vine to send out their own messages for whatever reason they want, and the grapevine is the most deadliest thing in the whole world as we all well know. Good news travels fast, but bad news travels faster. And they know how and when to say certain things in certain company to cause complete chaos and unrest. They will fuel that fire because it is so much harder to get into and destroy a firm of chaps, if they are all quite comfortable in the fact that they can trust each other completely, than it is if they are all running around fighting and accusing each other. And they do this with the power of the media and the press. And with that power they manipulate and orchestrate things to happen that in normal circumstances wouldn't have happened at all. And in using this method and relying on the general publics imagination as it is, it appears they had no involvement in it at all.

And also relying on the fact that the average criminal only thinks of tomorrow and the police think long term, and sometimes their goal is not to put you in prison at all, but to let you run and run because you are an endless source of information about criminal activities, by unknowingly revealing all in everyday conversation to someone that is in fact a police informant that has been tasked to befriend them for a period of 5yrs or more, that they all inevitably get shafted.

I am also fully aware that lately what has been looked upon as clever policing, is nothing more than learning a suspects everyday movements, and purely inventing a crime, and with a little help from someone or something, just wait for the right time to arrest him in his most embarrassing position and know that in investigating the crime his lifestyle will look very suspect, and inevitably secure a conviction. As simple as just putting one of his dog ends at the scene of a crime, and with DNA evidence against him, even his own solicitor would advise him to go guilty.

Now I am not saying at all that every CIB and police officer use these tactics, but obviously as the police force grows in size every year, common sense will tell you that it would be impossible to keep the same standards as you can with a smaller unit. Instead of combating this by making the examination and the physical requirements harder and bigger to get into the police force, they have in fact made changes in both these requirements, by considerably lowering the standard so now you can be arrested by a retarded midget, (what the fuck is that about?).

I'm very lucky that lots of people knew what I had done to get information, but if it hadn't been for the fact their plan may have worked, with the amount of time and effort put into it. They did not expect me to have a TV crew following me before the arrest, during the trial and after I got not guilty.... And me cockily predicting exactly what was going to happen, well it was easy. I was told that they were very concerned over what was happening and fully intended to stop it whatever way they could, and they did for a complete year. The week my book came out I could have no press at all because I was on bail. If only the public were allowed to see his bank statement, then I think they would know who was the informer and who was the handler.

As for the CPS and the CIB trying to say they didn't know I was going to get not guilty, and the CPS also thought there was a good case against me. Why did they then, when arresting me for not being a grass, but for actually doing exactly what I said I did with him, did they ask me to come back and sign on in February at the nick if I was going to go to prison in November? I am also aware that since the Russian invasion of very hi-tec surveillance gear they only need a warrant if they intend to use the surveillance tapes as evidence in court. But to just listen to whatever is being said on your phone and in your home for a year and then nick you when they hear it's the right time to hit you, and then putting it down as good police work, and an informant told them it all and he wants X amount of pounds.

But I want you to know just what they all got up to with me and why they did it to me. And just in case I happen to be the one telling the truth, which with not a lot of effort you'll find out, you'll of course understand my feeling of urgency when I ask you to investigate what I am telling you. By publicly saying I'm a real informer, they give themselves the cover to do to me whatever they want, and it would look as if the criminal fraternity had done it.

It's not the newest of tricks in the book, but as I said before, it works, and your safe in the knowledge that the public wouldn't believe a word of it, it is all far too JAMES BONDish for them to comprehend. But I know different and I'm sure you do, but to put my family and me in such a vulnerable position, and that is exactly what they have done, is evil in anybodys eyes. And just in case it was meant to stop me talking about it to anybody, I'll make sure I let someone know and that someone is you.

From where I am standing, it is not actually asking for the help that is a crime, giving it away when you aint suppose to, might be. Surely the crime for someone like me was, if I knew a way to keep one of my friends out of prison, and I didn't use it, then that is the crime.' Not being allowed the opportunity of using the actual people involved to stand up and give evidence for me and an awful lot of other reasons, that they all had a hand in orchestrating a situation that was meant to get me shot.

Viv - The Final Chapter

Knowing that the judge had all this information in front of him for weeks, and allowed it to continue as well as helping out for future arrests with the odd hostile comment, makes me wonder. Which brings me nicely to the very big question mark that surrounds the decision the CPS made in allowing this case to go forward and including me with absolutely no evidence whatsoever, in order to validate my continuation on these charges, and leaves me no option but to believe they were all equally involved in this conspiracy. Because without the CPS' decision to give the go-ahead to continue with the charges against me and give the CIB3 their very public platform to orchestrate my assassination, after investigating everything I had said and finding it all to be fact, this whole event could not have happened.

Now please forgive me if I sometimes appear to be needlessly spiteful, but after having the police want me for so many years and I've only ever answered their feeble attempts to rope me into things purely down to my name, with what I consider 'jovial banter". Like bringing the surveillance men beers, giving the front door key to the police station, fliers, posters and cheeky literature in the tabloids and the odd "not guilty" when I was. But now I feel that without any shadow of a doubt, they have tried to get me killed, I have no option but to fight back and quickly make public what they are trying so hard to keep under cover, that they would completely mislead the public by using the powers of the press, which I know only too well; into believing I was an informant. And to go to such lengths as to threaten potential witnesses including myself, that we would be arrested if we told the truth about Austin's corrupt dealings, just to keep it under wraps. Thank fuck Mr. Tucker called their bluff in admitting that he had received help from Austin, whilst in the dock, and on investigation, it was proved that he had. The robbery and kidnapping case that Austin had attributed that I had informed on.

The authorities knew that it was always going to be hard for me to produce the witnesses to substantiate my claims, when they were under the impression that they would be arrested if they tried to help out in this case. By them proving that Tucker did actually receive help but was not going to be charged for exposing them, it gave the green light for everyone else to come forward and tell the truth without the fear of being charged. While on the subject of witnesses, here is a list of witnesses both the judge and the prosecution ruled as being irrelevant to my case.

*The evidence from a doorman of a fetish club, that Austin had at one time frequented quite often, that he had boasted of a catalogue of goodies that he could obtain from the police stores, such as bulletproof vests, night sticks, pepper sprays and complete uniforms for both men and women, please tell me how that was ruled irrelevant to my case, where I was saying that he was a corrupt policeman, nearly everyone I know got their vests from Austin.

*A leading crime correspondent for a daily newspaper, who while undercover doing research for a crime book, witnessed Austin asking for more men to be informants for two of his friends. This was eight years ago.

*Also a journalist who had broke the Kenny Noye story and was prepared to say where he had got the information from.

*The newspaperman that I had approached and asked to help me try to expose Austin trying to sell me quantities of drugs with a colleague, and after alerting my solicitor that he'd tried to set me up, I was advised to go to the newspapers, but was refused help.

*A representative from Virgin publishing and from Front magazine, both whom have had phone calls from a man claiming to be a serving policeman, and was not happy with what was going to be done to me prior to my arrest. Also after the first week in court, I realised just how easy it is to portray a completely different outlook on something by bending the truth, and felt I had to do something drastic to prove was not lying with my claims. So I rang and spoke to CIB3 and informed them of another corrupt officer who had come unstuck with a fit-up, and was looking for a fake informant to justify his actions, I also informed my QC, who in turn informed the prosecution and once again it was ruled irrelevant.

Also a witness who was found to be not guilty in the trial concerning the leaked documents from the CPS containing the 20 top informants, (which I wasn't on by the way), explaining how Austin was very instrumental in this case as well. The police losing all records of my numerous complaints of harassment, the letters lost by CIB and the refusal by the judge to allow the jury to see literature where I had exposed these corrupt officers before, in newspapers and magazines. But what I feel to be the biggest injustice of all was being refused to bring up as my witnesses, the people they said I'd informed on, which would have completely destroyed their ultimate goal. Also deemed irrelevant, was the passages from both my books that were withdrawn by the Virgin publishing team, prior to them being published, that also exposed the corrupt ways in which the police operate. These books are on sale in any good bookshop (£16.99, Stop the ride I want to get off and Raving Lunacy. But I think you will be more interested in the book about the case, which will be exposing everything, it will be called '*The Ride's Back On*'.

When my witness Mr Smith revealed that he had been paying Mr Warnes £500 a week for advanced knowledge of any future raids on his unlicensed nightclub, and Austin had approached him to be a fake informant to make it easier for Austin to help him, they couldn't shut him up quick enough. Also the man they flew to New Zealand to find because of an accusation I made, that Austin had tried to bribe him into placing a package in the safe of my pub, The Albion, also turned up and said exactly that, he too had been approached and asked if he'd be a fake informant, and was treated with a gift of a large wad of fake fifty pound notes. The final straw for them was when another businessman also admitted to using Austin's resources for any colleagues that were in need of his help.

The fact that Mr McGirr explained in his evidence that the invaluable information he had received from Austin had enabled him to expose another large police corruption case in Bexleyheath concerning false allegations and fraud which is still being investigated. As a long term friend, had witnessed many of the corrupt goings on using the 'fake informant' system, and was in fact the witness that I spoke to on the morning that I met Austin, and to whom I'd fully explained my intentions to. He also witnessed the event from afar, due to my concerns as to what had made Austin so panic-stricken. For whatever strange reason, the press failed to report any of these facts, but the jury had to sit there for almost 8wks, having the facts drummed into them, and on my acquittal, the complete jury took it upon themselves to come into the pub, opposite the Bailey, and explain to me that after the first three days, they knew I was nothing to do with this case whatsoever, and it wasn't until mid-way through that they had realised why they had brought me here. Not being one to miss an opportunity, I took full advantage of the fact that there was TV cameras, photographers and journalists from all over, made sure that I got all their thoughts on the trial recorded, and a couple of photographs with the jury for good measure.

You must already know the trouble I'm having, legally trying to publish these interviews and photos. Their main question was that they had always thought that the police would rather drop all charges than produce an informant, and no one had ever heard of a case where a man was being tried for being one, and if I were a genuine informant, at my level, why on earth would they want to expose me? How lucky I felt to be so important. The fact that everyone had been mislead, misinformed and manipulated into a situation where they thought I was a real informant and not someone who had been lured into an evil trap; which is exactly what I truly felt had happened to me, and is the reason that I refused to get in the dock with any of the other defendants, especially Austin Warnes, who had helped in this plan, and also why I knocked him out 'on sight' in Bow St. magistrates court, and I wasn't surprised at all that he did not press any charges, because I still think he'd had a touch, considering what he was prepared to help instigate, have happen to me. Don't you?

It's easy to see, if you think about it, why the embarrassing factor helped to keep it such a big secret from the public. Obviously the informant can't tell everyone what he gets up to, to earn all his money, as the very word 'informant' sends shivers down peoples spines, he'd be far too embarrassed. The corrupt officer can't let it be known to anyone else, except another corrupt officer, because if caught, the embarrassment to the police force would be immense, and when CIB investigated it and found how incredibly easy and widespread it was to gain entry to the police computer and relieve the Treasury of millions of pounds each year, they were too embarrassed to reveal to the public, the lull extent of this problem and decided to completely deny that any of these practices existed, and to make sure I can't broadcast these facts, they created the life threatening situation I faced after my acquittal. Maybe they thought that I would be too embarrassed to admit what I'd got involved with, in order to have the edge for me and all my colleagues, but how wrong they were. This is once again, a prime example of why it is wrong for the police to investigate the police. An independent body would have seen straight through this from the start. What the CIB and Austin have conjured up for me in the near future I dread to think. To receive just 4yrs for his major part in this hideous crime, he must have agreed to help them an awful lot in something, perhaps he is already exposing more fake informants to ensure he gets his appeal granted speedily."

There you have it and now that's out in the open let's hope the police can clean up their act on the fake informants scam. I've published what Dave has said because I don't believe many other publishers would publish this sort of thing apart from Blake Publishing who would. The Masonic movements of the judiciary are very clever indeed and their connections go deep within the publishing world so a few words in the right place can stop this sort of thing from being published.

I should know especially when Jack Straw had me in court and managed to get prison CCTV footage showing prison officers in HMP Birmingham beating Charles Bronson black and blue removed from a video documentary I directed about Charlie. It showed what really goes on yet no one has been prosecuted for this violent attack on hard man Bronson yet I was given a three week suspended prison sentence if I didn't stop advertising the video. The footage had to be cut from the video; it's still on sale minus the prison CCTV footage and can be ordered in the rear of this book.

Dave's got another book coming out next year called *Dave's Little Black Book* and of course his video due for release soon called *Dave Courtney's Underworld*. Don't forget that you can book Dave for an Event/Audience With/Act in your film on: www.crimebizz.com

5

Phil Berriman – Captain Hook

I hope that you are a little wiser after having read the previous chapter as to how informers are used by some police officers and how police use propaganda to set the wheels of retribution in motion.

On 4th September 1994 Philip Berriman was caught bang to rights, or so HM Customs Inspectors thought, when he was found to be in possession of some £15m worth of Afghan cannabis on board the 'Melanie'. Crime Squad Detective Constable William McDougall questioned Berriman after the Melanie was towed into Falmouth harbour after a perilous nine-week voyage to hell and back. The repercussions from the lies and deceit concocted by the police are still felt now nearly a decade after the event – Berriman is a remarkable man with a story to tell.

What followed was a whirlwind nightmare of hell for Phil when he faced charges of smuggling drugs into the UK. Had Berriman been a lesser man then he'd have been banged up for something in excess of ten years but something saved his bacon, something that led to a police officer being arrested on the directions of a judge during the drug trial, which started in October 1995.

When Detective Constable William McDougall of the Crime Squad lied and lied and dug himself deeper with every lie he told into a very deep hole and when a tape was produced that proved him to be a perjurer it caused a little upset between HM Customs officers and their working relationship with the police. This all stemmed from a prison visit McDougall and Detective Sergeant Hans Kitching made on 29th November 1994 whilst Berriman was on remand.

Viv - The Final Chapter

Little did McDougall and Kitching realise that Berriman was recording the interview on a recorder he'd secreted away in a box file, all from within a maximum-security prison!

The trial judge, Judge Taylor, asked the Devon & Cornwall police to investigate into the evidence McDougall had given and he promptly slapped a gagging order on the trial. A file was sent to the Crown Prosecution Service (CPS) relating to McDougall's perjury, the CPS claimed there was insufficient evidence to charge McDougall? Cleveland Police Force has disciplined neither McDougall nor Kitching. Last heard McDougall was working on 'Administrative Support'. After reading the interview Phil Berriman gave me I want you to decide, along with the other evidence, if the CPS were right in their decision not to bring charges against McDougall, to me and others, the evidence is as plain as the noses on our faces but obviously the CPS and Cleveland Police Force do not work on the basis of hard evidence, which supports the claim that freemasonry is involved somewhere along the way.

The Observer newspaper gallantly fought for the lifting of the judge's ban and it is as a direct result of that ban being lifted that you are now being told the full story of Berriman's plight. You will notice Paddy Conroy's name cropping up more than once and on the face of it you might believe Paddy to have been fully involved, I want you to remember though that Paddy has not ever been charged in connection with this matter, but Phil claims Paddy helped him out with a few favours when he was having trouble prior to the Melanie saga and there was a level of indebtedness to Paddy for the help he'd given to Phil. Other than that it would seem that Paddy has been used as a pawn in a life size game of chess.

Phil Berriman reveals some eye opening stuff in this interview and it's not without some pain that he recalls the set of events that started him off on a journey of misery with little hope of survival when he was forced to travel 10,000 miles in an unseaworthy vessel. You would expect drug dealers of such mammoth status to be like a well-organised team of drilled SAS soldiers, Phil tells me the startling truth of it all.

"When I was nicked, halfway through my interview, they said to me it was Paddy Conroy, I said, 'Look you know who it is but I won't tell you.' It was about four to five months into my remand when I said to my Barrister, 'How far can I go in court, you know what I mean, without dropping Paddy in it? He replied, 'You can do anything you want. Anything you say in your own defence cannot be used against any other person.' I didn't realise I could so that was when I applied for all of Conroy's papers and documents relating to his kidnap and torture charges to be released to me, but there was Public Interest Immunity (PII – means a trial judge can slap one of these orders on certain evidence and it never gets to see the light of day in the courtroom or outside of it.) and there was a lot of stuff held back but, I got basically everything he was charged with so I got a full copy of his deps (depositions).

Because we had to disclose my defence (Defence was of Duress – forced into doing it and was in fear of his life.) in order to get these documents the next thing I know is the police and Customs come to visit me with my barrister present and try and charge (Paddy: Why didn't they charge him then?) me with aiding and abetting Conroy's escape. I sailed Conroy to Spain on the Michelle Louise.

(Author's note: Paddy Conroy and David Glover escaped from custody whilst being taken from prison to court to face kidnap and torture charges in a very lightly guarded mini bus prior to this drugs swoop by HM Customs. If I am led to believe what really happened then it is startling that David Glover, Paddy's co-accused, could set Paddy up for something he didn't even know anything about.)

They were furious I was going to lay it bare in public court, I was offered a deal, six years for a guilty plea. Yeah, like I'd trust them, and anyway by now, I was sure I was going home. I mean they knew it was him on the boat because they'd photographed him getting on it. By then I knew that Glover had been the principle informer so I said it was Glover and that he'd threatened to shoot me if I didn't do as he told me and take Paddy on the boat. Then I said that everybody else on the boat didn't know who Paddy was, he was under a different name. By saying I was forced to do it by Glover, this put it back on their toes so they couldn't charge me with that.

As far as I'm concerned the whole thing was a conspiracy, they arranged with Glover the escape from jail. I was right in the middle of it. At the time Conroy was arrested, I was being set-up by the undercover Customs and I've never been that stupid, they had me in Turkey looking at 830kg of cannabis and would have had us all bang to rights with a light plane and the Michelle Louise to boot if Paddy had not been arrested. I sussed it out and had dealt with it by the time Paddy and Glover escaped, (got off the bus).

That deal I was nicked with, Conroy never had a single shilling in it and he was on half. That stuff had been bobbing about off Dakar (Africa) for four months and three firms had tried to get that far down to get it and I was conned into going and getting it, totally conned.

Going back, Conroy's now out of jail and the next thing you know, 'We want your boat!' This was my motorboat the Michelle Louise (46 footer). I told them it didn't have the range but they started to get a bit shitty with me and the next thing I went down to Hartlepool and I said to my dad, 'Look, just get the boat sorted out and get it away' because I wanted to go to Majorca. I was finished with my salvage business and the daily crime that went with it, I just wanted out of all this shit (He who rides the tiger can never dismount.) At this stage it was being watched (thanks to Glover), they were taking photographs in the marina. The boat was made ready in two days and we got it all finished off, I had no intention of using that boat for anything dodgy anyway. I was under pressure to supply another boat because a boat had gone wrong from the year before which I'd supplied.

So they were taking photographs and that so I just wanted them to get it away, my dad and his pal and a couple of the other lads, I just sent them off and I said, 'I'll pick it up down south,' because I knew Conroy wanted to get his hands on the boat. The next thing they turned up here when the boat had gone, he turns up here at three o'clock in the morning saying, 'Where's the boat?' long story short, I got him into the jeep, Jim, and me and drove him down to Torquay to get him away; he had a beard and all that.

When we arrived in the green jeep the customs, unbeknown to us was taking photographs, and when the photographs were produced the title underneath Conroy read: 'Unidentified'. They even gave us a dodgy weather forecast (Customs) and sent us out into a storm into the Bay of Biscay this was the sort of people they were. I wasn't a particularly good sailor and it was a motor boat as well, I said: 'What's the weather forecast...' they said, 'Oh yeah, no problem, no problem.' Four hours later we're in the eye of a storm, it was the Harbour Master that sent us out into it!

We'd pulled in at Brest and even though Paddy was on the run he'd applied for a passport in his own name and they'd sent him a passport while he was on the run! My girlfriend drove it over at the time and met us in Brest with it; from there we sailed down to La caruna then flew to Malaga. The Customs knew where Paddy was all the time."

When Phil is pressed on how the customs knew where Paddy was he says: "We'll go one step further, when I'm in jail I'm looking at all the different statements and checking all the airline manifestos and a Customs officer called Bashier, I think it was the 10th of July 1994, travelled to Malaga and sat alongside Conroy's right hand man who does not wish to be named and he's bigger than me so we'll call him Bloggs, at trial the prosecution denied Conroy and co were involved, (so why was a customs officer sat next to his right hand man who was on his way to see him).

And what had happened Bashier had watched my house the day before; I didn't have any evidence...only the manifesto. So what I did was get my barrister and say to him, 'When you question him (Bashier) about that...' because he didn't know why he was being called, he thought it was just a daft observation that he's put in, '...when you get him he'll read out this from his note book saying he'd watched my house, etc, etc then pretend you've got the next page relating to the flight. (Paddy says: How did Berriman know to tell his barrister this, Berriman would say from flight manifestos, but Berriman would have had to know what was on the next page to get his barrister to question it?)

So my Barrister asks him to read the next page, pretending to have it in front of him. And all the Customs in court are freaking out and my barrister said, 'Come on what's your problem?' He had to read what was in his notebook and he said, 'I was given instructions to go to Manchester airport, and follow Joe Bloggs and he was there sat right next to Bloggs.

My barrister said, 'You were there right next to Bloggs, who's Bloggs?' He replied, 'I don't know,' 'He's Paddy Conroy's right hand man, the man the prosecution would have us believe was not involved', that's when they put the late statement in about me having informed (Proved later to be lies).

They knew exactly where Conroy was all the way through the operation and I was supposed to supply the boat, I was under pressure to supply a boat in the past and things had gone wrong. And then Conroy had thought the firm had dealt him out, he demanded I come to Spain to see him. I flew over for three days just to sort him out and tell him the score. I had a boat organised that was sat in Gibraltar, the Melanie, I put my own boat up as security for it.

His skipper, a guy called Jeff Berge was one of these guys that Conroy had been paying for, a dead game lad and he seemed really good, a Scot's fisherman off Alnwick. He was supposed to be coming over, he turned up at Gibraltar and he was a different bloke, he was late and he was sitting there gutted and I thought, 'His bottle's gone,' it was really strange. I said, 'Is there a problem, what's the crack? If you hadn't turned up they were going to make me sail the bloody boat,' that's exactly what I said to him.

I went through to Conroy in Spain to pick up some details of where this gear was, the Moroccan thing had fell through. He was offered half of the cargo, if it got in! But really it was on top that's why nobody would go and get it; everybody knew it was on top, it was being watched, everybody but me that is.

He didn't tell me it was off Dakar, what he said to me was to get the boat down to Tenerife. So I said to Geoff Berge the skipper: 'The gear's down in Tenerife, you've got to go down and pick it up, it's all sorted there's a boat going to pick it up from you at these secret co-ordinates. When I came back to Gibraltar, he'd just gone, he'd done one. Now what actually happened was that Customs had got hold of him and had made him go through with it because one of their firm, Gary Parkin had been nicked and had turned informer. They held him until he agreed to go through with it and when he heard I would have sailed it myself (only to where the crew would pick it up) he told customs who told him to do one.

Because I'd told Berge they were going to Tenerife that's what he told the police and that's what Paddy had been told. So I had to meet this guy in Casablanca because there'd been all this messing around with different people not turning up and this boat was there and we said we were there. So I picked this guy up in Casablanca and said we were supposed to go to Tenerife and he said: 'No, we're going to Dakar.' I had no charts to go to Dakar and the boat wasn't fit to go there.

What I did was call in at Morro Jabel, a port in the south of Forta Ventura in the Canaries and told the Spanish there was an engine problem, I got on the phone to Paddy and said, 'What's going on, you want me to go to Dakar?' He replied, 'Just go there and we'll have a crew sorted out by the time you get there.' So I sailed down to Dakar and we had gearbox failures, you name it, unbelievable. The boat just wasn't capable of doing that, it was all right to go to Tenerife and back up, but that was about it.

We went to Dakar and the firm based there wouldn't even pay for a GPS aerial, you know what I mean the lads are there sniffing coke up there noses and having prostitutes and running around in Mercedes and like we were botching stuff with soldering irons and things like that, it was pathetic. They'd like to make out it was no expenses spared but he hadn't put a penny in, I supplied the boat, I'd lost my own boat, £180,000 worth to get this one. I sailed this boat down there and they were stitching the sails, there was a GPS there and it was $400 for this aerial and they wouldn't even buy it, the other GPS broke down twice on the way down so there was no positioning system to meet this boat which was critical.

I was just kicking off and he said: 'Look, we'll give you a million quid.' I had no idea he was on half and that the chances of us landing it safely were just about impossible, I found out this myself afterwards from a south London firm, it was their cannabis and they knew all about it so when I was in jail I knew exactly what had happened. Going back to Dakar, they told me I could have as much diesel as I wanted so I had it all worked out, I got fresh water in bottles so I could fill the water tanks with fuel, the Melonie had a decent engine so I filled the boat full of drums all on the deck and everything because I was supposed to get them filled up from the supply ship so I could get back.

Eventually after a while I tried to get away, we got threatened and bashed off these blacks that were watching the boat and it was just all a load of bollocks, I said that the boat's there and I'd done my job but they went, 'Ah well its not that easy, we can't get a crew now, its down to you, we'll give you a million quid, but if you don't we're going to do...'

We set off from Dakar with this skipper guy, a Cuban bloke, to meet this boat and when we got them on the radar and talked to them on the radio they said; 'We'll come to you.' Now the reason I was told this boat was stuck down there was because the engine was knackered, but he's doing about eight knots coming towards me and I thought, 'There's nothing wrong with his engine.' They just wouldn't go into Senegal's waters because it was all on top; this is what I found out later.

I met this boat and I threw a line and said: 'This is an aluminium yacht, I'll never be able to go alongside with the yacht fenders and all that.' The next thing the rifles are out and they said: 'YOU WILL.' And the minute I pulled alongside this boat the fenders just splattered and it smashed all the side of the boat, the cross trees on the mast and everything including the bows and I just cut the line, shoved it into reverse, the line went around the propeller as we backed off and they had the guns on us. So after I got the propeller shaft out I spent all day making a rubber coupling joint for it.

Then they loaded one hundred bags, just kept loading it and loading it and it was up to the gunnels, it was just everywhere so I went, 'Right okay.' They had little food or coffee, they just came on board and took most of our supplies and then when I asked for diesel, 'We've got no instructions to give you diesel, we haven't got any diesel.' Instead of 600 gallons I could have taken because I was going to have to motor against the tide and the trade winds to go back up I was only given about 140 gallons of sludge, that's all they gave me and it wiped the engine out in two days. The boat was listing and everything. Does all this sound like they thought I had a chance or does it sound like they knew I was fucked and on my way to jail?

In the meantime they (Customs) still knew where Paddy Conroy was, in Spain, and they'd gone looking in Tenerife for me because they knew I was on this job so they had gone looking for me with a spotter plane and everything. Geoff Berge and Paddy Conroy were the only persons that had the co-ordinates where this boat was supposed to meet me. (Paddy says: How, if so, did Berriman know?)

We had a hell of job on the return journey running electrics on a petrol generator with only 5 gallons of fuel and eventually that was off, I was nine weeks at sea, when I'd left England, I told my bird I'd be back in three days. We were starving; we stopped two ships for food and water on the way back. 3.7 tons of cannabis and yet I had no fuel, they took my supplies, they wouldn't fix the boat and we sailed straight into a trap!

What happens in all these big drug deals is that they, the money men, all put their money in a pot, there was a few lots in the pot for the job I was on, it's bought in Pakistan for next to nothing. One firm's responsible for bringing it so far and the other firm says, 'Right when we get it we take it to here' And what they do is say, 'I'll have £500,000 in that,' and then a few others put the same or less in and they have a few jobs going at once so if one gets caught then they've got the other ones running.

These guys on the Costa they set up these deals and that's what Paddy was trying to get into and they were trying to keep him out of it. The year before they ripped him off and they had no intentions of getting him into Morocco with these guys, no intentions at all. He wasn't in their club if you like, he'd then been given the opportunity to get this stuff in and it was just a fanny, it was on top before it even started and don't forget it was on top for him, they knew where he was, they knew where I was, they were watching me. He would have had to pay the south London guys for the stuff he sold; there are only a few people who can organise that scale of job on the Costa del Sol.

When I finally got back and got to the spot I was supposed to be met at we fire up the generator until the batteries are charged and then we got the GPS on and then we've got to turn them all off again so I'm in the channel approaches we've got no radar, no lights, we couldn't put the navigation lights on because we had no power left in the batteries. I got to this spot where we were supposed to meet, 120 miles from France and England; these were secret coordinates that only the other skipper had.

There was nobody there apart from a trawler and eventually when all came out it was revealed that this trawler was full of Customs and was trawling in a four-mile square around the spot where I was supposed to meet this boat. I went back the next night and still nobody there so I thought 'Bollocks, I've got no food, I've got no petrol left for the generator, if I dump it they'll kill me.' I couldn't do anything, anybody else, the problems I had with that boat, they'd have dumped it. All the things that went wrong with this boat could never have gone wrong, I'd have bet some of the stuff would have lasted twenty years, steering bosses falling off and it just went one thing after another, and another. The gearbox first, then the engine, sails, electrics, everything, food – anybody else would have just dumped it, but I couldn't, I couldn't.

So what I did I got the pilot book out and had a look at this place called the Helford River where about fifty people live in the village…no navigation, no lights, I thought that was the perfect spot and if I could get in there I could get a diesel pump, some diesel and then make arrangements to get it in (the cargo of cannabis) myself.

There was no contact with anybody, it had all gone pear shaped, the reason being, I was supposed to go to Tenerife and back, no more than five weeks at the very, very most…three weeks probably. They were sitting there watching Conroy, they knew exactly what was going on (initially when they all left England), they were all sitting down at the south coast watching this lifeboat, (the pick up boat) they knew exactly what the score was because of the informants and when it didn't turn up they thought Conroy had got it in somewhere else. I'm still out at sea, they think I've already got it in and they think they've been mugged and that's when they nicked Conroy again in Spain, this was two weeks before I got nicked.

In these two weeks I was still merrily sailing around with no engine or nothing against the tide and the winds. After they've nicked Conroy back in Spain he's looking at extradition and now on extradition they can't charge him or investigate him for any other offences, so he was saved from the cannabis job.

After they've nicked Conroy the operation's back on, whether they've realised or what I don't know. (Author's note: This is not inferring that information came from Conroy but merely stating the set of events leading up to Berriman's arrest.) As I sailed in they were all over me and the searcher was there and they just followed me in, the skipper (Berge) told them I had it wired with explosives and all sorts. I went into the Helford River and the reason I ended up on all the front pages was because it was called 'Smugglers Creek', they'd been using it for three hundred years to smuggle brandy in. There was seventy armed police, customs, all the boats they were just waiting for me.

When I was interviewed by McDougall I said, 'You look tanned,' he replied, 'Oh yeah I've been to Tenerife looking for you.' I knew then straight away I was set up and on the interview they said, 'We know it was Paddy Conroy,' I replied, 'I wouldn't tell you if it was, I'll take responsibility, I did it, I was under duress off some people and my two crew members did it because they didn't know any difference.'

It was then I realised why everything had gone wrong with that boat, it was my spirit guide trying to stop me getting back and then from that moment on I knew I'd get off. I was remanded and spent a week in Exeter prison category C and returned to Truro court and I couldn't believe there was armed police with fifteen vehicles in convoy; there was a helicopter with armed police the whole shooting match. I went from there to Bristol prison and was now a category 'A' (high security risk), I didn't know any difference, I'd never been to prison in my life, jail was jail to me. Then I was called down an hour later and made double category 'A'. I was the only double cat 'A' man in Bristol prison until two weeks later when Tony White and John Short were in for cannabis and cocaine. Tony White was involved in the Brinks Matt robbery; the insurance company has since sued him in civil court for it.

They couldn't prove it criminally against him over the Brinks Matt robbery because he'd been fitted up with a document and they verballed him when he was out the cell for 45 minutes. And how he got off with it was his solicitor, Henry Milner who I ended up using, they got the document and in court he said, 'Right is this a true statement,' and the coppers said that it was and that they had wrote it down question and answer style so Mr Milner says, 'Right okay start from scratch, you write that same document out in 45 minutes without any pauses because that document has taken nearly everybody in our office at least an hour and three quarters to do.' It was impossible to have done that in the time he was out of his cell. Yet none of the police that lied in that trial was charged with perjury.

I bumped into these two in Bristol prison and they were cat 'AA' also, we were out in the exercise yard the three of us and they told me, 'Oh yeah they didn't give you any fuel or anything and they took your food,' I thought what's going on here, they knew all about it, even things we had told nobody and that's how I got to know what had gone on. These guys were bank robbers when all you needed was a ford Zephyr and a shotgun but now with all of the technology and cameras and everything else it has all changed.

It was Tony who told me I should try and tape the coppers after I told him they had arranged to visit me regarding a CS gas gun they had found in my house. He knew the dance; he knew they were coming to see if they could get me to grass in return for a letter to the Judge. In '84 a bank robbery trial was scuppered when a tape was produced of a prison interview with the arresting officers. I had nothing to lose, I hollowed out a whole ream of depositions and hid a £25 realistic tape recorder/player in my (defence file). I was strip searched in and out of every visit but the screws knew it was coppers I was seeing so the search was not as it should have been. I will be grateful to Tony White for the rest of my life.

After I had got the tape out through my brief I was quite confident I was going home at trial. I could not tell anyone but for sure my phone calls (which are all taped and sent to customs) must have got them so worried as to what it was I had, they had me 'ghosted' to the special secure unit at Belmarsh. That day I had just got returned three small pieces of cannabis when the screws burst in at lunchtime and ordered my bags packed. Now nobody told me I was supposed to wrap it up before 'botting' it.

By the time we got to Belmarsh I was taking the piss out of the screws and fanning cannabis and cabbage farts around the van. I was completely stoned until I was about to be put into my new home. My property bags had the seals removed, which is against regulations. I kicked off and refused to enter the spur until I had retrieved my defence file. IT WAS THE ONLY THING MISSING FROM MY PROPERTY. There was murder on; I got it back two hours later. Next day Governor Carol replied to my complaint with the most pathetic excuse imaginable. Get this, my bags had been 'opened in error' and then when they were in the x-ray machine my file fell out and was trapped by the curtain and remained undetected in the machine for two hours. Strange that, I would have thought the machine would have detected a full defence file and displayed it to the operator.

After ten days on a hunger strike Frank Cook MP came to see me and instigated an investigation by the Prison Ombudsman whose report concluded my file had been removed illegally and the explanation given was not possible. I was not allowed to mention or produce the report in court? There was never any mention of the tape in the file but there were a couple of things I did not want to disclose. They assumed they had found my reason to be confident but they were wrong.

When Conroy had been nicked then why didn't they just send a boat out and come within fifty miles of me (radio range) and tell me to dump it and get off, they just let me get on with it and I sailed straight into a trap. They're not bothered, I was just one of their soldiers, I'd been a dodgy person for twenty years and never been convicted I had a 120ft yacht in Spain out of a salvage business. I was good at what I was doing but it was when I got involved with J Deplege, he and a pal attacked me and I battered him in a nightclub and I'd had to get Conroy involved after that to frighten him off because he was getting silly and that's when I owed them a favour, they did that for me because I knew about boats.

This guy was taking over all the doors around here and I'm well known, I don't look it but I'm a bit tasty, I went out to a nightclub and the man and his pal attacked me, bit my ear off and I battered them, bust their noses and cut them both, then I was getting death threats. I wasn't bothered I wasn't interested. It was my girlfriend who asked me to get it sorted, as she was worried all the time.

I used this in my defence because to use duress as a defence you've got to show you were in fear of your life. I had to show why I got involved with Conroy and how so I used this carry on with the guy running the club doors and how he'd shot my car with a shotgun and all this sort of thing and I used statements as well to show why I got involved with Conroy and then I became indebted to him for the help he gave me and in the trial I gave that I was in fear of my life from Terry Rich and Davie Glover and just kept laying it all on Davie Glover. To have the defence of duress you've got to have all these things in place and I just happened to have and made things fit from 1990 to 1994 and it all fitted together perfectly.

When I got the gear (cannabis) it was all mouldy, it was in sacks, it was all wet, it was green, it was soft black from Pakistan. It was just a complete and utter farce from start to finish after he got nicked where were the people to meet me?

I used to have parties at my home and you could reckon on at least six or seven of the top villains in the north east would be here and the reason being I was a good villain, I'd never informed on anybody and they knew if they came with me everything would be sorted...the buck stopped with me. I was good at what I did, I covered myself for every single thing, they couldn't get me, they used to have surveillance on me and all sorts but they just couldn't get me. I can tell you if my phone's tapped now, just put a meter across it, it's dead easy.

You have people who have no telephone etiquette. I've watched certain people talking on the phone, literally talking openly. They (Police/Customs) just have to listen to one or two peoples' telephone conversations and they've got all of the information they need, they know exactly what's going on so they just let these people run and do what they do. It makes no difference who the phone is registered to if your ringing home, your bird and your mates with it they will get the number instantly and tap it digital or not authorised or not. They may not be able to use it in evidence but they sure know what's happening, when and where and who's doing it. The mobile phone is a godsend to the agencies but the crooks don't even want to think about it, so sometimes they talk in daft codes until something goes wrong and the phone etiquette goes out the window.

The fact that only two crew and myself were charged with this cargo speaks for itself, normally a job this size nets between ten and twenty people. I was the target they wanted but there was not a single piece of evidence or observation on anybody else, which they could use to charge them. I would rather drive to Blackpool for a face to face than use the phone. And if it weren't for the informants in Paddy's firm that gear would have made a lot of potheads smile.

When I got nicked people I knew came into my home and took everything, they took the doors, furniture, every single thing, they took everything out of my salvage yard - £250,000 worth of stock, they even dropped the steel buildings and scrapped them they supposedly got £20,000 for it all. They did it because they said the customs would take it all anyway, they wiped me out within a week everything had gone. This went for my defence as well because it was on record and everybody knew. The jury were gob smacked, this was a yard making five grand a week and it was just levelled, it was people thinking I was going to do 14 years, what difference was it going to make, they just went like vultures and ripped me to pieces. This is a shame these people also have to live with.

There was this Columbian, supposedly the top man in one of the cartels, I read all the papers involved in his case. He was claiming duress and he would have got off in the retrial but he did a deal on ten years and they said on TV he was the most senior man ever caught yet he only gets ten years? The people that set him up got £150,000 and you've got people who pose as drug dealers, not undercover Customs, and they go and broker the deal in Spain or Columbia or wherever and then they get the Customs involved and the Customs give them £150,000 or £100,000 or so much per kilo to set them up. They instil fear that's why people don't mess with the VAT people, they don't care and they have to act like that so people know who's in control.

Viv - The Final Chapter

This guy from Columbia Frank la Pera Soto was actually a chicken farmer, I got very good friends with him, he was an interpreter paid £3,000 to come over and talk for the guy he was with and customs put him up as the main man and he was just a daft chicken farmer from Columbia and there they are on television saying he's the most senior man from the Calle cartel ever caught yet in reality he was under duress because of the money he'd borrowed for his chicken farm.

The Customs are only interested in public opinion, they put somebody in jail for 15 years, I mean I was just driving the boat for god sake and all of a sudden I'm the mastermind behind it all, and they have to give somebody 14 years for that amount of cannabis on a private boat. So it was, 'We can't get Conroy we can't get the people behind it, right Phil Berriman's the man, let's have him high risk, armed police escort, the full shit,' and that's exactly what they tried to do. If they'd said to me, 'You're driving the boat take a deal, six years,' I'd have taken it. Like McDougall said on the tape they're interested in results & amounts and what the public see, nothing else. To get me on high-risk category they told the Devon and Cornwall plod that they had information that I was to be sprung on the way to court. (Who pays the bill for this circus? Look how easy it was for Conroy and Glover to escape from a prison to court mini bus and yet the previous run to court was helicopters and armed police escorting them? Glover led Conroy into the perfect entrapment situation designed to get him locked up for twenty years.)

What happened was once the tape was produced by me they'd already printed in the newspapers what McDougall had said, that I'd offered to be a supergrass, they printed all of that and then soon as the tape comes out and proves the opposite the judge puts a gagging order on the trial so the truth couldn't be told. When I came out people thought I was going to be killed because I said it was Paddy Conroy but they don't understand the double jeopardy law or anything like that. Paddy got no grief over any of this job, I was the target! I used all I could including his deps to scare the jury, it was no skin off his nose, I made sure of that before I started!

The top and bottom of it all is I came out but instead of coming out to a hero thing it was all, 'Oh, he's going to get killed now,' and all that. That's why I got the pub in the town so everybody knew where I was, I was frightened of nothing, because I had done nothing wrong, and that was like throwing it in their faces. Conroy's firm didn't want to talk to me and I had all these papers as evidence and I was trying to say to them, 'Look, they knew where I was going, how did they know?' (Author's note: Paddy has specifically made it clear that Phil Berriman has already claimed he was like Tom Hanks in Castaway – no one, not even Berriman, knew where he was to end up therefore the identification of the Helford river as the place Berriman finally landed had to have come from Berriman's quarters and since Paddy claims not to have had any involvement then it would seem logical in what Paddy says.)

When I got the beating from the three masked men (and an other party that shall remain unnamed to save him the shame.) I was lured to a workshop by Henry Nixon (who I had regarded as a friend for 15 years and done untold business with) under the pretence of helping Paddy with some deps for his appeal covered in overalls and big gloves they beat me with chunks of wood with nails in and a ball peen hammer to smash my legs it lasted for $2^{1/2}$ hours and all this was about was that these rumours were flying about that the Customs had given me a million quid's worth of cannabis and that I must have grassed my way out and all that type of thing.

A dealer (name withheld for legal reasons) had fifteen kilos of Moroccan soap bar and was knocking it out. They thought it was mine and wanted the money saying it must be from the job. They didn't even know that the gear on the boat was soft (paki black). I didn't get the chance to talk, they smashed me up first. One hero then went to call xxxx xxxxx to verify what I said telling the two to leave me alone. While he was gone another of the firm arrived got dressed up and tried to break my legs with a hammer just for fun. All he got when the leader came back was a slap. They threatened to kill my kids before dropping me off.

I know that all this was done without Paddy's knowledge and I know he was furious but, even when the Observer got the gagging order lifted and told the full story I still have not had any apology. It may have been the case that they just thought I'd gone into dealing and with Paddy locked up things were tight and they used this bullshit as an excuse to 'tax' me. These days if a firm gets wind you are sitting on a bag of cash you cannot account for there is a very good chance you will be taxed, (taxed actually means robbery with violence) but you can't report it to the police so beware your associates whatever you are up to.

I'm at a five-week trial, I got two coppers suspended so I'd like to know where they got it from, they haven't got the brains to work it out. They beat me senseless, I knew they weren't going to kill me because they were masked up, if they weren't masked up then it would have been the end for me. So the gagging order was a nightmare until the Observer brought the story out 14 months later the truth came out and this was only because the copper hadn't been charged and yet he's committed blatant perjury for three hours in the witness box and he was asked three times on every point, the judge saw it, the jury saw it, all the legal team saw it, the judge ordered him to be arrested for god sake.

How on earth can't there be no evidence, the tape recording was verified by the Home Office, every word he said was written down and recorded so he'd lied and lied and if I hadn't of had the tape I'd have been convicted and branded a grass and maybe I'd be dead by now, how many others has this happened to? The coppers should have been charged and got three years, the Home Office authenticated the tape I made as not being made up or interfered with and they've got every word he said in the witness box, the two are completely different and at odds with each other.

Look what they've just done to Geoffrey Archer for perjury and this copper's just stood there and lied, my barrister said to him, 'Hey do you know about the laws of perjury in this land,' and he said, 'My client's got a tape recording,' and he still went on and lied. He stood there in his big blue three-piece suit and when the tape played he obviously thought I'd got two cons to pretend to have a conversation. But, when his unmistakable voice came over his suit got bigger and he shrank under the glare of the jury, as the lies were uncovered one by one. I was giggling throughout and the jury got on it. The more the judge tried to control me the bigger the impact the tape had.

Because they'd made me double 'A' I had to stay in Bristol prison but if I'd had the trial in Belmarsh I wouldn't have had to have all that security. So we're talking about five weeks of a 100-mile dash every day from Bristol to Exeter court because the judge wouldn't let that trial go anywhere outside of his jurisdiction. The security alone would cost the tax payer millions and on the tape it is confirmed the crime squad had told Devon & Cornwall plod a crock of shit in order to get me the double 'A' high risk circus which is meant to sway the jury, imagine what the jury thought when they discovered this.

Looking at 14 years you're bound to have a QC (Queens Counsel), the judge wouldn't let me have a QC, he refused, refused, refused because he didn't want to have somebody more senior in the court. I even appealed and he said I could have QC but I would have to pay for one, he wouldn't release my money so I couldn't have a QC. There's people on £20,000 and £40,000 worth of drugs charges have a QC but I couldn't and they wouldn't let me have a trial at any other place than Exeter, we went for a judicial review and got refused.

The two that were charged with me made a plea of 'Guilty' and they were brought back to give information two weeks later, the judge shouldn't have done that. When the tape recording come out he even threw my dad's pal out of court, a 70 year old five foot tall straight hotelier, he tried to make out he was intimidating the jury, they tried to knobble the jury by using their own Customs people.

What happened was the jury came in one day, this was after the tape was revealed, and the judge knew this trial was scuppered he tried everything in his power to shut me up and god knows all sorts. And when it looked like it was going my way the jury complained that they'd been getting followed in the lunch break and they were going on about a retrial it was all dead serious and everything.

One of the jurors suddenly stood up and said, 'Excuse me,' and the judge went, 'Sit down,' and the juror said, 'No, the people that were following us were talking to that man this morning, the Chief Customs officer Peter Hollier.' So it was Customs blokes following them around trying to make out that they were getting knobbled and intimidating them and all that and trying to get the judge any excuse to stop the trial and then there wouldn't be the surprise of the tape, they tried all sorts. If I had the money I'd get the transcripts from that trial because they are unbelievable.

I named the two grasses to Conroy's firm but they weren't interested, they weren't interested in who grassed them up from their firm. And yet the shit was beaten out of me based on public opinion and when that story come out I went up to Talltrees and showed one of them the Observer piece and he didn't want to know and that's the reason I wouldn't get involved with anybody ever again because at the end of the day they're criminals. I didn't even get any support in jail from them, not the slightest bit of support at all. I still have friends who are villains, some are active and some are not, but I will never get involved with any criminal in crime not after what I've been through.

People close to me knew I was going to name Conroy, it was blatantly obvious, I mean the police had allowed them to break out of jail and he's photographed on my boat, Bashier's sat next to Bloggs and they knew where he was in Malaga so they couldn't do Conroy because he was on extradition. When I went in court I said, 'Yeah, it was Paddy Conroy.' He's already up for kidnap and torture because I've got all of the paperwork, it was perfect and of course it was possible I'm frightened of this guy and he was on trial the same time as me and I'm giving that to the jury, it's no skin off Paddy's nose.

The Customs even tried to make out that a song I'd written while on the voyage to hell proved I wasn't easily frightened and I said, 'Is that the best you can do, I'm nine weeks at sea, I'm sitting in the cold and damp with no engine, no lights, no nothing and I've got two crew members wanting to commit suicide and we've written a few words to a song and you want me to go to jail for 14 years for that, is that the best you can do? You're losing it now,' and the jury started laughing at him.

I had a pub after the trial and I opened a back yard in it and called it 'Smugglers Creek' and generally since then I've been inventive, we got £150,00 last year to develop a machine that recycles cooking oil, works on a centrifuge. I worked on an invention, a babies bottle that cures colic, Boots are now selling it, made in Taiwan, the company I showed my idea to screwed me and I haven't got the financial clout to take these people on, I will eventually.

I've invented the spring-loaded fishhook and this time I've got it patented and it looks likely to take off in a big way, would you believe I invented it while at sea during the nine-week drug caper and now it looks to be paying dividends.

I'm writing a book at the moment explaining how I turned into a criminal and within it I tell of a few run ins I had with Robocop Ray Mallon he's been my arch-enemy for 20 years. The Huntingdon police when they were investigating Mallon for the Lancet Inquiry came to see me. The Lancet Inquiry was about Ray Mallon and corruption within Cleveland Police Force. The Lancet Inquiry will never be made public, never. There's a few people in this town that have a made a lot of money and they've never been touched, a lot of money. I would not put anything in my book that the police don't already know.

There's a fight between the Yarm Lodge and the Stockton Lodge in the Masons, that's the key to the Lancet Inquiry. What happened was they got Mr X for this and that and the other and all these allegations. The Yarm Lodge said, 'Right okay if you've nicked him for that....' And they all started reporting each other and it was tit for tat. It was a fight between the two lodges Yarm and Stockton.

Mallon was tipped for the top and he was a rising star and there's other people been left behind that are still sergeants and he was moving up to Inspector, Chief Inspector, Superintendent, and that's what it was over. They're bringing them back into play but it'll never come out because it's far too serious. The public don't know that Conroy and Glover jumped off that taxi minibus when they escaped, they don't want to read stuff like that because they think it doesn't happen.

I was raided by the police last year because they thought I had a skunk farm in my home after the spotter plane noticed my new sunbed (how daft do they think I am) 20 plod kicked my door in, within 2 minutes they realised the mistake and were gutted, they said they found almost an ounce of cannabis in the living room but my friend another ex hash smuggler Boris who also had defeated the customs complained that he saw the plod take it out of his pocket and plant it.

There was hell on, he made a proper complaint. Plod was furious; they nicked him straight away then searched my house for five hours before taking me down the shovel. The interview was a laugh, it lasted 26 minutes during which I never shut up slagging them off and dared them to charge me. I said I would ring the papers myself, what a story, 'Man not guilty of 3.7 ton importation is charged with 3.7gram possession.' Later a club manager friend of mine was at the licensing sergeants leaving do. I asked him to find out what they were looking for (skunk farm under my sunbed).

One of the coppers said, 'I know him, he doesn't do anything,' and another one turned around and said, 'Look, Phil Berriman owes us millions and millions of pounds and he will re-offend, we've had a psychological profile done on him and he will re-offend,' but they're wrong and I won't.

The only way I can beat them is to stay out of jail. Whatever I did the attention I would get, it would be on top straight away. They do not forget, look at Charrington, they chased him and had three or four different countries involved. The Customs have unlimited resources and what they did with me was to put me in a high risk category, I've never been to jail in my life, and they stopped me communicating with people because they knew I was clever enough to find a way out. I was told by the coppers from Huntingdon (Lancet Inquiry) that that was part of the investigation the main thing and it was to do with policemen's connections with all these top villains."

With that we end this most revealing interview and I see Phil as having gone through the mill but one thing is for certain and that is he is a most remarkable man to have come through all of this and remain sane, I wish him luck in all that he does as I would hope all of the people that once supported Phil but turned their backs on him would also wish him luck in order to make things right. Certainly what Phil says of the laws of double jeopardy are true and if Paddy Conroy's legal team had of advised him correctly then he'd have had nothing to become concerned over, all good and well looking back over it but damage has been done.

I was given three chapters of Phil's book and found it to be a very interesting read indeed and I believe it would do very well in book form especially the chapter relating to the time Phil bought a ship called the Aubriender an ex Royal Navy mine sweeper some 117ft long. Phil certainly knows how to put a story across and I really hope he gets a publishing deal because the book, which he says might be called 'Captain Hook', is the dog's bollocks. I've included a few extracts from those chapters for you just so as to whet your appetite.

Robocop v Phil Berriman

(Items prior to this in this extract have been omitted for legal reasons)

A few weeks went past and we had stopped talking about it when I was driving a Lotus Cortina along Bishopton Rd, Stockton. A police panda, blue flashing lights, I stop and who walks up to the car, Shining Buttons. I wound down the windows, "What's the problem officer?" He was half smiling, and I wondered if it was the same copper. "Its OK you've done nothing wrong," and before he could say any more I said, "I know that". He went on, "You know the other week, well the bloke has made a complaint against me because his..." (Items omitted for legal reasons, although omitted it does not mean they are factually incorrect but simply that supporting evidence has not yet been given at the date of publication, although it is claimed to be in the possession of a firm of lawyers.) Well, I could not believe my ears, I was furious.

The next thing I said was to have a massive impact on the rest of my life that is how I remember it word for word. "Listen mate..." (Items omitted for legal reasons, although omitted it does not mean they are factually incorrect but simply that supporting evidence has not been given at the date of publication) His face changed back to the one I recognised and he glared at me like I was shit. "That's all I wanted to know, bye". And off he went.

A few weeks later I had gone to the Incognito nightclub, when I left I discovered my car; a Triumph convertible had been stolen. As I reported it the police told me it had been found only five hundred yards away in a side street. I recovered the car and everything seemed all right, no damage, I checked the glove box, a chequebook was still there so I assumed it had been taken as a joke. In those days almost any key would work on a worn lock. I drove home relieved and thought no more about it.

A week went by until one night I arrived at my parent's home at about 11pm with my old school pal, Wayne Wrangham. My mother informed me the police had been and could I go to the Station as soon as. I was interested not worried; I had never done anything wrong. We hot footed it to the cop shop and walked into reception at about 11.15pm. As soon as I got in, Shining Buttons and a charge sergeant called Horrocks grabbed me by the arms and said, "Philip Berriman I am arresting you on suspicion of theft of an excise licence." "An excise licence, what the fuck is an excise licence?" "A tax disc you have stolen". It turned out that who should have found my car, before it was reported stolen but Shining Buttons, what a coincidence. He had been in the glove compartment and found a tax disc belonging to a Cortina, which was parked in a bus garage owned by my father's friend. The drivers were all thieves so I had taken the disc for safekeeping. I relayed this to Shining Buttons and the diligent sergeant who seemed none too pleased but dispatched a plod to my mother's house where I told them they would find the documents. Meanwhile I was thrown in a cell but actually thought it was funny, how pathetic of Shining Buttons to go to the trouble he had, sad bastard I thought.

Around midnight I was let into the charge room still chuckling to myself. Plod had returned with the documents and produced them as I grinned. "I'll be going then lads, if you don't mind." Shining Buttons was beetroot, "Your going nowhere till I get you for something. Get him back in that cell". I was thrown in the cell until the door opened and I, the prisoner, was taken into the charge room and questioned in relation to a very heinous crime, they actually suspected me of.

At a time and place they had no idea of, driving a car without an MOT or perhaps road tax. I was in and out of my cell until 4.30am when I found myself stood in the charge room with Shining Buttons, Sergeant Horrocks, another sergeant and a plod. I was tired, sick and stood in my stocking feet. They had tried all night to intimidate me but I had done nothing wrong and, I was in a police station what could they do? I got cheeky and to all the stupid questions about cars, I replied, "On a trailer." "Who's?" "I'm not telling you." And so it went on until I decided to give a little back.

I stated there had been £8 in the glove compartment and intimated Shining Buttons must have stolen it.

(This piece has been cut but what Phil Berriman claims is that Silver Buttons became agitated and as a consequence Phil and a number of police officers including Shining Buttons became involved in a fight, which resulted in Shining Buttons being injured as well as Phil Berriman)

I turned to sergeant Horrocks and told him I wanted to make a formal complaint. "Oh do you now?" As I was grabbed on each arm and held so that (Name changed to - Constable X) Constable X had an easy target. I actually thought for a few seconds I was having a nightmare, but it was true. I also was aware there was some commotion outside of the charge room.

Constable X launched into me punching my abdomen as hard as he could, his face was contorted. I could hear my father's voice outside of the charge room, he was shouting as the plod outside were stopping him coming in. Wayne had told him the dance and after getting the run-around from the desk had got an inspector from nearby Middlesborough to accompany him. He could hear what was happening and like the sort of guy he is, he was battling outside to get in.

Meanwhile inside the Gestapo were busy administrating their "punishment beating" I had my own problems. I knew I was getting it whatever and fuelled by the noise of my dad fighting I decided, whatever happened I was going to hurt Shining Buttons. The thing about cowards and bullies is they only do it when there is no danger to themselves. The last thing they expected with four against one was a fight.

I planned my move and it went perfectly. I pulled my head to the right and nutted plod holding my left arm, he left go to defend himself and I crossed my left right into my charge sergeant's nose, as he left go of my right, Shining Buttons was a clear target as he was stood gob smacked. I connected his jaw with a right hook and he fell down putting his arm down to break the fall. I had lost it by now and could see my chance. I snap kicked his arm and later discovered I broke it, then as I was hit from behind by one of the heroes I grabbed what can only be described as a big tin telephone and smashed it into his horrible contorted face as I fell on him under another blow. The batons were raining hard as I did my best to destroy his face, I knew I could take no more but had got the timing right. I moved to the side and dodged what would have been the last blow I would have known about, it landed right on his face. Fucking good shot! I thought as I lost consciousness.

I came round in my cell as the inspector from Middlesborough came in, I could hardly comprehend what he was saying as I became aware of more and more injuries about my head and body. For sure they had carried on braying me long after I had gone out, there were lumps in places they could not have seen during the fracas, they must have turned me over and danced on me. One thing I do recall is the inspector went ballistic when he saw me. He promised there would be no charges and it would not be covered up. All I asked for was a doctor. I passed out again but no doctor came. At 6.45am I was hauled out of the cell and charged with the following; Assault on four police officers, violent disorder in a police station and criminal damage. Oh! And, reported for possibly driving a car without MOT.

I was thrown out semi conscious to find my own way home. My father picked me up and he was visibly shaken at the sight of me. All I could tell him was the truth but he could not believe me. And why should he? This was not Turkey or Bosnia this was Stockton on Tees. "You don't get that for a bloody tax disc I know," and "You had better tell me what you've done," he balled. When I told him the story from day one he still doubted me but had to act.

We got doctor reports, photographs and a good solicitor called John Hill. We made an official complaint. It was then I discovered the identity of Shining Buttons. His name was Ray Mallon, a shining star, tipped for the top. He was in the England water polo team or such like. Anyway, he was a hero on a mission to cut crime so much that he eventually became famous and become known as ROBOCOP, challenger of evil, champion of justice and the future of British policing.

Time went on and as it did I seemed to become more popular with the police. They seemed to be concerned for my safety. Whenever I ventured out in a car they would take time to stop me to make sure it was road worthy and also they would breathalyse me to make sure I was OK to drive, how considerate of them. I started to get sick when they started arresting me because it was positive, (I never got to see the tube) after many fruitless trips to the police station and mad endorsements on my licence, they included two for fog lamp brackets protruding more than 3 inches from the car they were Ford's own but if a traffic cop who has done his 14 day course in car safety says they are dangerous then you get three points and a fine.

At court it appeared I had no chance, my word against four popular bobbies? The place was full of top brass; it was a big case, their shining star and the reputation of the force was at stake. As usual the complaints against police cannot be dealt with until any criminal proceedings connected with the complainant have been dealt with. During the prosecution, which, is always first my brief cross-examined the witnesses against me. It was during this time the judge had already grasped what had really happened that night. I was first up after the opening speech, I got to the bit about me still being there at 4.30am and the judge stepped in and stopped the trial. He ordered the charge Sergeant Horrocks back to the box and demanded to know why I had still been there. "We were trying to ascertain if Mr Berriman had driven a vehicle without proper documentation at some time in the past." The judge knew he could not let the details of this farce be made public by allowing my testimony to continue so he stopped the trial and directed I be found not guilty.

He was scathing in his remarks to the senior policemen present and demanded action against the pathetic pieces of shit sat at the front in their shining buttons looking confused and hurt. They were so thick and arrogant they could not believe a court had found against them. My complaint was upheld and there was harsh action for most concerned.

Viv - The Final Chapter

General Background

I decided after much consideration that I should leave the country. I had built up a decent few quid in business. I bought a classic Crayford Ford Cortina convertible and set off with my girlfriend at that time Jill. We ended up in Jersey where I blagged the best job on the island. I was the lifeguard/blue coat at Pontins holiday camp. There were only vacancies for waitresses for females and Jill did not last long before she ran home to her rich daddy. I had a ball; I could not get to the bar for people buying me drinks. A lot of husbands send the wife and kids to theses places while they work or holiday with "The lads" they assume its all bingo, kids and conga. There is more sex goes on in those chalets than anywhere I have ever been. Carry on Shagging would have been made in a place like this.

I had a great time until the assistant manager (entertainment) developed a crush on me. He was a big guy, camp as you like but took it too far at the dinner table. It was his day off and he was pissed, after an hour of listening to him whispering all the things he wanted to do to me, he grabbed my hand and forced it up his shorts. It was like arm wrestling in secret, I was trying to maintain a normal presence in front of five hundred guests and the other blue coats at the table. As soon as I touched his bollocks I gave him a kiss, a Glasgow kiss. His eyebrow was split and he rolled around the floor screaming like a camp stuck pig for maximum effect. The best job on the island slipped away. But hey, there is a limit to what you will do to keep your job, right girls!

THE AUBRIENDER

The ship was laid alongside the old customs quay, which had been sold to a company who were busy building high-rise waterfront apartments. She was a 117 feet ex Royal navy mine sweeper of the "fairmile B" class. Built of mahogany and stuff. She had been converted at various times in her life for use as a "Boozer cruiser", rum smuggler and more recently a houseboat. To cut a long story short I had all sorts of ideas and plans for this vessel and my head did not stop buzzing until the auction the next week.

We arrived back in Gibraltar with plenty of time. The auctioneer had informed me the ship had been used as security with a bank based in Gib. The owner had defaulted leaving it in the hands of sitting tenants who lived on board and sold various bits of it to anyone who wanted them. The hull and machinery were all there but there was no steering or controls, just an empty wheelhouse. I expected it to fetch about £30,000. I knew I could raise 25k and at a push the 30k. A handful turned up in time for the start, including the bank manager and auctioneer.

I was well nervous; I'd been to many auctions but never one for a ship. Off we went and the bidding started at £3000, up went my hand and that was the last bid, everybody else had come out of interest only and I discovered I was the only registered bidder present. A very embarrassed bank manager and auctioneer hastily conferred then offered the ship to me for £4000. I couldn't believe my luck, shook on it and gave him a cash deposit in exchange for the receipt.

Soon after, as I was trying to contain my joy, a car full of businessmen turned up in a serious panic. They had come to buy the ship but had been delayed at the infamous Spanish frontier. The bank manager tried to get the auctioneer to restart the auction. After a torrent of abuse and threats from myself, the sale stood and I owned a ship. I was offered £24,000 for it there and then but refused. I liked owning a ship, which I now described as a 120-foot motor yacht, which was nice. I used a whole roll of film and took many notes. I allowed the "squatters" to stay on board until I returned on condition they sold nothing else and cleaned up some of the mess while I was away.

Back in England I sourced much of what I needed to make the thing habitable and jammed it all into a transit van. As usual everybody thought I was mad but with a couple of pals to help me we set off with a huge wad of cash with the sole intention of getting this "yacht" to move under its own steam from the quay where it had lain for 6 years. Some 1,700 miles later we arrived at six in the morning. The squatters had taken advantage of my kindness, as I discovered by comparing photo's I had taken of various bits and bobs. Lots of stuff had been sold or taken off. I woke the motley bunch, who informed me they had not found anywhere to live; they had rights and insisted they were allowed a few more weeks on board, rent-free. They obviously had no idea who they were messing with, but one hour later we had wired up our generator to the main circuit board and started it without consideration to the exhaust fumes which smoked out the whole ship from the engine room. Thirty minutes later we were throwing the last of their belongings alongside, cheeky bastards.

****

There ends Phil's story and to round off the Robocop situation to date Ray Mallon has tendered his resignation because he claims fighting Operation Lancet has become too costly therefore he wishes to pursue a political career in running for the job of Mayor.

His resignation was declined and to date he remains suspended. The CPS decided there were no criminal charges to lay against him, but he does face disciplinary charges for which he will be dealt with at top level. Had Mallon's resignation been accepted then of course such disciplinary charges would have been discontinued so we have to consider that he might be made an example of.

An uncanny death caused a stir when the former Chief Constable of Hampshire Police Force, Sir John Hoddinott, 56, was found dead in Middlesbrough's Thistle Hotel. Nothing uncanny about dying in bed, but when you consider that the retired officer was appointed in May 2000 to investigate operation Lancet because of his known tenacity for getting to the bottom of such things it does seem rather bizarre that he should die whilst visiting Middlesbrough to hold preliminary meetings relating to the £7m inquiry into allegations of corruption within Middlesbrough's CID and its chief - Robocop.

Police have claimed there were no suspicious circumstances attached to Sir Hoddinott's death and when he failed to turn up for breakfast it was his colleague, Detective Chief Superintendent Keith Ackerman, who found him dead in bed.

Sir Hoddinott was not conducting the Lancet investigation but he was there to ensure the operation had been carried out properly, but as Phil Berriman claims the likelihood of such an investigation being made public as to what was discovered is highly unlikely considering the overall depth of cover ups we've had from many a past inquiry into such corruption in various other governmental agencies.

An interesting point to note is that the death of Sir Hoddinott has put doubt on the future of a review of Operation Lancet!!!! His review was to have helped a government case study on police complaints reforms – his sudden death now casts doubts over such reforms taking place. A new police complaints procedure was being looked at by the Government, which would have meant replacing the Police Complaints Authority with an independent police complaints commission – no doubt run by retired police officers? The Government must learn that the police cannot investigate the police due to freemasonry having worked its way into the system as well as the judicial system being heavily infiltrated by masons. Serious flaws were exposed by one of Britain's biggest anti-corruption enquiries and as an act of protest Barry Foxton a member of the Cleveland Police Authority stood down.

Operation Dollar was set up to examine claims made against other officers in Cleveland force by Superintendent Ray Mallon. A further £326,000 was used in investigating claims of assault, conspiracy to pervert the course of justice, falsehood, neglect of duty, improper disclosure of information, improper treatment of witnesses, incivility and discreditable conduct. Three officers in particular had these allegations levelled at them. After lengthy investigations it was disclosed in early 2001 that the result of another farcical inquiry led to one officer receiving a severe dressing down.

Robocop Mallon fired off some sharp shots when he said: 'One of my statements also raised very serious concerns about the management and control of the Lancet investigation by senior members of Cleveland Police Force and the Complaints Authority. It would appear these concerns are shared by the Home Secretary (replaced in Summer of 2001) Jack Straw, who has asked a retired chief constable, Sir Hoddinott, to review the way this costly inquiry has been run.' Ray Mallon had hopes of Sir Hoddinott revealing improper conduct by senior officers involved in the inquiry and given that Jack Straw has departed from the post of Home Secretary it may seem there is little hope of all being revealed.

6

The Berriman Files

What follows is the taped conversation between Phil Berriman and two police officers. Whilst this was taped there was only one person aware that it was being taped and that was Phil Berriman. He asks me to point out that all what he said was said with some pre-planning.

Statement of Philip BERRIMAN

Age if under 21 over 21 (if over 21 insert 'over 21'). Occupation Businessman. This statement (consisting of 7 pages each signed by me) is true to the best of my knowledge and belief and I make it knowing that, if it is tendered in evidence. I shall be liable to prosecution if I have willfully stated in it anything which I know to be false or do not believe to be true. Dated the 13 day of March 1996

On 30 January 1996 1 was seen by Detective Superintendent FURZELAND and Detective Sergeant WARREN at Stockton-On-Tees Police Station. The purpose of the meeting was to allow the officers to speak to me about the background of my recent case at Exeter Crown Court, the making of a recording of an interview which took place at HM Prison Horfield, Bristol between myself and two officers of the Regional Crime Squad and to enquire into an allegation of perjury committed by those same two officers. I was asked if I had any objections to my witness interview being tape-recorded. I had no objections provided that I was given a copy of each tape. In fact I had brought along my own small pocket tape-recorder but did not use it. At the conclusion of the interview I was given a copy of each tape.

The whole of the interview was tape-recorded and the three tapes each bear a label marked NICW12 and then 1-2-3 respectively. I have signed each label.

I am able to say that this statement has been formulated from a transcript of the tape recordings made on the 30th January 1996 and the 13th March 1996, and I have agreed to this course of action.

On 5 September 1994 1 was arrested at Durgan in Cornwall in connection with the importation of cannabis resin. I was subsequently charged together with two other men and remanded in custody by the magistrates' court. During my remand time I was variously at HM Prisons Exeter, Bristol and Belmarsh.

On 2 October 1995 my trial commenced at Exeter Crown Court and continued until 2 November 1995 when I was acquitted of the charges.

During the course of a conversation at Bristol with another prisoner unconnected with my charge I mentioned that I was expecting a visit from police officers to interview me about a gun found at my home address following my arrest. As a result of what he told me I decided to try and tape-record the interview without their knowledge so that I could not be blamed as an informant and for other reasons detailed in this statement.

I could not get a small tape-recorder into the prison because I was a 'high risk' prisoner. So I decided to secret a tape-recorder which I already possessed in prison inside a hard cardboard box file. I obtained such a file and a sheaf of A4-sized paper and cut out a hollow big enough to take the 'Realistic' make tape-recorder which I owned. Having cut out the hole I glued the A4 paper together with toothpaste, put the tape-recorder into the hollow and then covered it over with sheets of paper with holes in where the microphone was and put some sheets of paper from my defence papers on top. In all the thickness of the paper was about four inches. This consisted on the top of the front sheet naming the defendants and the second sheet, page 86 of the Court bundle. The remainder of the papers were committal papers of another prisoner.

On 29 November 1994 whilst at HIM Prison Bristol I received two visits from police officers. The first in the morning was from a Chief Inspector ALLDAY and his colleague concerning a complaint which I had earlier made and the other in the afternoon from Detective Sergeant KITCHING and Detective Constable McDOUGALL. The morning visit enabled me to put into practice my plan to tape-record the interview. I did not know who it was who would visit me firstly.

I have been shown by Detective Sergeant WARREN on 30 January 1996 a tape cassette bearing the label PJD/1 which I have signed. Stuck onto the cassette is a white label which bears the legend '29 November 1994 - 2 pm'. I can say that I wrote the time and date upon the stick-on label in my cell at HIM Prison Bristol at 14.00 hours on 29 November 1994 and I identify the writing as mine, thus I can positively identify the tape cassette as the brand new unused one which I inserted into my 'Realistic' make tape-recorder and then switched it on and recorded a short test message upon it before switching it off. I did all this because I did not know the time that the visit would start.

The actual sequence of what happened is that some time after 2pm that day, 29 November 1994. 1 was taken from my cell by two prison officers and at the entrance to the wing two further officers with dogs joined us to take me to the visiting block. In the block I was strip searched and then dressed in prison clothes. The box file which contained the tape-recorder was looked at but not thoroughly examined.

As I walked into the visits room I switched the tape recorder on. I then had about 45 minutes of taped conversation. The two officers were waiting for me in the visiting room. I searched them by tapping them down to make sure they were not 'wired up' in any way. They allowed me to do this, I was aware they had a tape-recorder with them but this was not used in the interview. During the course of their interview I allowed my tape to run continuously, I did not switch the recorder on or off nor did I press the pause button. The interview lasted almost an hour. I knew that I didn't want to be sitting there having a conversation any longer than I really had the tape, because it would be a pointless exercise. I didn't want to be in that room for any length of time without the tape playing.

The Berriman Files

When I put the tape-recorder down on the floor and closed the lid of the box so that they couldn't hear it switch off and I was sure it was switched off then I made a conscious effort to finalise the interview. I wanted to be out of there. I knew that the time that they entered and left the prison would be recorded and I knew that it wouldn't be much use me having a tape if I had been sat in the room with them for two hours. It took me about ten minutes to wind up the interview without making it too obvious.

After the interview I was again strip searched, redressed in my own clothes and returned to my cell. The box file containing the tape-recorder was not examined. In my cell I copied the tape (PJD/l) onto another tape using a Panasonic tape-recorder which I was also in possession of. On the other side of the copy tape is the tape-recording of the interview which I had had with Chief Inspector ALLDAY that morning. I have arranged for the police to recover that tape from my father. I would emphasise that the tape PJD/l is a genuine recording. I have not edited, wiped off or cleaned anything from it. It is a continuous recording with no stops or 'pauses' after the test message.

Having recorded the tape PJD/l within the following few days, I prepared type written excerpts from the conversation which I thought were relevant and gave them to my solicitor. Henry MILNER along with the tape PJD/I. I identified who was talking at any one time on the type written excerpts to assist my solicitors in drawing up a transcript. I saw the transcript for the first time on 16 October 1995 before Detective Constable McDOUGALL gave evidence.

I now return to the interview which I had with Detective Sergeant KITCHING and Detective Constable McDOUGALL on 29 November 1994 at Bristol Prison. The interview covered a number of issues. Firstly I was aware through my solicitor that I was to be interviewed about a gun found at my house after my arrest in September 1994. Whilst in custody in Camborne McDOUGALL said to me that I was under arrest for possession of a class one firearm or something similar to that. He said there was a loaded handgun found at my property. I said I have never had a handgun and told him it was a CS gas gun which I had for protection. I was not charged with any firearms offences in September 1994. Then on 29 November 1994 at Bristol Prison after meeting them I later said, "I THOUGHT YOU'D COME ABOUT THE GUN" and McDOUGALL said, "NO, THAT'S JUST AN EXCUSE TO GET IN TO SEE YOU". I was not interviewed further about the gun, nor did I decline to be interviewed on tape, but before the officers left I handed them a type-written statement I had earlier prepared regarding my possession of the gun. At the end of the interview I was handed a charge sheet with two firearms offences on it. I told the officers I had cleared the gun with Customs through Dover. Those firearms charges have never been pursued.

Secondly, again whilst in custody at Camborne, I recall I had two conversations with McDOUGALL which were not recorded on tape as part of a taped interview. One was when McDOUGALL came to see me without my solicitor, Mr HART or Mr BARBER being present and told me to give the police any information, not the Customs as they couldn't be trusted. This conversation took place between McDOUGALL and myself in my cell before any formal interview took place. The second occasion was a short conversation with McDOUGALL and BARBER but in the absence of my solicitor Mr HART. This was to do with two Customs men in Hemel Hempstead whom I'd met in March 1994. 1 asked whether they were aware that somebody had already had a word with me and BARBER said, "NO". That was the end of the conversation.

The meeting was in relation to a different job. I was approached by two guys to put heroin onboard a boat. To me it was obvious these two were undercover Customs men. I won't get involved in heroin and in the end I thought this is ridiculous because if they wanted to they could have stitched me up for something so I thought I am going to cancel this out and I rang Customs and I went down and I gave them information. One of the two Customs men in Hemel Hempstead was called John McELLIGOTT. My diary contains a yellow 'Post-it' note bearing the phone number of Customs House in London which was the number I used to make contact.

I was not invited to sign any note made by either McDOUGALL or BARBER relating to either of the two 'off the record' conversations at Camborne at any time. At no time did I say anything about wanting to give information either then or in the future.

Whilst in custody at Camborne I didn't speak to KITCHING at all apart from maybe "HELLO" or something like that. I am not sure if he charged me or not.

Thirdly, going on from this on the subject of giving information, on 29 November 1994 at Bristol Prison, McDOUGALL reminded me that I'd offered to give information to him whilst in custody at Camborne. This was not true. During this interview the name CONROY was brought up by McDOUGALL, I said nothing about CONROY. McDOUGALL then brought up the name of BROOKS, this was after my tape had finished. BROOKS is an acquaintance of mine whose phone number was in my diary which Customs officers had seized. The only thing I said about BROOKS to them was that I thought he was involved in putting people together. I have met the man but that was to do with a rigid inflatable boat. I did not give any specific information about BROOKS. The officers said to me that I'd be better off giving them information because they were going to say that I did anyway and destroy my defence of duress and make me out to be a 'grass'.

They said they'd get me some time off my sentence and put a letter into the judge. I made it clear I wasn't going to give information because these people just kill people. I just wanted to get out because the tape had ended.

I was also asked by the officers for information about others involved in drug smuggling. I gave them no names nor did I name those responsible for threats to me and my family which were ongoing.

I have never given any information to DC McDOUGALL or DS KITCHING or any other officer on the Regional Crime Squad or any other police officer anywhere in the country.

Fourthly, I have been asked if I have any knowledge of a boat called Miramar or Miramar II. I do not know of a boat of that name but I know of a hotel in Mohammadia, Morocco called Miramar.

The tape I made at Bristol Prison does not reveal that I spoke about my father being made drunk on a boat in order that the people who did it could break into his boat the Michelle Louise and take his telephone book. This was done and my mother received a phone call to say that my father had had a heart attack and they wanted to know if she could get hold of me. I mentioned to DC McDOUGALL and DS KITCHING that the boat my father was taken to was moored behind the Sea Witch and I seem to recall my Father mentioned the name LORIMER or LORIMER II but it was definitely something 'II'. This boat was registered in London to a Dutch man. This was a conversation after the tape had run out.

There was a card on the Melanie, the boat which was used to bring the drugs into Durgan referring to the phone number of that hotel from a time when I used the phone in Mohammadia. That card was seized when the boat was searched. I believe the card was subsequently returned to me but I have since disposed of it.

Finally, I have been shown by Detective Sergeant WARREN an exhibit used in my trial at Exeter Crown Court. This is a copy of page 86 of the court bundle and is exhibit NLD/2. I knew that this document had not been in my house when it was searched following my arrest as the prosecution alleged. I knew what I was involved in at the time so I made sure that there was nothing at all in my house relevant to anything because I did not want to be connected to anybody. When I showed this document to DC McDOUGALL, I recall he read out the words "BRIBES PAID" which appear on the document.

By 6 September 1994, when I was still in custody at Camborne, anything to do with cannabis or anything else was faxed down to McDOUGALL and BARBER for the purpose of the final interview and that document was never mentioned. A few weeks later, four or five weeks later when I got the court bundles, that piece of paper turns up. That's when I knew they were fitting me up. So when I knew the police were coming, I decided to pull them about it. This was one of the pieces of paper I had on top of the tape-recorder. When it was coming up to the end of the 45 minutes of tape I opened the file and took out the piece of paper and said, "WHERE'S THAT FROM?" I wanted them to admit that they hadn't seen it, that it hadn't been at my house and what was going on with it.

McDOUGALL picked it up and read it and said, "I'VE NEVER SEEN IT". I was trying to get him to say they've done that to incriminate you or whatever and in the trial when McDOUGALL was on the stand he lied and said, 'I HAVE NEVER SEEN THIS DOCUMENT UNTIL I CAME TO COURT THIS WEEK," when the tape proved that he had. They had known since 29 November 1994 that I disputed where this document had been found. I would add that KITCHING also denied ever having seen the document. I believe the handwriting on the document is mine but according to my evidence I gave the document to the Customs Officer McELLIGOTT in the March before I was arrested because it was to do with these Turkish people I spoke to McELLIGOTT about. During the course of the trial McELLIGOTT was asked about the document. He denied ever having it.

I believe that after he had given evidence at my trial, McDOUGALL had told KITCHING that there was a tape of the interview on 29 November 1994. That was blatantly obvious.

After the judge warned him not to, McDOUGALL had been in touch with KITCHING and forewarned him that there was a tape of the conversation. Specifically, I think KITCHING didn't do a lot of lying in court apart from the fact that he said he hadn't known about the tape as he hadn't been warned. McDOUGALL was challenged on point after point, "DID YOU SAY THIS?" "NO, I DIDN'T." He was asked to repeat it two or three times and warned about perjury. He said he'd reminded me that I wanted to give information at Camborne. That was absolutely untrue.

In conclusion I believe McDOUGALL and KITCHING came to see me in Bristol Prison to recruit me as an informant and a 'grass'. McDOUGALL said the interview about the gun was just an excuse to come and see me. I refused to be an informant and I gave him reasons why I wouldn't be an informant. I recorded the interview because I wanted them to admit to me that Customs were withholding evidence, the threats to me and who was really behind the job. I knew that they were on the main firm (people involved in importing drugs) and that they had two informants. Customs pulled one of these men out of the job knowing I would be forced to sail the boat. I was trying to prove they used *agent provocateurs* and I wasn't the main man as they were trying to make out. Also I wanted to include on the tape page 86 of the court bundle as I have already mentioned.

What McDOUGALL and KITCHING did for the sake of a conviction is to put my life at risk because what they said in court was printed in the newspapers and it was also on the television. The prosecution's case was put forward that I offered to be a 'supergrass'. That was a deliberate lie which they threatened me with in Bristol Prison on 29 November 1994 to make me plead guilty or do a deal and give them information. What they have done to me is basically tell the whole criminal fraternity in the North East of England that I am a 'grass'. They put my life in danger. I was in hospital on 24 January I had twenty odd staples in the back of my head. I've got hammer marks all up my legs, I've got broken fingers, bashed elbows and bruises. I have been unable to walk and am on painkillers. I believe McDOUGALL and KITCHING deliberately told those lies as part of a threat they made to me on 29 November 1994.

I have read the original statement of my Counsel, Mr. Trevor BURKE, dated 12 March, 1996, and I have no objection to that statement being adduced in evidence.

TRANSCRIPT OF MR BERRIMAN'S TAPE OF 29TH NOVEMBER 1994 AT 2PM.

B = Phil Berriman M = Det. Constable McDougal K = Det Sergeant Kitching
Testing one, two, three. Three, two, one.
Ten, two ....testing one, two, three, four, five. Five, four, three, two one.
This is the 29th November in Bristol Prison.

B	Alright,
M	**Hi Mr Berriman, how you doing?**
B	What's happening then?
M	**We've come to see you.**
B	I thought you'd come about the gun.
M	**Oh, that's just an excuse to get in.**
M	**Someone came this morning you know.**

114

The Berriman Files

B   Err, Chief Inspector Allday.

K   Bastard.

M   I know him he's a cunt, what did he come for?

B   He was the one who investigated the Porsche thing, when my Porsche turbo was bumped outside the yard and even the insurance investigators, their own engineer and their valuer valued the car pre-accident, seen it, they knew about the car, knew about the accident and he said he agreed with it and told the insurance company it was 100%, but it was an ex-copper that was investigating on behalf of the insurance company and he got D.S. French in Billingham to do an investigation and they arrested five of us, bloody dawn and everything, dragged us out the bloody house at seven o clock in the morning. And I put a complaint in but they didn't know that I had the original car that had been smashed they thought I'd got rid of it you see. And with me having it they reconstructed the accident and proved it had happened exactly as I said so they were fucked, and now they come to try to get me to drop the complaint but they won't give me information I want. I've already wrote them statement there.

M   So the complaint was against them?

B   Yeah, well against the actual, the fact that they brought an investigation on, when it shouldn't have been.

M   Cos we were supposed to come and see you this morning and were told that he was coming and he said that he wouldn't change it.

B   Well he didn't get it finished but I wrote the statement anyway because he didn't get it finished to get a statement out because the legal visit was over. So I just said "that's what it's like mate, he came all the way from London, my solicitor yesterday for an hour....

M   Is that your new one?

B   Yeah, Henry Milner

M   I've been on the phone to him loads of times but he wouldn't talk to me until he had the legal aid papers.

B   He won't.

M   I'm lucky if I get as far as his receptionist.

K   How did you get in touch with him then, someone just told you he's a good un?

B   He's the best in London

K/M   Is he?

B   Well put it this way he got John, er Tony White of the Brinx Matt robbery he was the only one acquitted.

M   How did you get onto him then?

B   They put me in high-risk category mate, Tony White's in for

the same thing and he's on our landing.

M   Ah so he put in a good word? I wondered why you'd sacked the beatnik.

K   You have to admit like he was a fanny wasn't he?

B   He is an idiot.

M   He represented you initially so he was alright (unintelligible) how's things in here, looks a bit fucking dismal from outside.

B   About the worst nick in the country apparently

M/K   Is it?

M   Well someone rang up.

B   Who?

M   I haven't a clue.

B   So if anybody rings any police station and says anybody on remand is going to get...

M   Somebody... somebody knows who it is but I don't.

B   Surely they're going to have records of it?

M   Someone will probably know.

B   So, somebody rings up and says that and because of that it's like twenty odd grand or something to take me to court every time.

M   No, it's not somebody ringing up, somebody has spoken to a policeman and said "Berriman's going to get fucking sprung on the way to court."

K   And it's not the Crime Squad either.

M   It's a detective in Stockton.

B   Somebody?

M   It's a detective in Stockton, I'll tell you who it is, I don't know who the bloke is. (?)

B   Who is it?

M   Haven't a clue, I dunno.

B   Well who's the detective?

M   I don't know who the detective is.

B   Well you've got to know, you can't, you can't expect to spend hundreds of thousands of pounds running me down to Truro without knowing who it is, surely it's to do with case. It's bloody ridiculous.

(Other conversation partly intelligible concerning the same subject)

K   Well it's stupid man.

M   Well it's custom's case.

K   It's their case.

M   This detective's got some information from somebody in Stockton and he's gone to the customs and said, "such and such is going

to happen." So customs have said "right well get him put in category A to make sure it doesn't happen."

B   High risk category A, high risk category A, like I can't ring anybody, I can't call anybody, I can't do anything, I'm banged up 23 hours a day.

K   **Well you see what would we benefit doing that to you?**

B   (laughs)

K   **Well I've got no gripe against you.**

B   Er?

K   **I don't even work in Teesside.**

M   We might be able to do something about changing that for you.

K   **I don't know, I've go no idea.**

M   Well you're getting remand on Thursday aren't you?

B   **Yeah but at the end of the day, what's it going to look like in court. You've shoved me in here, there's only three in place and the other two are ex-Brinx Matt and three famous London bank robbers and you've got me in the same category with my record, negligible, it's a joke man.**

M   Well its got nowt to do with us, its a customs case not ours.

K   **They do all the running around from the moment I saw you down there we've had nowt to do with the case and neither has Billy. (Unintelligible) Their getting a right good fucking run out of it aren't they.**

B   Have they charged anybody else?

M   **Just the three of you as far as I know, they haven't told us.**

B   What a fucking nightmare.

M   **How come the other two have been committed and you haven't yet?**

B   Well because I changed my solicitor, not only that they shifted them from here now and they split them up as well.

M   **Yeah they're in Oxford.**

B   Yeah, but they've put them in different wings as well. Like I said they're obviously not happy with the solicitor I've got and stuff like that. What we are alleging at the moment is that the customs and or I don't know whether it's the police or not but the people involved have deliberately put me in this category to impede my ability to be able to get my witness for my defence or mitigation because we can't have legal visits here - it's well known. It's exactly the same for the other two cat A high risks, they've been put up here when the case was supposed to be held in London, they have been shoved up here because there's no facilities for, umm, legal visits.

Viv - The Final Chapter

M   So, you're not allowed any visits from your family or anything?

B   One of each, an hour, that's it! And I still can't ring my kids. I've sent two sets of papers off, I complained about. I've had two visits from solicitors, one hour each, and they travel from London, and they just say "out" and there's hell on. I can't get evidence and witnesses organised because it's not fresh in my mind.

M   I would have thought that was contrary to some rules.

B   It is contrary to all sorts but I complained about it because I complained about it last week, I put a proper letter in a request complaint form, they shoved me on the filthy cell where I can't get the TV or radio so I'm sat banged up 24 hours day. They have deliberately put me in Bristol prison because of the regime, then they can blame the governor. It's bent; it's a proper conspiracy man. It's Customs; they do it all the time. The other two people, the gear was pulled in Dover and all the people are from London, the Customs are London, and they ship those two up here and put them on high risk.

K   Well, you talked yourself into that. It is the customs that are doing it.

B   I know.

K   I mean you sending that card, I'd love to see it when it goes up there, I mean he is a cunt. They won't believe it up there we have never done a fucking thing, honestly. I mean, you see your fucking case there, I mean customs are reveling in this, their still fucking jetting all over the world. But can you imagine going on an inquiry to Gibraltar or fucking Africa, I could do with a bit of that.

B   Well, I hope they catch something in Dakar.

M   Well, they will go to Gibraltar for one inquiry about the Melanie but the can't just go for a day can they?

B   You should be charging the bloke that gave me the Melanie, he's trying to nick my dad's boat and everything. He's a bastard.

M   That's right yeah, I heard about that.

B   He's given them a statement, an affidavit that I have a copy of, that can be proved with their own surveillance, will prove the total opposite. He's saying that he didn't go out on the boat and this, load of bollocks. The Melanie had left Gibraltar before he signed the contract. He took the bugger out and came back in with a zodiac in full view of Shepard's marina and the observations and they haven't charged him with it!

M   Like I say they don't tell us anything they are doing at all. I mean, that boat has obviously been used on runs before.

B   Yeah, it was all done and dusted man, it had extra diesel, it had extra food on it. It was ready to go, push the button, untie it and gone. It went before he signed the contract, he took it out with the crew and came back with the zodiac. There would be observations on that, and the fact that they would not charge for the days he was gone. It's all there, all the evidence is there and they've just took his story, it's a load of bollocks! If I'd known what he'd tried to do when I was being interviewed by you I would have put him straight in it because he's bang out of order.

K   Well who? He's already made a statement but they are still over there, customs went to Gib on Tuesday last week so they will be due back tomorrow.

B   It might be now that the Gibraltar police have got involved they've got him now and realised that he's telling a pack of lies because the statement that he's made, his affidavit to try and nick the boat and it was only there as an alibi. It was only left there as an alibi. It was only left there as an alibi in case anything came on top, and he was well in the job, he was part of their crew and he was getting 40 grand for the use of his boat and his boat back.

M   So, what I'm thinking of is what happened is when the customs had put a restraining order on the Michelle Louise so nothing could happen to it.

B   He'd registered it in his name.

M   Yeah and he went to a solicitor in Gibraltar and he made an affidavit saying it was his boat.

B   You look at the affidavit and all the observations and all the rest of it that affidavit is absolutely backward, it can't possibly be true. Even with us flying out on the day he was supposed to have gone out on it and all the rest of. The boat's only left the marina once since it was there the Michelle Louise was days and days before he says, totally wrong and all the evidence is there to be got.

M   Would they have found this out?

B   Of course they would.

M   Them being there now, the customs?

B   I'm taking him to court to get the boat back for my dad.

M   Taking him, Lara?

B   Yeah, we've seized the boat, it's registered in my dad's name as a British ship. Now, he's blatantly made an affidavit that can't possibly stand up with all the evidence from the marinas and the observations, everything will prove he's telling a pack of lies. Me, my dad, Billy Winspere, and others we flew from Gatwick the same day as we took him out on the boat, we'd already signed the contract three days before. He said he'd never met my dad till he went to the solicitor's office sign the thing and that what five days before.

M   **So your dad has met him?**

B   Yeah, my dad met him in the solicitor's office and that was it. He signed it over, I told my dad we were registering the boat in Gib to save the VAT in Spain, and the solicitor was in on it as well. We went in and discussed it all, I gave the papers to my dad, they checked his passport, my dad signed the papers and my dad thought he was registering the boat in Gib and that's all he thought. And in fact that was their concoction to get an alibi because the firm, with the boat already been used before; he wanted an alibi in case anything came on top, that was part of the bargain. A bunch of cunts.

M   **Is his solicitor bent as well?**

B   Yep.

K/M   **You knew his name?**

B   Louis Triay.

M   **Cos, we wanting to get a trip out there weren't we?**

K   Yep.

B   **Bent as fuck.**

M   Well, we won't be going now, not with them fuckers.

K   **They've certainly done the dirty on us.**

B   So, what do you want then?

M   **Well, what do you want, do you want any help with your sentence? If you're convicted, basically.**

B   Well I'm going for a serious mitigation, as you know.

M   **Well I don't know what you're going to do, I mean you might have told customs or you might have told your solicitor, no one has told us.**

K   Have customs been to see you?

B   **Customs requested they want to see me.**

K   Well I thought they would be fucking sneaky like that.

B   **They told my solicitor they could consider me extremely helpful.**

M   Your new solicitor?

B   **Yeah**

M   So, it's in the last few weeks then?

B   **Well it's in the last month.**

K   They are fucking cunts.

B   **I know.**

M   Out of courtesy I said to them months and months ago…

B   **And my solicitor was told not to tell you.**

M   By the customs?

B   **Yeah**

K   Customs told your solicitor not to fucking tell the police, who was it, do you know who made the request?

B   **I saw my solicitor yesterday and he told me that customs had made an approach yesterday telling him they want me to work for them. The customs are cunts, you know what I mean they don't give nothing to nobody, I know they don't.**

K   Well, they are even deceiving us.

B   **I know they are.**

K   They fucking shit on us.

B   **The customs have got proof, I know for a fact, certain things in the case, customs have got proof of the intimidation I had, they have proof of that. It's as simple as that and it won't come forward in court.**

K   Well it should do like.

B   **All I would want is, what about the phone taps? I know that the only reason you were waiting for me in the Helford River was the phone, which I accept and understand but if the other phone taps came to light they would also be of me getting threatened. And that's it, they ain't gonna do it. There are threats on the phone about the 4th and 5th of July. I was rung up and threatened with my family and me, and that's on my own phone at home which is very unusual for them, and there was threats on that phone. If they have got phone taps anywhere they would have them of that. And that would be my mitigation.**

(Paddy Conroy says: Berriman says they were waiting for him in the Helford River because of the phone taps but since he was only going to the Helford River on a last minute decision that he might get help to repair his boat then this sounds wrong. How could they have tapped any phone when he was out at sea with no power and no nothing, who would he have called and what for. Berriman blames a phone tap for his own mistake!)

M   I don't think there was any wires there.

K   **I don't know.**

B   There was, all I'm saying is they couldn't possibly have been waiting in the Helford River for me because I did not know I was going there, I had no idea I was going there I just couldn't get any further and the nearest place I could get into the little river was the Helford River and it was in the pilot book that I actually thought there was a bloody yacht yard at Durgan.

(Paddy Says: See, Berriman admits no one knew.)

M   **Who was this for, Paddy?**

B   You might be bloody wired up you two.

M   No, we've got a tape recorder but it's on the floor.

B   Lets have a look then.

M   It's not switched on, it's not plugged in. That's in case I had to interview you about the gun.

B   I've made a statement about the gun if you want it.

M   Why, well we don't really need it, it was just an excuse to get in and see you.

B   I'll give it you later on and you can have a look.

K   So was it Paddy then?

B   You know all the people involved in this case, right, you know that. I haven't got the fucking bottle, I've got as much bottle as anyone I think, but I haven't got the bottle to name the people in the case. You know who it was; you made the mistake of picking him up before the job was over not me.

K   Who's this Paddy?

B   What?

M   Paddy Conroy, who else? There's no one else whose been picked up.

B   Maybe, I don't know, I haven't got the bottle to name anybody, I refuse to name anybody right, it's as simple as that.

M   So are we right saying Paddy Conroy's involved?

B   It's up to you to work what you've got, you've obviously got information, you've got surveillances.

M   There's that many fucking rumours going about?

B   Let me tell you now right, there's more than one firm, all this gear is nothing to do with one firm, this gear, no, its a number of firms it doesn't work like that you have no idea about what goes on, there's different firms along the Costa. All ex this, ex that and all the rest of it. They just put money in and the other firms, the suppliers and stuff like that, they come along and they organise a job. The likes of Conroy or any of them, all they do is they say, "Ok, we can get that in," and they use everybody else in the way that they used me and other people to get the stuff in through threat or by favour. That's what he was bloody kidnapped when he kidnapped the kids in first place in London, because the fucking guy wouldn't come across the border and drive it across. It's common knowledge man. You have those types of people in that category as being the main men and they are not, they are not the main men.

K   That's what we certainly thought they was.

B   Yeah, but they are not, its big the people who get them to shift 20's and 30's and 50 tons in a year. They come in all sorts of different places, they come in all sorts of different ways.

K **And they go undetected.**

B   Exactly, because they only deal through them. Now, what happens is people, the likes of the Newcastle firms and stuff like that who get a hundred kilos dropped off or whatever on account, they knock it out for a couple of hundred quid a kilo on top. They get greedy and they want to get involved in it. So they tell them they've got the facilities to get an X amount of shipment in. When the shipment comes, they say they've got the facilities to get it in. So, they get a chance at it, see what I mean? I mean all them firms up in Newcastle have been bang at it. They've been trying for bloody years and failed because they won't employ professional crew and they won't give them the money to sort things out. And they won't give anybody what its worth to do it.

K **What would you get out of that?**

B   All I was doing was paying off a debt, and there was a £100,000 sweetner because they had been taking money off me for the last year.

M **Oh, I know you were in a lot of debt as well, weren't you.**

B   Yeah, I haven't paid a bill in a year. Every week they have been coming down. Who do you think got all the money for all the gear from my yard? You have no idea what goes on.

K **I didn't know this, I knew you were in debt but you've always looked good, you know what I mean.**

B   I've always earned good money, up until a year ago mate last September or so, I used to earn two grand a week stood on my head and I spent it. I haven't paid a bill in a year. I've got bailiffs at the door but you know all that by the documentation that you've got. I've been paying a debt that they discovered I owed about a year ago. And this was a final way of getting out of paying, it was that or be hurt.

M **Have you had any threats since?**

B   Oh come on, me bloody girlfriends living at her mother's house. She can't bloody do anything. Of course I've had threats since. You know what I mean; it's as simple as that. It's not my job to put people away. I've done what I've done for my own sake and my own family's sake. The people concerned are not opposed to be pulling kids out their beds in the middle of the night and taking them away. You know that, you know they've done that.

K **Aye, I know.**

B   This is the situation, it is down to you people to put them away, not me. You know yourself you can catch them bang at something and by the time somebody gets to court they have been in touch with the witnesses and there is no case to answer. And that's what's happening in this case now.

M **You know yourself they are hard to get at.**

B   Of course they're hard to get at, because they have got everybody feared to death. You wouldn't go and pull him on your own; you wouldn't go and pull any of them on your own. Only pull them if you have an armed carry on and that. It's horrendous what goes on and other people have to take the fall for it. There's no way in the world people can make statements against people or any of the crew. I'll tell you what, there was a kid in here, a German kid, he brought some gear into the country. It was only 30K or something, he grassed the people up. He got out of here 3 weeks ago to day because he only got 15 months and he served some on remand. He'd grassed people up and people got arrested. He got on the plane; he got off the plane in Germany and was shot through the head in his hometown before he got to his door, dead! From the same landing as me, for grassing on 30 kilos, for naming the people. And the other kid he has grassed is on the other wing. That's what your dealing with man, your talking about some serious men. They do anything!

M **I mean what we are after, we are not after a fucking statement.**

B   Well, what are you after?

M **We are after what you can just tell us.**

B   What's in it for me?

M **Well, what we can do if your convicted cos you have been warned your going to be convicted, what your looking at is 12 years no just say 10 to 12 years.**

B   There's a bloke just been done with 17 ton and he got a 12 and his crew got an 8 and he was part and parcel of the whole organisation. How the hell can you give me a 12-year? I'm looking at 6 to 8.

M **Say we are looking at 8.**

B   Yeah?

M **Right, I'm sure you'd rather do a bit less than that wouldn't you?**

B   Of course I would.

M **Well what we can do is put a letter into the Judge, saying you have been very helpful to us and we've had such and such results out of it, and it lessens your sentence, and nobody gets to know. Your solicitor doesn't get to know, anybody. A sealed letter goes to the Judge; I mean you've heard of it happening before haven't you?**

B   Yeah, but what information could I give you that you could actually use in court?

M   **No, not use in court, it's to start inquiries off you tell us John Smith's financing a big importation, we start working on John Smith and we get the evidence but nothing you tell us will be given in evidence.**

B   And this is legal?

M   **Yes, it's legal.**

K   It happens all the time.

M   **Yeah, well aye.**

K   A letter to the judge, it happens all the time, but it's mainly that (unintelligible)

B   **Well, I would be happy with just the phone tapes were brought forward that would prove the intimidation and then I've got half a chance. They can help even if I go guilty, at least I'm only going to get a couple of years aren't I with mitigation?**

M   Well, that could be mitigation for you I suppose.

B   **Well, that's what it is, mitigation.**

M   Well like I say, that's in the customs hands. I mean we can't do anything with what customs have got cos they wouldn't tell us, you know yourself by us coming here today.

K   **They've not fucking told us. It's their case now and we just can't get anywhere near it. The only thing we can do really is put that letter forward which happens all the time and it works, I mean if your going to get convicted your going to get convicted, there's nowt we can do about that. But, at the end of the day if the judge reads this in his own chambers.**

B   Yeah but what I'm saying is if I go on a mitigation thing as a guilty with mitigation, obviously just production of the evidence that exists would help me. You know what I mean and the type of mitigation that I can prove already, even without your phone taps or without the information that I know they have got would help me tremendously.

M   **It's very unlikely, if they've information like that.**

B   Well, you must know that they've got phone taps because they wouldn't have been in the Helford River that morning.

(Paddy says: come on now, you can't believe this when he's only gone and said earlier on that even he didn't know he was going to end up here.)

M   **Customs do things and they don't tell anybody. If they got phone taps, they won't come out.**

B   I've been studying this lot and they haven't half got some power.

M   **More power than us, more power. Now if they did have something like taped conversations of you on the phone, there's no way**

whatsoever that will ever be released in court.

B   But why?

M   Because they don't.

B   But how they gonna prove where I was coming in with the boat?

M   They don't have to prove that, the fact that you came in, they don't have to say how they knew, do they?

B   No, I suppose not.

M/K   (Unintelligible).

B   So, if I'm in a position to give you information, what's to stop them blocking whatever information you give to the judge?

M   Can't do that.

B   But you said yourself.

M   We approach the judge ourselves, not them, nothing to do with them.

K   See at the end of the day we are going to be at your trial, we will be there with the customs and there's nowt to stop us putting that letter in it happens all the time, every day, and it works. I mean it's not going to get you off. You know, the type of thing it does do recently there was a guy looking at 5 years, he was convinced he was going to get 5 or 6 years and he got 15 months which was a result of a letter.

M   That was my job and that was 4 weeks ago.

B   Yeah, but how's that going to look if I get convicted of that amount of cannabis and I end up getting 3 years?

K   No, nobody knows. I mean the judge might not have got his leg over the night before or he might have you know he happy. I mean judges you know what they are like, their up and down, there's not one of them uniform are they? They're all bloody different. You know one judge might give you 10 years another judge might give you 6. There's just no guidelines for them, they do what they bloody want, don't they?

B   Obviously, from me standing here in a high risk situation you can understand from my point of view that all this looks a bit pie in the sky to me.

K   Oh yeah of course, but the thing is we're not asking you to grass on people where it's obvious that a grass has been involved, I mean CID would say, "Right, you're give you information where there is stolen property." CID knocks on the door, you lock the cunt up and the lad says, "Fucking hell I've been grassed, somebody has grassed me." Well with the Crime Squad that won't happen because if you put us in the direction nobody knows because then it would start the operation (unintelligible) and the sole reason for the Crime Squad doing that will be that somebody in the

Criminal Intelligence Service has informed us of the target.

B **Yeah but how then do you transfer all that, obviously by the time I get to court none of it will transpire and how the hell do you know then what's going on?**

M Because, say you give us something to work on and we're working on it and it hasn't come to a head by the time you come to trial, then what we mention in the letter as well as that (unintelligible) and we tell them like this is happening, John Smith's going to do a big importation and we're waiting for it coming in, this is all the result of what Philip's told us.

K **No Solicitors, nowt, Billy and me and no customs either.**

B Yeah, but you know I've been to bloody customs and that, you know what I mean it doesn't come forward like that does it?

M **Well we don't know what's happened do we; I mean they won't tell me about this.**

B How on earth without anything official, it's like me being up there on high risk, how does it look, if I'm getting no favours? You know what I'm saying and if I go to court as a high risk and I get convicted of all this cannabis and I can't prove duress.

K **If you're on high risk you're a high risk through no fault of your own, now I mean if you're on high risk because your going round stabbing prison officers but you're in here through no fault of your own, aren't you? That will not go against you, not at all, that will be all taken into consideration.**

M Have you thought, I mean, I don't know but this is something that could have happened if this person that's told a policeman at Stockton that you were going to get sprung on the way to court, have you thought that person could be one of the people involved in the case and wants to keep you on high risk?

B **Yeah that's what I believe.**

M That could be the case.

B **Somebody's done that. The simple reason is there's stuff going round in this trial that people don't want me to find out about. I can't get information about it, even my pals daren't talk to me, they've dropped me in the shit. I tell you what my whole view on the public, on all the people that I've always respected has totally disintegrated. What's happened to me has been the best lesson of my life I appreciate it, honestly. Because I've been pulling people out of the shit and helping people out and not doing this and not doing all that for years and years and years and the minute I'm in the shit, I tell you what they won't even go and get me addresses. I haven't got my phone book, I can't ring any-**

body, I can't write to anybody, I can't do nothing. My girlfriend's frightened to death she's been told by the customs that if she contacts me or discusses anything at all to do with anything she'll be arrested and charged.

K   They can't stop her.

K   No, it's just a threat.

B   I know it's a threat, I've told my girlfriend that and I've told my solicitor to tell her that, but the same thing is she's frightened to fucking death. I'm ringing up and saying can you find out when such and such happened or what date that happened and all the rest of it and because people have been approached by the customs and told that they can't do it, it's as simple as that. You wouldn't believe the conspiracy that's gone on with the customs; the power they have got is fucking horrendous.

K   Aye now, but we are fucking police and we're complaining, you know what I mean.

M   I tell you what we could try and do, it might work, it might not work is get you taken off cat A. Because the threat's not there you're not being transported to and from court.

B   Well I am.

K   Well only once more.

B   Yeah.

K.   Once you're committed.

B   Yeah, but what I'm saying is if I was to give you information regarding other people and all the rest of it, and I stand up in court and I get fucking 8 or 10 years, regardless of what you say, how the fucking hell do I know what you can and what you can't do, you hear about it.

K   Well I think the best, well you don't know about me from our Ann you've known Billy for many years; he's potentially the more trustworthy policeman that you know of. It's basically down to trust, we've got nothing I don't even work down in Teesside, so whatever you...

B   But you must know for a long time, I've always been in the grey area of the law, and a thorn in the police's side in our area, from years ago when I complained about the police assaulting me (talk over each other).

K   I'm told by Billy, I've been down there a year and I've moved around Teesside, I haven't a bloody clue about you or what have you, I just know about the case but I mean if (unintelligible) I wouldn't ask you to say something but Billy, Billy is straight as fuck. (Extraneous noise on tape - discussion mentioning Berriman's phone book)

B   See me being in the motor trade and that sort of area, and I

have parties in the home and stuff like that, the amount of people that come down with dodgy connections you know, I've always been very well trusted in our area it's as simple as that. So what are we actually talking about?

M   If you can give us a nice tasty job it's something that's going to help you. That's basically what it's about, it doesn't affect us one way or the other (over-talking) whether you get something off.

B   **As far as you're concerned I'm guilty of importing cannabis.**

M   You took a risk it's as simple as that.

B   **The risk wasn't there, listen I wasn't meant to be on the boat.** (Paddy says: Well if he wasn't supposed to be on the boat then that explains why it was pulled in. Because only Berriman knew where the boat was going or so he says.)

M   What I'm saying   (interrupted).

B   **I'm not prepared to go on board a boat like that, my sailing experience, although I consider myself to be competent, my sailing experience is nothing like what we did on that job, I mean nothing even approaching that. You can go to any port in the land, in the world and you never have me coming in or out other than the times I've already stated to my solicitor. I haven't got qualifications or experience to go on a trip like that, to go 10,000 miles on a boat like that without help (unin-telligible) is bloody suicide. I didn't go on that job by choice.**

M   That's good mitigation for you.

B   **I know (all over talk) but at the same time, at the end of the day if I get a guilty of it, it's still going to be an importation of bloody 3.7 tons of cannabis.**

M   At the end of the day, if you get a guilty on that, with your mitiga-tion, which you're relying a lot on, and a letter.

B   **So I can rely on.**

M   And a letter, that goes some way, it may not be a lot but it can cer-tainly get you a couple of years knocked off.

K   **And from the outside, it will look as though it's the mitigation that's done it.**

M   It's possible, I mean it's grasping at straws but it's there to be grasped if you want it and only you can do that, we're not asking you, we're not CID, we're not asking you to grass some…

B   **But there's no guarantee, as I say, there's no guarantee that you will do what you say. The rest of it is look at the bloody risk you're putting me under.**

M   But it's not so much as a risk.

K   It's not going to come from just you.

B   You're not talking.

K   But it's not going to come from you.

B   It's not about petty villains.

M   But it's not a risk, as much as an informant would, or CID, it's totally different.

B   Well what the hell are you telling me to do? If I'm an informant I'm an informant.

K   But there's no way anything we do could ever be traced back to you, come on we wouldn't tell the customs. I wouldn't tell the customs, not after what you've told me they...

M   Billy will be looking to talk for months and months and months and that has arisen because of someone who told us that this man might be worth looking at or something like that. That's all that will come out; it cannot possibly come back to you not in a month of Sundays.

B   So what's to stop me giving you spurious information?

M   Well you see once you've given us information

B   And you turn around and say, by the time they get it to court what he has given us is a load of bollocks, I'm going to recommend to the judge that you've just wasted a load of police time and we want him in jail.

M   No, yeah but we don't like going to you once you give us something if you, if you do, he'll be looking into it and he'll soon find out.

B   What happens if I was able to give you information and I get off? Off the court, through duress, cause we haven't decided which way we're going to go with it yet.

M   There's no way you're going to get off completely is there? I think you're duress could mitigate it but there hasn't been a fellah out there with a gun to your head all the way.

(Paddy says: Too true mate, too true.)

K   You know what I mean, you were terrified, but the amount.

B   Three quarters of the way there was, not to my head.

K   But the amount.

B   The quantity itself, there's nobody in their right mind that would shift 3.7 tons. They wanted to put 5 ton on the fucking boat, the boat was listing that badly, I wouldn't let them put any more on.

M   At the end of the day, that is the reason you did it, it's no excuse in the eyes of the law.

B   Duress is a defence.

K   Mitigation.

M   Mitigation.

B   **No it's a defence, read Stones manual mate, it's a defence.**

M   I think you would be taking a hell of a risk if you're just going to go on that.

B   **Well that's down to you's.**

M   It's up to you.

B   **Well ok, lets say we do, it's up to my solicitor. If I had the phone taps I could do duress as a defence.**

M   If they've got that.

B   **If I had evidence of phone taps, those phone taps, which I know that they've got right, because of the statements that I've made and because of the things you've said and the customs said, I know that they've got phone taps, it's blatantly obvious, they're got phone taps, if I get those then I can prove the threat, and at least get a serious mitigation down and be able to stand a reasonable chance of not doing the 8 years inside.**

M   But they never tell us anything.

B   **Obviously from the statement and information they have got they've got to have the phone taps. If you haven't got the (says something not understandable).**

M   If they've got it, then you ask them about it.

B   **Well there's no point in me asking about it is there, you can see by the information they've already got, that there has to be phone taps - there has to be phone taps.**

M   But it won't be out, they won't tell us, they won't give it out in court it's not in the public interest. Civil rights and all that shit you know. We're only assuming you might be right, we're only assuming.

B   **I am right, there's no two ways about it.**

M   But the question you rose there was, well what happens if I give you something to lead me in the direction of someone and I get off. What I'm saying, we'll be happy for you, you've got off, but we cannot help you, but at least we do an inquiry on the British side that doesn't come back to you anyway.

B   **Yeah, but then I gain nothing from it.**

M   Well that's right, you don't, but at the end of the day that's you personal it's a lot to think about.

B   **It's a lot to think about mate.**

K   It is a lot to think about.

M   **I appreciate you being sort of insistent, but I mean if customs had come to you or if they have arranged through your solicitor, they're**

going to do exactly the fucking same, but we've tried to find now.

B   Yeah, but the customs are in a position to do more for me. Because if their controlling the case then they can come.

M   Aye, that's the fucking thing. I mean that's what we're taking about here ain't we? It's all down to trust.

K   What did I say to you, in Durgen, when me and Bob Barber interviewed you, when he wasn't there, what did I say to you?

B   You said to me, don't do anything, unless you speak to us.

K   Exactly, I said if you want to talk to somebody come through me, don't go through them because you can't fucking trust them.

M   At the end of the day, who would you rather deal with, Billy or the customs, deal with the people who are bloody having a conspiracy around you?

B   They are, there is a bloody conspiracy, they know what's gone on man. They know exactly what's gone on, they'll keep this stuff because they haven't got the people responsible for doing it and they want me to make statements against people, that would make me fear for my life, in fear of my family's life as well as for the rest of my life.

K   Don't that show how stupid they are.

B   Well they are stupid.

K   Asking you to make a statement, we wouldn't dream, we wouldn't ask you for a statement.

M   I wouldn't insult your intelligence by asking you for a statement. And I certainly wouldn't give one anyway. Cause in two year's time I might be the person responsible for putting a gun through your head.

B   That's exactly right.

M   That's why you wouldn't be asked for it.

K   It is a lot to think about.

B   You thought I was going to the Canary Islands to pick the gear up.

K/M   Well no, that's a possibility that was just in own minds. But we didn't know where the gear come from. (Talk over each other) Customs didn't know. Once you left Hartlepool we was out of it.

B ·   Customs had the observations in Gibraltar.

K/M   Who did?

B   Customs.

M   No.

B   No!

K/M   They didn't know where you were.

B   Bloody hell, the Michelle Louise pulled into Gibraltar and dropped in at the customs man.

K/M   **Well you eventually they would have known but I don't think there's been anyone watching you.**

M/K   There wasn't in Gibraltar.

B   **Then you want to get your act together.**

K/M   Well maybe there is, if there has been they fucking haven't told us.

B   **You'd have had two guys stone cold, as wanted as anybody in the country (unintelligible) they come on board and held a gun in my mouth mate, they give me a slap because I wouldn't (unintelligible). I'm serious.**

K/M   Well obviously they haven't been watching you.

B   **That's what I'm saying, that's what I couldn't understand. I could not understand what they got out of that (over talking) I knew I was being watched in Hartlepool in fact further down on, the house down on the left hand side. I clocked it through my binoculars. (Unintelligible) Where all the boats were out of the water you were parked there for a while, then you were moved up, you know you were being watched.**

K/M   Didn't you know, when all this was going on, did it never enter your head to get in touch with a policeman you knew, and you could have done exactly what you've (unintelligible).

B   **Yeah**

K/M   So there was really nothing you could have done, what went on?

B   **The depths of what went on you wouldn't believe me. Do you know what I mean, I didn't go into this in the way that you think at all, because I was doing alright, I was happy alright and I know that I've had people come to me and say all by the way we've had the police think you're doing this with your boat and all the rest of it. The Michelle Louise was never intended to do a job, the Michelle Louise hasn't got the range to do a job right, it's got a range of about 600 miles which means you've got to stop, even then there is no way in the world you could Morocco (unintelligible) it just hasn't the range.**

B   We got a tug in the Michelle Louise probably because it was a Newcastle firm that we bought it from.

B   **We've got a tug in Lacarona on the way back with it, then we got a tug again in Southampton because the delivery skipper that we employed has rang the customs and excise, I'm sure this bunch are into drugs (unintelligible) we were just a bunch of lads having a sail back, you know having an adventure. And we had the boat out of the water, they searched it, and tested and everything. The Michelle Louise was already on top years before when I first bought the damn thing. And** because everybody in Teesside because nobody else has got boats or anything and my reputation they obviously think that the boat was bought for drugs. The same with the Aubrienda, the big boat I had that I was doing holidays in down in Benal Madena, everybody that ever came on the boat and went back through customs got pulled. And all the vehicles that went down there supplying the bits and pieces and all the rest of it, they all got searched, never once (unintelligible). We were under observations right - (unintelligible) where's this come from that was supposedly found in my house in a file according to the evidence. (Unintelligible)

B   I'm saying that was in a file in my sideboard, now I ask you who would be stupid enough to leave that in   (Unintelligible) According to that it was found in one place and found in another place, according to Isla Skelton and somebody else they reckon they found it in a file, just that in a file in my cabinet with all these documents in. (Unintelligible) She's served some things on me months and months ago.

The remainder of the tape is mostly unintelligible. END

This chapter and the previous chapter has raised allegations against Paddy Conroy and as I've always tried to secure some comment from Paddy in other matters and particularly in relation to the chapter I included in the Viv 2 book relating to Paddy's kidnap and torture conviction I feel obliged to be give Paddy the final word relating to these matters herein. Paddy says: "I totally refute the claims made by Berriman and I can tell you that I had no involvement in any such deal involving Berriman and the £15m of cannabis he tried to smuggle in to the UK. Fucking hell I couldn't find my to the Canary wharf never mind the Canary Islands so for me to be involved in this sort of thing is a joke.

Basically it all boils down to Berriman giving me a lift over to Spain when I was on the run and when I got off the boat over there then that was it between me and him. If as has been said that I was sprung from a prison escort to court by a plan involving Glover just so I could be let loose to get on with this so called planned job then why was I nicked two weeks before Berriman sailed into England with 3.7 tons of cannabis, wouldn't the Customs have left me alone, wouldn't they have told the law to leave me alone until this job was done? I was nicked in Spain and extradited to stand trial for the charges I'm now serving my time for, I wasn't nicked on drugs charges.

What's happened is this, Berriman has heard about me being nicked when he got back and he too was nicked so he decides to put it all on my toes and as he said it was no skin off my nose for him to raise my name in his defence of duress when he blamed me for threatening him into doing it. He says he was the patsy, it's the other way around and he used me as the patsy in order to get off with it all. Who knew that he was going to the Helford River, certainly not me because even he didn't know he was going to the Helford River or so he says. But if he didn't know he was going there and nobody else knew he was going there then how can you account for all these Customs people being there in wait for him to turn up there?

Berriman says he shouldn't have been on the boat, well if that's the case then maybe he was nicked by mistake but how did they know he was landing there, there were certainly no phone taps on him when he was doing a Tom Hanks act as a castaway so only he can tell you how they knew the boat would be landing there.

What's happened is he's met Tony White the Brinks Matt robbery guy inside and maybe he's had a few pointers in how to get off with it and he then sacks his brief and employs Tony White's solicitor to represent him because this solicitor is the same one who got Tony off with the Brinks Matt charges. Berriman concocts this story about me giving him the threats and the likes but only after he's told I can't be charged with any of the things he's charged with. Why did he grass me up for something I didn't do or have no involvement with, he was throwing me to the wolves in order to save himself and that makes him a grass.

Berriman says: *'I could not get a small tape-recorder into the prison because I was a 'high risk' prisoner.'* Well how the fuck did he manage to get a BIG tape recorder in to the place then if that's the case. Look if you've ever been on category 'A' status in prison you'd know what I meant but since the majority of you haven't been in prison then I can tell you it's nigh on impossible unless you stick it up your arse. You're not allowed to even have a blank audiocassette tape yet Berriman goes on to say: '*I can positively identify the tape cassette as the brand new unused one which I inserted into my 'Realistic' make tape-recorder.*' Where did he get this 'brand new unused' tape from?

Then he says he taped the conversation in case the two police officers asked him to grass up and he didn't want to be accused of being a grass so he taped them. What's happened is that Berriman has fell out of a bed of shit and into a garden full of roses and he's used me and the police to get off with these heavy charges. The jury believed all the shite his defence spun about me threatening him and then the coppers were double dealed by Berriman when he produced the tape in court.

When Berriman says: '*All I would want is, what about the phone taps? I know that the only reason you were waiting for me in the Helford River was the phone, which I accept and understand but if the other phone taps came to light they would also be of me getting threatened.*' How can a phone tap have led the Customs men to the Helford River when even Berriman didn't know that he would end up there, the way he says it no one knew he would end up there and yet the Customs men are there waiting, come on pull the other one Berriman! I mean look what Berriman says: '*There was, **all I'm saying is they couldn't possibly have been waiting in the Helford River for me because I did not know I was going there, I had no idea I was going there** I just couldn't get any further and the nearest place I could get into the little river was the Helford River and it was in the pilot book that I actually thought there was a bloody yacht yard at Durgan.*'

What else does Berriman say: '*You know all the people involved in this case, right, you know that. I haven't got the fucking bottle, I've got as much bottle as anyone I think, but I haven't got the bottle to name the people in the case. You know who it was, you made the mistake of picking him up before the job was over not me.*' And then D.S. KITCHING replies: '***Who's this Paddy?***' And Berriman plays for time by saying: '*What?*' Detective Constable McDOUGALL says: '*Paddy Conroy, who else? There's no one else whose been picked up.*' Berriman makes a big play of saying to the law that they

made the mistake of picking him up before the job was over. How did
D.S. Kitching pluck my name out of fresh air like he did, that's
because Berriman had been talking to the coppers long before this
and had thrown me into them because you see the coppers would
have been saying to Berriman 'Who's the person you're on about,
who do you mean by that?' But they didn't say any of that and were
talking casually and all knew my name without it being mentioned
by Berriman.

And what does ' Detective Constable McDOUGALL say to
Berriman: *'There's no way you're going to get off completely is
there? I think you're duress could mitigate it **but there hasn't been a
fellah out there with a gun to your head all the way.'** Exactly!
Berriman was told: '**You took a risk it's as simple as that.'** And what
does he say to that: *'The risk wasn't there, listen I wasn't meant to be
on the boat.'* Ha, ha with that sort of original material the man should
be a comedian, Chubby Brown move over mate. As far as I'm
concerned Berriman is a grass and will always be remembered as a
grass. I hope I've rested my case because if I go on and on like
Berriman then maybe you might not believe me."

Well there you have it, two sides of the coin and who am I to argue
with either story, make your own minds up, what a pity we didn't
have a vote line for you to phone in order to register your votes, let's
make it a premium rate line. Putting the jokes to one side this is a
serious issue although Paddy Conroy cannot be charged and in all
fairness the Customs denied the involvement of him and others from
the outset of the case. The Observer newspaper covered the story and
claimed Conroy had involvement in the duress side of things but
unless that can be proven then it cannot be claimed as being
absolutely gospel. What won the trial for Phil Berriman was the tape
recording and I believe without that then he'd be looking at double
figures and just as equally this applied to Dave Courtney in his trial
when he was able to back up what he said with a tape recording of a
conversation with a bent copper.

7

Unforgiven...not

Ernie Bewick has been called a 'gangland killer' and an 'enforcer' but I can tell you he's one of the most forgiving men I've come across...okay that might shock some of the family of Tony Waters and it might shock the people that have been spoon fed lies and deceit, but it's the truth and I always try to give you the truth until I find out otherwise.

For those of you that might not have heard of Ernie Bewick I'll fill you in with the details, although I've covered some of them in a previous 'Viv' book, but I feel I may have missed some points out and for that reason it's now all in context.

December 7, 1997 was to be the last day in the life of convicted drug dealer Tony Waters. As a result of a fight Waters, 44, lost his life outside of the Eastender pub, in High Street East, Sunderland.

Waters deliberately went looking for Bewick with the intention of doing him some damage over an incident that took place the previous night between Bewick and two other men in Sunderland's Luciano's restaurant. Ernie Bewick was pursued head on in a confrontation that was designed by Waters and for that reason it goes against all of those that have advised since the death of Waters that he just wanted a quiet life since his release from prison some four years earlier. It would seem that some would want to paint Waters as a whiter than white character and if that had been genuinely so then you'd be reading a very different view point here but as it goes I cannot write anything else.

Waters left behind a family that grieve him to this day and of course the time of year (Christmas) of his death compounds the pain and hurt they must feel for the loss of their loved one, but without fear or favour such sentiments should be put to one side for a moment in order to reveal the depths of Waters' resentment for Bewick. Bewick was and still is anti-drugs; Waters was pro-drugs and was well known within the drug fraternity of the north and saw Bewick as a stumbling block to dealing his drugs in the pubs under Bewick's charge so any excuse for a confrontation would help in ridding Bewick from the area.

Bewick, not a man to underestimate, was fully aware of the way Waters was dealing drugs and knew that he was the difference between Sunderland being flooded with drugs or being kept relatively drug free and so long as he was in charge of certain pub and club doors it would remain that way. In a similar way to how Viv frowned upon drugs so did Bewick and just as similarly as others wanted rid of Viv so that they could deal in his patch on Tyneside it looked to be the same way in Bewick's territory on Wearside. Bewick and Graham had a lot in common although I would have to give Bewick the slight edge over Graham in his handling of matters and his ability to sense danger.

Waters, a terrier tempered person, met his untimely end as a direct result of his desire to wheel and deal drugs in Sunderland, although first I give you an insight into Ernie Bewick so that you can make your own mind up as to whether you agree with what I write. Directly from Ernie Bewick the story unfolds with his account of the two fights he had with another northern hard man, Billy Robinson, from Gateshead. I've covered the Bewick v Robinson fight in another Viv book but here is the more exciting update directly from Ernie Bewick when he accounts for the night he was working on a door when Billy Robinson and his party turned up:

"That night I was called to the door (The Blue Monkey – rumour has it that Ernie started working there because of trouble with a well known drug dealer selling drugs and because someone had been murdered outside of the club) and they said that Billy Robinson was at the door and he wanted to come in. Well on that particular evening it was the type where everybody had to pay when they came in so I went up and I really didn't know Billy at the time and I explained that everybody had to pay to get in. His henchmen standing beside him said, 'Do you know who you're talking to,' and things like that. I said, 'I'm sorry you know but you've got to pay in.'

If anybody had of asked me the same thing I'd have said, 'Fair enough,' so then I was being called a little shit type of thing and abuse like that thrown at me so I said, 'Look you can't come in.' So he said, 'Right you little thing get round the corner you little shit,' I said, 'Well, fair enough.' So then Billy slapped me across the face and I went forward to go into him, he tried to punch me so I ducked over the punch and gave him a right cross and an upper cut and knocked him out.

Then his friends were there, his big henchmen suddenly seemed to deflate and I said, 'Right get him up and fuck off and don't ever come back here anymore,' so they went but obviously by then all the talk starts to generate so obviously there were a few scares that they were going to come through team handed at the door and there was a couple of times we had to prepare for what might have happened.

Months later I heard rumours that I was going to be set up and different things so one day Keith Bell (Changed his name to Keith Collins – see previous mention in Viv series of books where Keith gives his account of the fight.) come knocking on my door trying to go on as if though he was a friend and he says, 'Look, Billy wants to have a go at you and he wants to see you as soon as possible for a one to one (straightener) so I said, 'Fair enough I'll come now,' he replied, 'Well can you not make it later on tonight, you know where I live, you've been to mine before can you come through?' We went through and it went on a couple of hours while they were talking so I got something to eat at Keith's.

Later on the fight was arranged at a gym in Jesmond, which was owned by Andy Webb (Former Mr Great Britain). Andy Webb was a gentleman, Viv was a gentleman, they were all nice and friendly I came through by myself (Staggering to think that Ernie was fearless in turning up to such a venue on his own, but he did!) I never brought anyone with me I walked in their camp on my own, there was a few of them there and Viv got on the phone to tell Billy I was there and I was kept waiting a further hour and half to two hours before he came.

I remember feeling cold (due to the lengthy waiting process) and Andy Webb was very good towards me and he gave me a cup of tea to warm me because by the time Billy had arrived they'd been talking for about twenty minutes around the corner. So I more or less explained to Viv that if I sort it out over a cup of tea without any trouble then that's the way I preferred it. (Again, staggering to think that Ernie was as a calm as a cucumber wanting to talk things over a cup of tea and obviously the others there might have seen this as a sign of weakness, but Ernie's just that sort of guy and not for one minute should he have been underestimated – it wasn't for nothing that his fists were called the 'peacemakers'.)

I didn't want any trouble but at the same time I went through because if that was the way to solve it fair enough and Billy obviously wanted the fight on so fair enough. So I went through where they had the fight arranged, it was a small compartment, there was a little bank that went up and obviously I realise now that was suited for Billy's needs with me being a lot lighter he could get me into the corner or if I ran up the bank I would slip or fall over, which I did at one point when I was fighting but I got out of that anyhow.

Billy came up to me and he was a gentleman when he approached me. The first thing he said to me was, 'Ernie I want to shake your hands now before we have this fight and I'm going to shake your hands after the fight.' So I shook his hand then we got on with the fight.

Billy sort of stood in a boxer's stance, I didn't underestimate him because he's got a powerful punch and later on as we became friends we had a bit of trouble with someone and he has got a powerful punch. So my strategy was to wear him out and then go in for it, that was my strategy before I even went through there. I stood there and I jumped about a bit and I was flicking punches at him trying to egg him on to come forward. The punches weren't really very hard; to be honest I wasn't even properly warmed up because I'd been standing waiting all that time in the cold.

So Billy was throwing lefts, coming forward with lefts, straight lefts and trying to catch me with them but obviously I was jumping about a little bit, flicking a punch here and there, getting him to move and at one stage Billy got on top of me, but I managed to quickly escape from underneath his arm and I was back up on my feet in no time because I was only 13½ stone at the time and I was pretty fit and agile and I could jump about a little bit. (Wow – don't let Ernie fool you here, he's still very fit and looks like he could walk through a barn full of troublemakers.)

We stood, we bounced about a little bit again, he was trying to get his punches and I noticed he was open for a left hook. But something inside's telling me to hold that left hook back so now I'm throwing right hands all the time and now I'm warmed up and they're coming over strong and I even said during the fight as a bit of hype, 'Right I'm warmed up now, I'm starting the fight off now.'

I don't know how long I was fighting, I cannot say if it was five minutes, but it wasn't half an hour or three quarters of an hour, but when you think five minutes could be a long time for most fit fellahs. Anyhow I never took any punches, I might have had to a little bit but nothing really hard and I came in with a right hand all the time, I've thrown a right hand and caught him with a left hook, so now I'm coming in to finish the job off. (It would seem that Ernie was cruising in like a battleship.)

Billy's moving around but as he's staggering over I'm thinking, 'Whoa, I've been caught with an upper cut,' by then I fell over, it was a good punch, one of my hands was on the ground, in fact it was the left hand, and then Keith Bell come around and he got hold of my hand. I was embarrassed because I thought they were stopping the fight because I'd been knocked over, I thought Billy was now going to run in and kick me because he would have been desperate and I was going to roll around and spring back up, that was the theme that went through my mind, you're confident that that was the way it would go.

So I knew I was vulnerable because he could have run at me and kicked me. I got up and that was the point I went berserk, I tore into him, split all his lips and that and literally went mad and shouted, 'COME ONNNNNNNNNN!' and just literally went straight at him as if to say I'm not getting beat off anybody, I was really hyped up.

Then I went forward and Viv grabbed me shouting, 'HOWWAY ERNIE. HOWWAY ERNIE,' and things like that. So they stopped the fight and I was dead confused because I'd realised Billy had knocked me over, but they said 'Howway, you've beaten him fair and square.' So then Billy went that way and Viv went the other way and I was confused so I followed the way Viv went.

Remember, walking away from that I'd been involved in a fight and I'd been hit and things like that and for a minute my mind went a bit blank so as I walked through the door I remember walking into Viv and he was sitting on the seat and he was saying, 'Look, I want no trouble, I want no trouble in this gym mind.' I said, 'Look, I'll stand here with you.' I folded my arms and stood beside him. Andy Webb was standing there and Andy Webb's head was down like that, I don't know why. I thought it could be because of what Viv said or he was embarrassed with the way Viv went on because he seemed to be like a honourable type of person and was nice towards me and made me feel comfortable.

I can remember that I went to the toilet, came back and then shook Viv's hand and everything and we were alright, as I walked towards the door and went out I could feel Viv watching me from behind, I knew without turning my head. When I got out Billy was at the other side of the door so he must have walked around and out some other way. He come up to me and hugged me and I hugged him back and we shook hands and everything and just like what he said before the fight that he'd shake my hand after the fight he kept his word.

I'd previously boxed Viv Graham and I beat him in the ring, I was too strong for him pound for pound. I remember when I was young I used to idolise Rocky Marciano and when I used to fight in that ring I didn't want to box and I used to think it clever to take punches so I knew I could take a punch even though I'd boxed a few times. At that time I was silly, I was young and it was daft the way I went on at that time. At 17 to 18 we go through all sorts of phases when we grow up don't we. Looking up to Rocky Marciano gave me strength if I wanted to beat anybody I just used to think of Rocky Marciano, he had a head like a bowling ball and you couldn't hurt him and that's the way I thought so really a little bit of that was still in me.

Viv - The Final Chapter

Anyway getting back to the fight with Billy, as I was getting back into the car Keith Bell said, 'You know Viv shouldn't have stuck that sly punch on you.' I said, 'Ah, I see what you mean,' and then I realised that it wasn't Billy that gave me that walloping uppercut and it all fitted into place then. I got out of the car and went back into the gym and Viv was on the phone and I think Keith was in the other room although I'm guessing about that. When Viv finished he came over and said, 'Ernie, look Billy was like a dad to me he really brought me up when I was younger.' I said, 'Look, it was only a daft punch forget about it.' Viv said, 'Is it okay if I come through?' (To Sunderland) I said that it would be alright, but I'm always like that even when I got out of prison I forgave certain people for what they'd done against me, but I'll talk about that at a different time.

But I can forgive people and I realise everybody's got good points and everybody's got bad points, I try to motivate the good points in people which isn't a bad thing is it, but be careful because the bad ones will take over. Marciano is portrayed as a good man, his mother went to church and prayed for him, he come from an Italian type of family where his mother didn't like him getting into the ring and he didn't like his mother knowing he was getting hurt so I suppose in a way when you're reading books like that as a kid maybe it's been reflected in me and kept me off the drugs and off the streets and got me into the gym training. People wanted to be like Marciano but now people want to be like Tyson.

After the fight with Billy I maintained some links with Viv and we had a few discussions on the phone about it because I'd heard rumours going about that I'd been knocked out for ten minutes, I'd discussed that with Viv and Viv explained, 'Look I haven't said anything like that, Ernie.' He told me that he had lots of respect for me and I came through there on my own.

Billy Hardy went through to Newcastle and he met with John Davison and Viv and all them and he turned around and said, 'Look, all of them through there they've got loads of respect for you.' But I was also hearing stories, what happened once was that Gavin Cook was asking me about what went on and he said, 'I've been in his (Viv's) company and he says he knocked you out for ten minutes,' I

Stevie 'The Hammer' Eastland

Gary Ward - Innocent

Tommy Harrison, centre left Lee Duffy, centre right

Escape from death, a typical trip to the shops, ends in near death in
Murderers Square Mile

The back lane in which John Hall met his death. This photograph is reproduced exactly as it was taken from the negative. You will see a haze to the left which also appears on the negative. There is no explanation for this uncanny phenomenon that reveals something more sinister pervades the atmosphere of Murderers Square Mile.

The Avenues of Murderers Square Mile - A typical day

Murder Squad Police Offficers show stressful faces on an inquiry

David Glover Junior serving time for
kidnap and torture

Paddy Conroy denies all involvement
in the Phil Berriman drug smuggling
chapter

Phil Berriman stands alongside the chart that he used to help navigate him to Dakar and back to the UK in a nine week voyage of hell

Ray Mallon alias Robocop applied his Zero Tolerance policing on Teesside when he headed the CID. Now facing disciplinary charges as a result of the £7m Lancet Inquiry that led to one police officer being charged with stealing a boiler and being acquitted by Teesside Crown Court. Mallon hopes to go on to political career that may well see him in charge of his old bosses!!

John Henry Sayers fresh from his prison sentence served for robbery. Refused by Newcastle City Council the chance to run a taxi firm. Yet the same council can pay a security firm run by a convicted felon money to protect their sites?

Stephen & Michael Sayers May 1999
HM Prison Frankland.

Manchester's Paul Massey helped save Sunderland
from an underworld takeover

Bradford's Morgan Duffy convicted of the Raggalds
pub murder, now fighting his conviction.

Brian Cockerill was on the other end of Lee Duffys' fist to no avail
Duffy said weeks later: "Who in their right mind would want ot fight
someone the size of Brian".

Rich Horsley has had over 100 street fights and is a popular figure amongst the Teesside underworld. A former Heavyweight boxer now applying his time to the world of crimebiz.
Rich is typical of hard knocks Northerners and would give his last penny to help the needy but cross him and he's not a very nice chap.

Ernie Bewick could be considered to be Sunderland's Rocky Marciano but he would refute this because he is an understated man. He is a popular figure amongst those who have needed his services for club and pub door security throughout Sunderland. If Harley likes Ernie then he can't be too bad.

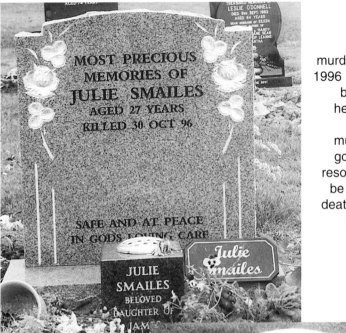

Julie Smailes murdered in October 1996 has not had the benefit of having her killers caught. This unsolved murder refuses to go away and until resolved will always be a reminder that death can still mock us from beyond the grave

Paul Logan was lured to his death by two men posing as pizza customers. £5,000 was the alleged amount paid to have Logan beaten up. His death was said to be a tragedy due to the severe beating. His killers are local men known to the Geordie Mafia and police sources know who they are.

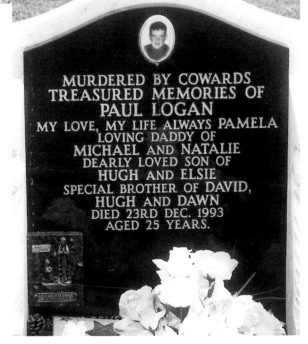

In Ever Loving Memory Of
LEE PAUL DUFFY
DIED 25th AUGUST 1991
AGED
A CHERISHED SON, A BELOVED
BROTHER, ... AND DADDY
AND A ... FRIEND.

Lee 'The Duffer' Duffy was killed in a violent manner. "He who lives by the sword dies by the sword." This was one of Duffy's sayings and as if though predicting his own demise this is how his life ended. Duffy and Viv never got to meet in that fight that was arranged for them. Maybe fate kept them apart.

Did the killers of Paul Logan continue their carnival of death by killing Viv some seven days later, some police officers seem to think so.
Viv and Duffy are united in death yet it was life that kept them apart. Two Legends the likes of which may never be seen again, the power vacuums being too big for any one person to fill.

IN LOVING MEMORY OF
A DEAR SON AND BROTHER
VIV GRAHAM
DIED 31st DEC. 1993
AGED 34 YEARS.
LOVED AND REMEMBERED
BY SONS
DEAN AND VIV

SIMPLY THE BEST.

Wheeler nightclub now in a state of deriliction was Viv's learning ground on Tyneside pictured here on the Gateshead side of the Tyne Bridge

Consider this to be a piece of sociological history steeped in history far beyond the comprehension of Gateshead Council. The 'Get Carter' carpark has been selected for demolition yet its beauty gives out a feeling of safety to those who seek its sanctuary on a cold winters day.

Viv was becoming, as some say, too big for his boots and was starting a road to bullying people he felt able to. From nothing to boxer to club doorman to death.

Stuart Watson was always the threat to Viv's machismo (macho image). When Viv failed to defeat Watson he always felt there was something in the line of unfinished business - Watson never flickered

Left, Joe Hunt his solicitor wrongly
accused underworld figures of
being informants.
Above, the Company featured in
Chapter 18

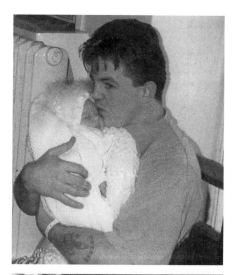

Above, Lee Duffy showing off his legs
Above right, Duffy holding Kattieleigh
his daughter
Right, Duffy & co chilling out.

John 'Mario' Cunningham is one of the old school of the Geordie Mafia. You'll not find him mentioned in the book in fact he warrants a book all on his own due to his exploits of robberies totalling some £500,000. When you consider John was at the height of his career in the 60's and 70's that would probably total well into the millions now. Mario is one of the staunchest characters you are ever likely to meet. The Geordie Mafia have a lot to thank this man for.

Harry Marsden a close friend of John Cunningham's was a proper handful when serving time. Always down the block and always ready to have a tear up with those out to harm him. He suffered abuse in the boys' homes of the north by those that ran such places of punishment. Harry has now gone on to overcome personal tragedy and his own battle against the big C. He was instrumental in training Viv as an amateur boxer and now runs one of the main boxing clubs in Newcastle helping society and thereby putting all the wrongs he's done to right.

Dave Courtney monarch of the underworld can be
hired from www.crimebiz.co.uk

said, 'Look if Viv ever wants his go at me...'

I heard Viv was very supportive towards me over a few things because I've had trouble with the Sayers'; we've chased them from Sunderland when they came with guns one night. There's a load of lads will tell you the truth about what happened there. They come barging in, it was Gary Rob who had the 'After Dark' (club), and what happened was Gary said, 'Look, they've all barged in.' Ashy (Paul Ashton – now serving a total of 31 years imprisonment) was there, I said, 'Don't worry we'll get them out,' I went up to the two Sayers' (Michael and Stephen) and said, 'Look, there's all of us, are you daft or something?'

There were some big hefty blokes with us so I turned around and said, 'If you want trouble we'll do it that way then!' They turned around and said that they had guns so I said we also had guns, 'He's got one there,' I said, pointing to one of the men with me, I was only bluffing but sure enough one of them did have one as well, he actually went to his car, came back and told me he had a one but I never saw it, but I spread that about. I'm not a bloke that would like to use things like that, but from my point of view it was a bit of bluff and I wanted to get them off the premises and they offered me violence and I said, 'Okay then I'll have you two together and I'm offering you two violence.' In other words if that's what you want, but there's loads of scenarios happened like that around the town. Anyway the bluff worked with them and they cleared off.

Some time later there was talk that one of them (Sayers) was going to come through and have a go at me now I heard that Viv went up to him and he turned around and told the lad that was with the Sayers' that he was going to get knackered if he had a go at me so one night when he come through to Sunderland I sat and waited and confronted him and said, 'I hear you're going to have a go at me?' 'Nah, nah I don't want any trouble with you,' was his reply so I just left it.

I built up a friendship with Viv and actually went through to his house and had a cup of tea with him and had a discussion over different things. I remember Gavin Cook was working with Viv through there (Newcastle) and he came through and said, 'I've told

Viv that you're not bothered about him and I'm keeping out of it so here's his phone number.' He must have been match making and I said, 'Look, I'm not going to back down from him, Gavin.' So I pulled Viv up and said, 'You're the one going around telling everyone that you knocked me out for ten minutes,' he replied, 'Ernie, I've never said that, I've got nothing but respect for you and all I want is your respect,' I replied, 'Look, Viv you've always had my respect, I've heard a lot about you although the only thing that put me off was when you punched me but you've always got my respect, but now you're going around saying you knocked me out.'

Anyway Viv denied saying it to the end. I remember meeting one of Viv's friends called McNally from around where Viv had once lived in Rowlands Gill and he said, 'Honestly, Ernie, Viv Graham had lots of respect for you,' and he went on to tell me that Viv was telling everyone I was 'a man' and how I'd went on my own to the fight. There was another lad training with me in the gym and he said, 'You know something, Ernie, you should never take notice of what some people say, I was training with Viv once and he's got loads of respect for you.'

I ended up getting on well with Viv but you've always got to remember that there's still a dividing line and you do hear Chinese whispers and all that. I'd heard stories, how true they were I don't know, but he'd come and have a drink with you, he'd take you to the bar when he was ready and as you go in he'll put his arm around you and all of a sudden it's BANG, BANG and he's on you.

Other stories were that he wouldn't take his coat off and stand in front of the man, it would be something like 'You alright, mate,' and then BANG so I was advised to be wary of that sort of stroke so I kept that little bit of doubt in my mind and I was very careful of how I went about it if I ever socialised with him because he did want to come through here. I'd also heard that Viv liked to have an audience around him when he kicked off with a couple of lads who he might knock out and then the word spreads, 'Viv knacked three lads the other night, you should've seen him.' I mean anybody can go and do that, but that's just the image...but anyway it mightn't be true because you hear all kinds of stories about me, you'll hear some good

146

and you'll hear some bad."

There ends the interview relating to the Billy Robinson fight and it goes to show what kind of a man Viv was in the sense that he broke a code of conduct for his friend and mentor, Billy Robinson, when he punched Ernie in order to give Billy some time. Billy wouldn't have approved had he had time to say so because afterwards he congratulated Ernie on a fair and square win.

Maybe that's not the way it was meant to go but it did and I believe that when Ernie felt Viv's eyes burning into his back after the fight that Viv may have been over awed at Ernie's resilience to his punch and it maybe showed Viv that if he ever had a toe to toe with Ernie then as had happened in a past boxing match between them then it would be Viv who would come off the loser.

Ernie was forgiving towards Viv and that clearly shows the type of characteristics he learned from his hero Rocky Marciano. As for Viv spreading rumours that he'd had Ernie knocked out for ten minutes it fits in with some rumours I'd picked up elsewhere but of course such bravado helps maintain a hard man image and what better way to do it than to perpetuate the hard man image by embroidering on the truth, as Viv seemed to do.

Ernie is the classic hard man, Viv was the new bread straddling the line between past and present but Viv didn't have the inherent safety reflex that's bred into city dwellers and that is what I believe Viv lacked and was to cause his eventual downfall.

The delicate matter of Ernie being on prison licence made it difficult to talk about the Tony Waters murder but the story I've heard time and time again was that Tony had it in for Ernie and he'd made a cocked gun gesture with his hand and pointed it towards Ernie indicating that Ernie was going to be shot. From a third party I was able to get the picture of the build up to Tony Waters' death. That night Ernie was hit over the head with a bottle and his head was bleeding. The night before that Ernie had a fight with Scott Waters when Ernie tried to eject him from a restaurant because he was being abusive.

Word was spreading around town that it had taken seven of them to sort Scott Waters out, a rumour apparently started by Waters. Ernie was in one of the pub's that Waters was in and people were looking to Ernie to see what he would do to scotch this rumour and it looked like Ernie was sucked into a vacuum of deceit and lies and reacted in a way that was out of sorts with his character and he decided to approach Scott Waters. Ernie was maybe forced into this option in front of the very same crowd that had told Ernie about the rumours Waters was spreading and because he couldn't back down he confronted Waters head on. Ernie, as a consequence, knocked out Scott Waters.

Further rumour has it then that Waters went back and told Tony Waters and a number of others that he was getting the better of Ernie Bewick and in fact had supposedly decked Bewick twice when seven others intervened and jumped him. This twisted story was to be the death of Tony Waters and the following day police intelligence reports suggest that people were walking about with guns looking for Ernie Bewick, looking in all the wrong places it would seem, which gives rise to the fact that they probably wanted word to get back to Ernie Bewick that they were looking for him over the previous night's fight.

They wanted to send a message of strength and into the bargain they wanted to frighten Ernie Bewick into staying away so that they could sell their drugs. Certain people were advised to stay away from the town centre because there was 'going to be trouble'. Ernie being Ernie wasn't going to stay away because it was his territory and he had to show others that he wasn't going to hide away over something like this. My own intelligence gathering suggests that Ernie Bewick was told that there was trouble in a pub, although there wasn't any trouble at all it was the perfect way to entice Ernie into another confrontation designed by Tony Waters in order to get Ernie Bewick to show.

On entering the Eastender pub Ernie saw Tony and they acknowledged each other and the story goes that Tony asked what had happened the night before and in Ernie's understated fashion he told the truth but Tony was having none of it and gave Ernie an insult that was designed to cause further trouble, he called Ernie a 'liar.'

Scott Waters wasn't a fighter and it would go against such a man as Ernie Bewick's own code of conduct to hand out the thrashing Waters said he received but it didn't pull any weight with Tony and Ernie was told to get outside the door, obviously for a one to one but as Ernie walked towards the door he had a bottle thrown off his head and a scuffle ensued but all was in control and Ernie then approached the man, Tony's stepson, who had thrown the bottle off his head but the man's mother got in between her son and Ernie and became protective towards her cherub of a son who had just stotted the bottle off Ernie's head.

The altercation seemed to have settled and one of the doorman, Ritchie Laws, had taken over the dialogue of settling everyone down but Tony's stepson had now thrown another bottle and this time it hit Ernie square on in his face, it beggars belief that Ernie didn't retaliate, he'd taken so much and yet here he was still in control, which takes some doing considering the force with which a grown man can throw a bottle off someone's head and face.

My inside source is able to tell me that Ernie pleaded with Tony to go and to forget about it. Surely two bottles stotted off Ernie's head should have been repayment enough but Tony was shouting at a lot of people and wouldn't leave and he was now making a show in front of people and was walking to go out and then would make to go back inside asking Ernie to come outside with him. Ernie by this time was telling Tony's wife the story of how it was only him and Scott Waters that had the tousle and that Scott had been lying about the 'seven' others.

Tony Waters came back in for the third time and during this time Ernie was explaining things to Andrea Chesum and remonstrating that she should ask the man that accompanied Scott about what had actually happened.

During this time Tony was shouting that Ernie was going to be shot and the argument continued down the stairs and when Ernie followed Andrea down Tony was physically poking his finger into Ernie's face and yet still Ernie didn't retaliate.

Outside of the pub...well, Tony Waters met his death in a fight that was ferocious by any man's standards but when you consider my findings as to how Tony had conducted himself and the provocation

Ernie was under I believe that was far more than my words can convey. Ernie didn't intend for Waters to meet his untimely ending in such a fashion and was genuinely taken aback when he was charged with murder.

Ernie was Sunderland's 4th Emergency service and the similarities between how he and Viv worked were uncanny, although no doubt every major city in the UK can boast a Viv Graham character I don't believe many can boast an Ernie Bewick character modelled on Rocky Marciano. Where the police couldn't protect people's businesses from being taxed by criminals Ernie Bewick could protect them and many a time the services of Ernie were called upon to resolve certain issues that the police stayed away from.

Ernie now faced a murder rap and his club and pub doors were open to being poached by others seeing this as a power vacuum that they could fill. Davie Binks was a name suggested as one of the people interested in taking over Ernie's doors but they were soon won back into Ernie's realm with the help of Ritchie Laws. One of Ernie's men was jumped on by five others and rumour has it that Ritchie stood up to Davie Binks, although for the sake of protecting both from prosecution let's just say this was a fairy tale I was told from one of my Chinese whisperers. We've got two very big men here as well as a man we'll call Wayne.

Wayne although young, 23, is very mature and powerful for his age and a fight breaks out where he ends up doing well and again rumour has it that he told Ernie on a prison visit that no one was taking his doors. Ritchie won some of Ernie's doors back in Sunderland and Newbottle and all of this happened during Ernie's period of prison remand, which was for a period of some 14 months. With such loyalty behind him Ernie had more support than Viv had when he was murdered and that indicates the difference in terms of Ernie and Viv.... yes Ernie was a lone wolf just like Viv, but when the cards were on the table Ernie's loyal supporters would always be there for him.

For those interested in further rumour there is a story that Ronnie Bestford went to a pub called the Sun Inn and told Davie Binks that he'd have to go and he wouldn't be picking money up anymore and with this Ernie's friends, continually of their own free will, gave their support to ensure Sunderland wasn't taken over by outsiders.

Initially when Ernie was on remand Joe Freeman and a few others helped secure peace for the city of Sunderland and eventually Graham Potts was brought in to work with Joe as well as Brian Loughlan and many others safeguarded Ernie's doors. Of course Ernie was still on remand while all of this was going on and little did he know what was to be the outcome of his trial where he was to face the charge of murder.

What I was able to ask Ernie was about the current scene and how things had changed and keeping within the confines of his parole licence he was able to tell me that a lot of the trouble has died down and a lot of the 'bad lads' have split up and how Paul Massey from Manchester (serving $17^{1/2}$ years reduced to $13^{1/2}$ years on appeal) had been able to help avert a gangland war in the city of Sunderland over the death of Tony Waters and because of this Paul Massey must be given credit for his part in smoothing things over in respect how people were fed rumours as opposed to fact.

I suppose while the police intelligence were oblivious to what troubles were brewing in Sunderland it was down to Ernie Bewick's ability as a 'peacemaker' to avert a serious takeover of the city from outsiders and with the backup and support of those brave enough to step out into a city ready to burst with violence a very serious situation was avoided.

Ending on a high note it would seem that Sunderland is a pretty well mannered city and things have settled down. Ernie Bewick deserves some credit for how he handled things when he was actively involved in running the doors, his followers deserve some credit for how they conducted themselves and maintained a calming atmosphere.

I could have plastered this chapter with violence, but you know sometimes it's better being understated than overstated and that's what I believe Ernie Bewick is all about, he's not a brash and egotistical man, he doesn't stick his chest out and spit on the path to give himself a hard case image, in fact Ernie is the total opposite of what you'd expect such a hard man to be and that's what makes him hard, he doesn't have to try, there's no need for such dramatics as I've often seen displayed by drug or drink fuelled louts.

Ernie doesn't even swear, he says f'd instead of fucked, which fits in with the way a lot of the London chaps go on. With Ernie you get what you see, there's no hidden agenda beneath his calm exterior and you can imagine him going about his business as if it was an everyday occurrence. Comparing some so called hard men to Ernie makes them look like common thugs and I feel we're not going to see the likes of these characters ever again. I mean what role model do kids use these days – steroid filled athletes, whinging and argumentative tennis players, booze filled darts players…you can keep the lot of them because there's only one Rocky Marciano in Sunderland.

Rocky Marciano helped evolve Ernie's style while a controversial character helped destroy it and because of that you'd expect Ernie to be a bitter man, but he's not. Throughout his prison sentence he only lost eight days of remission, that shows his strength of character and he did his time the right way, which I believe many could learn from.

Paul Massey is classed as the Godfather of Manchester's criminal underworld (see book 'Legends Vol.1' featured in 'Other Titles' pages at end of this book) and to many that is how he will always be remembered but to some a debt of gratitude has to be acknowledged towards him for his swift intervention on behalf of Ernie Bewick and the city of Sunderland.

Paul is serving 13½ years for a nightclub stabbing in which he denies all the allegations thrown at him, even though the injured party stood in the witness dock and told the court that the man in the dock, Paul Massey, was not the man that stabbed him, Massey was found guilty. The court decided that the injured party was far to eager to make his testimony in defence of the defendant and for that reason found against Paul, but just imagine for one moment that it was you, the injured party, wouldn't you stand in the witness box and strenuously defend an innocent party if you knew the man in the dock wasn't the man who had attacked you with a knife?

8

Lisa Stockell

Some of you may recall in the last Viv book I was in search of those connected with Teesside's Lee Duffy. I'm pleased to say that some three years on I've had more than just plain success in finding the people I needed to speak to then. I recall a journalist saying to me after I'd written the first Viv book that news on the book couldn't really be put out because of my writing style in that I'd only used one 'S' in the spelling of 'Teesside'…wow big licks! I love Teesside. Anyone who knows my writing style knows I'm a puritanical writer and that's part of my make up.

ALL mistakes have a subliminal hidden meaning and for that reason I'm loath to change them, fuck paying proofreaders, why take away my soul from what's written and leave you with the chaff. Do you know when you're reading something by your favourite writer the likelihood of you rereading exactly what they've written is about a million to one against and yet you merrily go on reading it believing they've written every single word of it, maybe there's been about four or five hands involved in the final result of it all, well with my writing it's left exactly as it was written.

Misspelling the word 'Teesside' must have had a subliminal meaning and now I know why. The missing 'S' out of the word 'Teesside' was for the 'S' in the name 'Stockell'…Lisa Stockell. Lisa, Lee Duffy's girlfriend, starts off by telling me I was quite fair with what I'd previously written about her and Lee and that I'd apologised in one of the Viv books if I didn't get the information I'd written right and now I leave the rest to Lisa:

"Lee wanted a quieter life than the life he was leading because he had kids and he wanted to settle down. He'd been in prison, he'd done it all and he'd had enough. He wanted to quieten down more instead of the fighting and all of the attempts on his life; he'd had enough of it. That's what I wanted him to do, quieten down and move away and I felt as long as we were around here that his life would never quieten down because of what he was. I just felt there would be more attempts to kill him, there'd already been so many.

I remember Lee saying to me, 'How do I get out, what do I do?' The first time Lee was shot was at a blues party when he was shot in the knee. He drove home and I was in bed, I heard a beeping outside and I went to the car, Lee was in the driving seat and he said, 'I've been shot.' I didn't believe him at first and then he fell out of the car and I just ran in and got my mam and we drove him to the hospital. I didn't think of anything other than getting him to hospital, I didn't have time to be in shock.

The second attempted murder was at another blues party, they'd come to my house but I don't want to talk about that part (see first Viv book pages 215-216) they then went on to the blues and they'd caught him inside and he was fighting with them and that's when he was shot in his foot. Lee wouldn't make statements to the police about these things, but this time he told me to make a statement to the police because of what they'd done to me and he said, 'Tell them everything.' But Lee said nothing and he told me not to worry about it and that he'd sort it himself.

I wasn't surprised to learn that Lee had other women because that's how I ended up with him. He was only young when I met him and he didn't have a name for himself then, he was only eighteen and I was only 15. When Lee ended up getting his four-year (1988) sentence for having a fight in a nightclub and doing something to someone's eye he got four years in prison. At that time Lee had a girlfriend but at the beginning of his sentence the relationship with her ended completely so then I helped him through his time and when he came out we had Kattieleigh and that's when it all started.

When he was in prison he trained and trained but when he was released he didn't do much training, he did it all in his four year sentence that's why he was so big. When he came home he used to keep fit himself, he never had a regular thing of going to the gym every day or every week. Maybe now and again he'd go with a friend but it wasn't a regular thing but he liked going to the gym and keeping fit.

He was only out for a year and a half and then he died, everything had happened in a year and a half. In that short space of time everything happened to him.

I remember we went out for a meal with the Sayers' but I wasn't aware they were a crime family and I wasn't aware of a fight going to take place between Viv Graham and Lee until after Lee's death, when Lee wasn't home he was completely different. We lived with my mam for a while because we didn't have our own house and he'd come in and bath Kattieleigh, take her out and do things, he was a family man and there was a really nice side to him. We'd take the kids out, including those from his previous relationship, to the park and do things together like a family.

I never ever knew Lee dealt in drugs until it was said in the newspapers, they said he was bullying this one and that one, but when I was with him he was never bullying. The only time I've ever known him to fight with people was with drug dealers and they've always had attempts on him, I've never known Lee go out and pick a fight on someone innocent.

When threats started coming Lee moved out of my mam's house because he didn't want our lives to be in danger anymore. We'd go and stay at different houses after that, we'd go and stay at friends. I just accepted it so everywhere Lee went I went. Even though Lee was threatened he still went out on the town, he still took me to Middlesbrough and still went to all the places he went, he never hid anywhere.

People showed him loads of respect, soon as he went into a pub they'd all come over and sit and drink with him and talk with him. The press said that when Lee went into a pub the place emptied and everybody stopped enjoying themselves, but that just wasn't true. Lee went to all the pubs and everybody stayed and had drinks with him and played pool with him. If people didn't want to be in his company then they wouldn't have stayed, but they did. He never drank much, he'd drink more coke than anything, he wasn't a drinker. Once he went drinking in the afternoon and the front door opened...he just fell in, he'd only been out a few hours and he was absolutely legless. All the lads had been drinking and he joined in, but he didn't usually drink.

Lee never had his own car, he'd borrow a car to get around in if he needed one or maybe he'd hire a car for a week or so if we were socialising and sometimes he'd go to the races and things like that.

After Lee had died to be honest I didn't read the newspapers because I was too upset to read such items, it was my mam that told me most of it. My mam told me not to read the papers because they'd put in that when he died people were standing around the street cheering, why put awful things like that in the papers, there was no need for it was there? At the end of the day the press wouldn't let you (Steve Richards) put an advert in to trace the family of Lee because they said it would hurt his family, what could hurt more than them putting that about the people cheering and holding parties after he had died? The papers were saying nobody would help Lee when he was dying and that no car would stop to help Lee and Lee was shouting, 'I'm dying,' this is what the Gazette put.

Lee's friend, Mark, was with him when he was stabbed and eventually he'd stopped a car and he asked him if they could get in and this lad let him in the car. Mark got Lee into the back of the car, Lee was still conscious at this time. Lee told Mark that he was dying and he told Mark to tell me that he loved me.

After Lee's death one or two people gave me support but not many. No one offered any real help, I don't think people wanted to and they said that the people involved in Lee's death would get their comeuppance.

Lee loved dancing, he loved a joke and he was really generous to his friends and it's not true that he had lots of enemies. When he came home he switched off and he was good to his kids, he had two children to his ex-girlfriend, we used to go and pick these two up and go out for the rest of the day to Redcar or wherever and then maybe we'd go and visit my dad at Liverpool, he remarried and moved there.

I remember that Lee once broke down, it was at a time when he was tired and worn out, and he'd had that many attempts on his life and there'd been three this time, I think he needed a rest but he couldn't rest. He was never ever in fear because he still got up and went out into town after he'd been shot so he can't have been frightened; he'd just had enough. He just felt like he wanted to settle down, but maybe he thought he couldn't with the attempts on my house and the attempts on his life, he'd just had enough. We wanted to settle down but everything happened so quick we didn't have time to sit down and talk, we were both young.

Lee once said to me: 'All I want to do is settle down with you and Kattieleigh, that's all I want, get the house together.' We'd got this house and the night before he died for some reason he just wanted to stay in this house so we went and stayed there and slept on the floorboards. Just the week before he was there decorating it, stripping paint, he wanted to do it all form scratch. He had no money, no car, nothing. He didn't even have a wardrobe full of clothes. He used to wear jeans and sweatshirts and his favourite was shorts, he liked to show his legs off, he liked his legs. He'd even go to the nightclub in his shorts.

When Lee died I was absolutely devastated, I lived with my mam for about a year after that because I couldn't go out, I couldn't sleep, it was horrible and I had nightmares about what happened to me and I still have nightmares now about Lee because I've never experienced someone close to me dying. It was awful, I've never gone through anything like that especially someone so close to me, I'd slept with him and I'd wept with him and he was took away from me and Kattieleigh hadn't even got to know him, she was only a baby. I don't think I'll ever get over it, you don't do you, you don't ever get over something like that especially with someone like Lee - he was one on his own. People have said that there'll never be another Lee Duffy never ever, nobody could ever replace him.

The people who were up for Lee's murder have had to pay a price because one of them, the one that was charged with hiding the knife, Lee King, was murdered.

Viv - The Final Chapter

My daughter, Kattieleigh, has kept me going over this, she knows they want to make a film on her dad and she asks why they're making a film, but I'll tell her a bit more as she gets older. Her bedroom's full of photos of her dad and when we go the cemetery she calls it her dad's garden."

There the interview ends and I leave Teesside feeling rather empty inside knowing that there's a ten year old girl who'll never get to see her dad, never get to be hugged and loved by him, never get to be protected by his strong arms, never get to be led down the church aisle by him when she marries and never get to see him help her blow out the candles on her birthday cake. Lee Duffy was someone's daddy, was someone's lover, was someone's son, was someone's friend, was someone's hero, was someone's guiding light, was someone's inspiration and now he's dead – killed.

9

The Duffer – Lee Paul Duffy

You can take the boy out of the city but you can't take the city of the boy, which was the comparable difference between Lee Duffy and Viv Graham. What I mean is Viv was from a little village and even though he tried to make inroads into the underworld scene on Tyneside he still had the village in him. Duffy though…you could put him wherever you wanted and he'd survive because of his streetwise instinct.

For those of you not familiar with Lee Duffy I suppose I'll have to give you the mandatory history lesson:

June 11th 1965: Lawrie and Brenda welcome newborn son Lee into the world, born in and raised on a council estate in an area of Middlesbrough called South Bank. His first school was Beech Grove primary and then he attended Stapylton School in the Eston area of Middlesbrough.

1979: Duffy was brutally assaulted by a hoodlum gang of older teenagers, he was knocked unconscious – he was awarded £80 compensation but the taste of blood was to start him off on the road to learn boxing skills so as to defend himself and later on when he became a strapping 6ft 4ins and 16 stone man mountain he dished out vengeance beatings on those involved in the attack. (West Indian Shandy Boyce is credited with teaching Duffy how to box.)

In later years what Duffy would do is go to the gym and train, if you were a boxer he'd go and spar with you. He'd turn up off the streets, go into the gym once every two or three weeks and knock you out. Senior night at boxing clubs was usually a Tuesday and a Thursday night, Duffy would turn up on one of these nights

Duffy often recalled the bullying from his early years and it's obvious this played a part in traumatising him. Psychologists say: 'The bullied become the bullies.'

1971: At the age of six Duffy was regularly assaulted by much older boys, if you can call 19 year olds 'boys'.

December 1980: It doesn't' take too long before Duffy's indoctrinated into the rough and tumble that these estates breed into children and he's now got convictions for burglary and car theft. The courts send him to a detention centre for three months.

1981: Duffy leaves Stapylton School with a grade three CSE in woodwork.

1982: Violence lands Duffy in a detention centre for six months.

April 1983: Duffy receives a 2½-year youth custody order after attacking and robbing a nightclub doorman.

1984: Charges of affray and assault dropped when no one would give evidence. Four similar charges were dropped on separate occasions, again, as a consequence of no one giving evidence at court.

1984: The Duffer meets single mother of one Carol 'Bonnie' Holmstrom, a South Bank girl three years older than him, when he comes out of prison. They spend five years in a relationship that is turbulent and leads to Carol having a breakdown.

March 1988: Duffy jailed for four years after pleading guilty for a vicious assault on a man in the Speakeasy nightclub (became the Havana club), the attack left his victim, Martin Clark, without an eye. During this sentence Duffy was moved to 18 different prisons. When asked for a strip search during these moves he would become very aggressive. He'd want to take over each jail and to be top man.

August 1988: His second child, another daughter - Michelle, is born whilst he's in prison and mother Bonnie tells Lee it's all over.

May 1990: Duffy gets out of prison and visits Bonnie in hospital; she'd suffered a breakdown because of all the stress. Duffy breaks down crying and then goes on holiday; on his return he breaks the news to Bonnie that Lisa Stockell is pregnant.

December 27th 1990: First attempted murder on Duffy takes place in Princes Road, Middlesbrough when he's called out of a club and dives over a car for cover but still gets blasted in the knee with a shotgun. He spends four days hospitalised but signs himself out.

When he gets out he goes to a pub called the Empire, which has then just been fitted with CCTV cameras to stop all of the drugs. Duffy goes up to the camera and blows smoke at it from a joint he was smoking.

(Anthony Cole, 28, of Blyth is acquitted of attempted murder in a trial that took place in **December 1992** when the court hears that there is no real chance of securing a conviction when vital witnesses fail to turn up.)

January 31st 1991: Second murder attempt on his life in a blues party in Harrington Road, Middlesbrough. Duffy fights with a gunman and deflects the gun downwards away from his torso and gets half his foot blown off. He had to have skin grafts taken from his thigh to close up the hole in his foot. As a party piece Duffy would show the sole of his foot, which visibly had pellets on view.

An hour earlier the same gunmen had stalked his girlfriend's (Lisa Stockell) home before storming it and holding a gun to the heavily pregnant Lisa and then demanded to know where Duffy was.

(All seven men accused of conspiring to murder (dropped to conspiring to commit grievous bodily harm) Duffy were acquitted in a trial that took place in **October 1992** when a witness refuses to give evidence.)

February 6th 1991: Daughter Kattieleigh born from his relationship with Lisa Stockell.

April 1991: Third attempt on Duffy's life when petrol is thrown over him in the Commercial pub in South Bank, attempts to light the petrol fail and as a consequence the man receives a broken jaw. Patrick Tapping was later acquitted of attempted murder when witnesses failed to turn up at the trial held in **May 1992**. Ironically Duffy who was charged with GBH on Tapping immediately after the petrol-throwing incident never stood trial.

April 1991: Wickers World pub in Middlesbrough was the scene for a violent attack on doorman Peter Wilson. The man, a kick boxer, was hit so hard that his neck was broken and many believed Duffy had used a beer can to smash Wilson with, but my own investigations indicate otherwise. Duffy was so powerful that a blow from his fist would probably have caused similar damage. I quote directly from a letter on the next page that Duffy wrote from HM Prison Durham dated Sunday 2nd June 1991 (8pm):

Now then, I thought I would write and tell you the crack of late. They've let me out of the block and back on the wing, so that's alright. I can get to the gym now and have a crack with the Boro lads. People thought I was on protection, all kinds of stories flying about. Well I'm here now so anybody's got a chance to see me, I'm ready and willing!! Everyone has been to my cell asking about me.

A million "alright Lee mates," half of them were slagging me off when I was down the block!! They make me sick, two-faced cunts...The idiot with the petrol is in here, I haven't seen him yet, if I chin him, I'll only end up in the block again, it can wait. Beefy, Paul and Nipper got bail. My Judge-in-Chambers was knocked back XXXXX!!! Bastards...I'm up at court on Wednesday 5th and Thursday 6th June – (old style committals).

The Wickers World assault is on Wednesday and that (Islam Guul assault) is on Thursday. I should get the Guul assault thrown out, which automatically gives me another shot at bail. And reading between the lines I think that Guul will sack it. We'll see eh? I have just received the statements from the petrol assault charge, they aren't too clever either, some woman says I punched the lad "10" times!! And another one says I went over the top!! What about me soaking in petrol I hear you ask? Fucking right. How can you go over the top when someone's trying to kill you? Let's see what a judge and jury thinks. Not guilty.

Duffy had spilled a bit of lager on a man on the landing below, the doorman came over and 'started being funny with Lee.' Duffy punched him once that was it. A third party was asked to see if Wilson would take a few thousand pounds to drop the charges...Wilson went straight to the police.

(A similar scenario to how Newcastle club doorman Howard Mills was offered money to drop charges against a man who had stabbed him in Bentleys nightclub in 1987. The stabbing resulted from when Mills had intervened when someone had thrown an empty beer can at a fellow doorman. Mills turned down an offer of compensation from the person responsible for stabbing him and people have suggested that as a consequence for turning down the money that is the reason Mills had his leg blown off in a shotgun attack.)

As a result of this attack on Wilson further charges of attempting to pervert the course of justice were fired off at Duffy when he attempted to bribe his victim with £2,500. In all Duffy had nine court convictions to his credit varying from burglary and motorbike theft to GBH.

August 25th 1991: David Allison kills The Duffer in a fight outside a club (Afro-West Caribbean Centre) in Marton Road, Middlesbrough. A knife was used by Allison to inflict the fatal blow and Duffy dies on his way to hospital after a main artery is severed near his armpit. The only money Duffy had in the world was that which was found in his pocket when he died...£60.

October 1992: (See Viv Vol.1 pages 215) Seven men acquitted of conspiring to cause grievous bodily harm to Duffy: **John Leroy Thomas**, 36, of Edgbaston, **Leroy Vincent Fischer**, 31, of Handsworth, **Clive Thomas**, 31, Sparbrook – all from Birmingham, **Peter Corner**, 23, of Eston, **Shaun Thomas Harrison**, 25, of Grangetown, **Paul James Bryan**, 31, of Eston and **Kevin James 'beefy' O'Keefe**, 32, of Teesville – all from Teesside.

The main prosecution witness in this trial, Ria Maria Nasir, was a former prostitute and drugs dealer of over 20 years standing from Teesside. She refused to give evidence against the seven men and was advised that she didn't have to answer questions that might incriminate her. This in itself is highly unusual for such a serious case and usually witnesses are held in contempt of court if they don't cooperate.

Anyone recall the case of a man who was severely assaulted, he was so frightened that he refused to give evidence against his attacker, he was jailed for three months for contempt of court and yet here we've got the prosecution led by Andrew Robertson telling the jury he was 'compelled to offer no evidence,' he continued, 'Miss Nasir is the main prosecution witness but her attitude shows her evidence isn't going to be forthcoming.' With this flagrant breach of court etiquette the trial collapsed and all seven men walked to freedom.

Tell me this, some sex pervert comes along and rapes a little girl and, say, you're a witness to this ugly crime and it so incenses you that you carry out the unlawful act of instant retribution by running the pervert over with your car, you can bet that you'd be up in front of the court and you'd receive the maximum sentence possible because you'd have committed a murder and that's regardless of what the reason was behind it or what the person was you'd run over and remember no one held a gun to your head to force you to do it under duress.

Why then should the attempted murder of Lee Duffy be so different, the very same people who attempted the murder are cold callous people, the very same people kicked in the door of a nine months pregnant woman and stuck the twin barrels of a sawn off shotgun into her mouth in order to find out where Duffy was and they then rob her and her sister of jewellery. This pregnant woman wasn't Lee Duffy the so called terminator of Teesside, she wasn't a threat to anyone and yet Miss Nasir can give an interview to the local press some four months later and tell them that she carried on dealing drugs in spite of threats Duffy had made to herself, her teenage daughter and her grandchild and a series of sinister attacks on her home, how brave of her to carry on under such pressure, what were the local police doing in all of that time about her claims of being victimised by Duffy?

The top and bottom of it all is Duffy taxed her, any such threats she says Duffy made against her family are not substantiated and certainly if such threats were made then she didn't go to the police. When Ria Nisar ordered the hit she said it was done as a favour but it is rumoured that she paid £1,500 - £1,150 of that was used by the hired assassins to buy an ounce of cocaine.

Again I say 'Hell hath no fury like a woman scorned' and this particular episode proves that. Miss Nasir put an awful lot of emphasis on her family being threatened yet when Duffy's own family and unborn child are traumatised the courts can turn their backs with complacency over such an issue. A contract was put on Duffy because he was stepping on the toes of other people carrying out illegal acts – two wrongs don't make a right.

Duffy and his followers allegedly broke up a blues party, the party organiser was then told to give the proceeds of the blues party to Duffy and this was the final straw that spurred Miss Nasir on to put

The Duffer - Lee Paul Duffy

a contract out on Duffy and it was claimed by the prosecution to have been organised for her as a favour by her brother-in-law John Thomas. On the other hand we have to look at how Miss Nasir became a prosecution witness in all of this and then boast of her 'contract' on Duffy and in the same breath claim that murder wasn't talked about in relation to the contract on Duffy, anyone in the real underworld will tell you that a contract is a contract – no messing! The other matter is this, I have been told that there is a taped telephone conversation in existence where a female is saying that she wants the blood of Duffy and can't wait, I have not pursued the matter but I have no reason to doubt the sincerity of what was passed on to me. Regardless of this tape though I feel Duffy, even in death, was given a raw deal.

The Crown claimed the two men allegedly responsible for carrying out the hit were Marnon Thomas and Leroy Fischer. These two men were picked out of an identity parade and fibres from Crombie coats the thugs were wearing were cross matched with bedding taken from the home of the victims, this is what one of the victims was told by the police. That in itself and even less if we look at the way Barry George the alleged murderer of Gill Dando was convicted on would have been enough to bring a successful prosecution yet against all the odds the case was thrown out of court all because the victim was Lee Duffy.

A paedophile would have stood a better chance of securing a conviction in Teesside Crown Court against these seven compared with the name of Lee Duffy...that beggars belief and I wonder if the anti-abortion campaign group would agree that Lee Duffy's life was worth less than that of an unborn baby because that is in essence what the law courts have implied by their actions. People fight for the lives of unborn babies yet a woman carrying a child is considered a worthless case simply by virtue of her loyalty towards one man.

After the trial collapsed Lisa Stockell asked the MP for Redcar and Cleveland, Mo Mowlem, to intervene and all seemed well until about a week later Mo told Lisa that she couldn't get the paperwork released to her. Criminal injuries payments for the loss of Lee Duffy were not pursued because Lisa was told that legal aid would not be forthcoming due to Lee having had a criminal record, again there seems one law for one and a different law for another. A top underworld figure gunned down and murdered on Tyneside had criminal injuries payments paid out on his behalf to one of his three girlfriends and he had a criminal record!

I accuse the police and the judiciary of gross neglect of duty in the case of Lee Duffy's girlfriend being let down so badly and nothing less than a full public inquiry should have been conducted into this total balls up of an affair by the CPS. I for one would not like to be pursuing such an action in Teesside given the state of past court cases failing to bring successful prosecutions against out and out thugs in relation to the attempted murder on Lee Duffy and not the basic charge of conspiring to commit grievous bodily harm. If you are to believe Miss Nasir that at the last minute the gun aimed to 'kill Duffy' (her very own words) was pulled downwards at the last minute by another one of the assassins then what she says is an admittance that Duffy was meant to be killed but one of them bottled it – one of them was the weakest link.

But if you hear the story on Duffy's behalf it was he that fought and grappled with the gun and managed to get it pointing in a downwards position before it went off blowing half his foot off.

Regardless of Miss Nasir refusing to give evidence there was enough evidence to convict the men responsible for robbing Lisa and her sister, Joanne, but the prosecution didn't even try to secure a conviction and even though Lisa and her sister were on standby as witnesses, kept nearby in the local police station, they were never called and one of the reasons given was that immediately after the robbery Lisa was asked if she's be able to recognise any of the men her reply was an emphatic 'NO' and even though she picked the men out a while later this shocked statement of one word would be the prosecution's reason for not calling her – bollocks is what I say.

Lisa didn't want to say anything until she'd spoken with Lee and it was when he told her to tell the police everything what happened on her behalf then she was able to act in more controlled manner, given the shock she was under after such an attack I believe none of that was taken into account, yet she DID pick out two of the assailants from an identity parade and her sister was also successful in doing the same. Now we're not talking about a pair of hardened criminals here who are used to getting guns shoved into heir faces and having their jewellery torn off them, we're talking about young females in fear of their lives and there was once an unwritten rule of the underworld and that was to leave the families of your enemies out of these ding dongs, alas we're dealing with unscrupulous drug dealers and all acts of chivalry are now dead.

In April 1991 when Duffy was in court for a bail application in relation to the Wickers World incident his girlfriend, Lisa, attended court to lend her support and while she was walking up the stairs of the court building she was confronted by the men charged with conspiring to commit grievous bodily harm to Lee and for some reason they were attending/leaving court in a pre-trial hearing. They started mimicking being shot in the foot and were singing some sort of song to her. Lisa was so distressed that the police let her see Lee whilst he was in the holding cells.

And, whilst the trial of the seven was waiting to go ahead some of the men were held on remand in the same prison Duffy was held in for his attack in the Wickers World incident. Duffy was put into solitary confinement whilst his attackers were free to wander in the mainstream prison. Many might say that it was in the interests of safety for all concerned but in reality it was further punishment for Duffy to endure.

No one would disagree that Duffy had taxed drug dealers and frightened the living daylights out of them, but would you want a drug dealer living next door to you or the enforcer taxing them?

After Duffy's death a national Sunday newspaper and regional newspapers were quick to put out the story that Duffy was an underworld enforcer and a drug dealer yet Duffy had not ever faced charges of drug dealing or drugs related crimes.

Lee Duffy's hero was another of Teesside's hard men Kevin 'Ducko' Duckling. Duffy was infatuated with 'Ducko' and as a kid he idolised Ducko and wanted to be like him when he got older.

As a result of being pushed to the ground and as a consequence hitting his head on the ground a partially disabled Sheffield man,

Viv - The Final Chapter

Paul Dallaway, 21, died at a blues party – Ducko was charged with his manslaughter in June 1988 and received a four year prison sentence.

Duffy had modelled himself on Ducko and similar hard men and maybe this is what helped mould him into the man he became although as a family man undoubtedly he was a compassionate man and he cared about his two daughters, he had from the relationship with Bonnie, and his daughter to Lisa, Kattieleigh.

For anyone not familiar with a blues party I'll explain what it is, no it's not a group of jazzmen playing the blues, it's a group of people gathering together in unlicensed premises, which are converted in a spartan manner from terraced houses, flats and disused commercial premises. Once the pubs and clubs were closed people would want the party to go on and that's how the blues parties developed, a few cans of booze and a few grams of white powder or cannabis would get things going but then they became more commercialised and people started to make money out of running a blues party where hundreds of people would pack into such premises and usually an old timer would be on the door taking the entry fee.

The kitchen would be serving curry & rice and plenty of drugs would be on sale to keep the party mood in full swing while reggae tunes blasted out at full power. Frequented by prostitutes and drug dealers - a proper den of inequity where illegal gambling would take place in the quieter rooms either upstairs or out in the back while usually an open fire was left burning continuously so as to consume drugs ditched when the police would raid.

Lee Duffy would use these blues parties as his hunting ground for the rich pickings drug dealers could offer him. Soon Duffy's reputation went before him and he was a formidable force second to none in the Middlesbrough area and no sooner was his name mentioned it would make drug dealers run a mile. There were however a few dealers that had no fear of Duffy and towards the end it was suggested that a consortium of dealers was beginning to get together to bring his reign to an end.

How ironic then that it should be Duffy's former friend, David

The Duffer - Lee Paul Duffy

'Allo' Allison, who should have the sword for his ex-friend to fall onto. As if in some Greek tragedy being played out to an audience of hundreds in some amphitheatre of death the scene was played out in darkness, shadowy figures dancing about to the tune of the baying crowd. Duffy was always the showman played his part as the gladiator Spartacus who was assured of death and this fight was to the death. Only one man walked away from the man made coliseum of bodies surrounding them and this was Duffy's swan song, maybe even the way he saw it in his predictions of death when he would say that he wouldn't see the age of thirty. One of Duffy's sayings was: 'You live by the sword, you die by the sword.'

When friends become foe such is life that tragedy often follows and the one to survive has regrets beyond comprehension, always reliving the nightmare, awakening thinking all is well and then realising it really is a living nightmare and for David Allison that nightmare goes on as tragedy follows him around. First the death of Lee King, blasted to death in the back with a shotgun closely followed by the death of his girlfriend, mother of three, Beverly Reynolds in January 2000.

Interestingly enough it was two days after King was blasted to death that Beverly hung herself and rumour has it that she and King were having an affair and it was said that she became so distraught at the loss of her lover that she took her own life by hanging herself. Again, it would befit any Greek tragedy if it were true that illicit love was to play a part in Beverley's suicide. If we are to go by what the Bible tells us and literally take the meaning of 'An eye for an eye and a tooth for a tooth' then it would seem something eerie happened, as if though Duffy was reaching out from the grave still serving up his brutal style of vengeance for the way he died and the way lies were told in court about how his death occurred.

Perjury was committed in the court that dealt with the men accused of murdering Duffy and that will be covered in comprehensive detail later on in the hope that it can finally lay the ghost of Duffy to peace.

What can be said of the police throughout all of this, apart from the fact that most if not all police officers in Teesside feared him it can be said that although they offered Duffy the chance of police protection they didn't do a comprehensive sweeping up operation in relation to what really went on, although I suspect that the police knew about the wheeling and dealing going on amongst the people involved in covering up what really went on prior to Duffy's death and during the fight and afterwards, but it suited them to have a nice neat bundle at the end of it all so the case would be finalised.

Similarly in the murder investigation of Viv's death there are many stones unturned and that is the same in Lee's case. Viv was murdered by police informers and as a consequence no action was taken and it suited the people concerned to have Viv tucked away so that dealers could go on dealing and that is so with Lee, the dealers wanted him put away and the police were kind enough to consider that the removal of Lee was for the better and therefore neither they nor the prosecution applied full power to the prosecution. The police are not stupid, they've got their informers and intelligence builds up in great big files and before long they've got the full picture, as I too have!

Viv Graham and Lee Duffy had so much in common:

Both were fond of women and had a constant stream of female admirers
Both fathered children to different women
Both predicted their own deaths in an uncanny way
Both were family men and dotted on their children
Both had a love of boxing, Viv competing while Lee would be using his skills on drug dealers' heads
Both men were accused of using weapons to cause an injury to their respective victims. Graham received a suspended sentence while Lee awaited trial
Both men had a vice – Viv's was gambling and Lee's was throwing his money away on his friends
Both men used drugs – Viv used steroids and Duffy used a variety of substances ranging from class A to class B drugs, a habit he picked up whilst serving time
Both men took their girlfriends to Blackpool
Both had a perverse sense of humour - Viv loved fooling around setting fire extinguishers off while Duffy had his glass trick whereby he would hold a pint glass and ping the rim off someone's head, the glass would break without damaging the person's head. Duffy would do this to a number of people then sweep the mess up and give the landlord £50 for the glasses

The Duffer - Lee Paul Duffy

he'd   smashed

Both received numerous death threats – Duffy had three attempts on his life while Viv had one attempt that was called off at the last minute

Both the homes of Viv and Lee were raided by thugs looking for them

Both were considered the hardest in their respective areas

Both went abroad – to Tenerife

Both started out working the club doors

Both died in a brutal way and had thousands of mourners attend their respective funerals

Both had a fear – Viv of the dark and Duffy of knives

Both had more than one girlfriend visit them whilst in prison

Both were lone wolves and worked on their own accord and neither bowed down to any other man

Both were accused, after their deaths, of being drug barons although neither had ever had a drug conviction

Both police forces in their respective areas said that no one would be able to replace them and fill the power vacuum and if anyone did then they knew what was waiting at the end of it all – which dissuaded anyone from taking up the cudgel

Both areas of Teesside and Tyneside have seen an increase in drug abuse and use since their deaths

Both men overcame propaganda during their reign

Both loved sport, Duffy excelling at swimming while Viv became an amateur contender at boxing

Both wanted to get off the tiger's back, but just how?

Both men were in Durham prison at the same time in 1991

Both suffered some sort of neurosis in that Viv would suffer crippling stomach cramps and diarrhoea while Duffy would break down in private when the odds were against him telling those he loved that he wanted out of it

Both men were matched against each other but it never come off when Viv stayed out of Duffy's way because he feared that even if he had of won then he'd have been murdered by those seeking to oust him from his position of Tyneside's top dog

Both men were held and comforted in the arms of their friends before they died.

Both men's deaths are surrounded in controversy that still goes on to this day

Both men's deaths allegedly caused people to celebrate

Both men were and are Legends, even in death they can't be matched

10

The Duffer is no more

There are two stories as to how Duffy met his death; I'll give you the one you've probably read of in the hundreds if not thousands of column inches of newspaper articles and features that have been written about it. I don't intend to rehash those features so I'll move through it as quickly as possible, but if you've ever read a fairytale then what follows is close to that.

August 1991: David James Allison killed Lee Paul Duffy on 25th August 1991 at 3.30am outside the Afro-West Indian Centre, in Marton Road, Middlesbrough. As a result of what is claimed to have been an argument in the centre both men became embroiled in a fight that took place outside of the centre.

February 1993: Allison, 26, of Overfields, Teesside, claimed he feared Duffy might have a gun when the pair fought and he said he swung out with a knife that was handed to him during the fight because he feared Duffy was going to kill him.

Allison said that he'd seen Duffy with a gun on previous occasions. Once Duffy, Allison claims, pulled out the gun in August and did not say or do anything and he believed Duffy was playing mind games with him. At the trial the jury heard how Allison had told police: 'I had to fight on; I was fighting for my life.' What is true is that when Allison said that he and Duffy had clashed several times in the past it ended up in him being given a good hiding in Blaises nightclub, in Middlesbrough.

Duffy gave the offer of a fight to him in the Afro-West Indian centre and Allison, not wanting to appear a coward, accepted.

The Duffer is no more

Allison claimed Duffy said to him: 'I'm going to bust your head in and kill you.' After that they started fighting and Duffy overpowered Allison and he says: 'I thought my head was going to split again, I thought he was going to kill me.' Allison broke free and he was handed a knife and he says: 'He came lunging at me; I was exhausted at the time and just swung out with it. He backed off saying, 'I'm going to kill you, you've stabbed me'. I used the knife to protect myself, to hurt him, to win the fight. If not he would have come after me, used a knife or used a gun.' Allison's particular use of the phrase '...to hurt him, to win the fight' is usually sufficient in terms of what the court would deem beyond reasonable self-defence since self-defence is not a defence for hurting someone needlessly. Self-defence is the minimum use of force required to defend yourself or your property from the real threat of an injury or further injury or even death. Using a knife to hurt someone or to win a fight with is NOT self-defence.

Allison was in the wrong place at the wrong time when Lee Duffy decided to pick a fight with him he told the court. Giving evidence in his own defence, He added: 'He put his hand round the back of my neck. I thought about the knuckleduster in my pocket I thought to hit him with it. Finish it at that and leave. I thought I might knock him unconscious. I would have to leave him unconscious to be able to walk away. I believed he could kill a person...he was capable of it. He started to beat me up. He came forward at me and threw me to the ground. I landed on my back. Duffy got on top of me. He was braying my head off the floor. I thought he was going to kill me, I thought my head was going to split open. The knuckleduster was in my right hand. I was hitting the back of his head trying to get him off me. He was butting me. I bit his cheek. Heard someone say, 'Shiv him.' I now know that means to stab someone.

Then for some reason he was off me. I was got to my feet by some friends and taken to the wall. When I was against the wall the knife was put in my hand. Someone said, 'Protect yourself.' I could hardly walk. I did not know where I was. I just wanted to get away from him and go home. I was terrified and semi conscious. I could not let myself go unconscious. He would have killed me there and

173

then. I took him seriously when he said he was going to kill me. Some people were shouting, 'He's got a gun.' I was terrified. I was confused. Duffy came towards me. He had an object in his hand. I don't know what it was. When he walked forward he raised it. I thought it might be a gun. There was nowhere to run. I was not in a fit state to run. I walked forward to get on to Marton Road and go home. He raised his arm so I lashed out. I did not aim for any part of his body. I did not intend to kill him. I did not want to cause him serious harm. All I wanted was for him to leave me alone.' Later that morning Allison visited Middlesbrough General Hospital where they were told Duffy was dead.

Allison told how he met King and Neil for drinks in Middlesbrough town center at a pub and then they went on to the blues party getting there shortly before Duffy arrived with some Geordie friends. Allison later described them as 'gangsters.'

The prosecutor, Jim Spencer QC, at the murder trial, which took place nearly 18 months after Duffy's death, said: 'Allison had been drinking for 12 hours before the fight while Duffy known as Teesside's top dog, had taken ecstasy tablets and cocaine. Seconds separated the pair into corners and when round one came to an end they had a minute's rest.' During the course of the fight Allison had a knuckleduster on and used this to his advantage and when Duffy spotted metal in his hand he said: 'You cannot do it with metal in your hand.'

In defence of his actions on behalf of Allison David Robson QC told the court that Allison was trapped in the car park and believing Duffy was armed with a revolver only acted in self-defence. 'He was like an animal in a cage; if there was an evil supreme in Middlesbrough it was Lee Duffy. Allison was the rabbit in the trap'.

The jury was given a graphic description of Duffy's last minutes by David Woodier, a prosecution witness, who told the jury that Duffy had punched him senseless two weeks prior to his death for no good reason and he went on to say: 'Duffy enjoyed the fear people had of him.' (Maybe he should have been a defence witness!) Woodier went on to describe how Duffy had come into the Afro-Caribbean centre looking 'stoned and wild eyed,' and he agreed

The Duffer is no more

with the defence QC, David Robson, that Duffy had 'poisoned the atmosphere' of the previously jovial and happy feeling in the place.

Duffy was then meant to have entered the club telling people to 'move' and to 'get out of my way now.' Woodier went on to say he could sense something was going to happen and that Duffy had approached Allison: 'Do people think we are going to fight?' With that he saw Duffy walk outside and Allison followed him.

Woodier said he went out about five minutes later and described how Duffy and Allison had a hold of each other in a sort of lock. 'I noticed Lee had his top off and was bare-chested. David Allison was covered in blood. Both seemed to let go of each other at the same time Allison looked tired and worn out. At that stage Duffy was jumping about looking really fit like a boxer.

I heard Duffy say to Allison: 'You had to use a knuckleduster, but you still couldn't put me away.' Allison answered: 'When it comes to bullies like you I have to use something.' Duffy seemed to get very angry. He picked up a bottle off the wall and said: 'You know what I'm going to do, don't you?' Duffy brought one of his arms round holding the bottle. Allison seemed to move to one side and pointed his arm out in a sort of roundhouse move. Duffy was facing him. That blow struck Duffy towards his left arm. Straightaway Duffy put his arm across his chest and said: 'Get me to hospital, I'm dead.' There was blood, a lot of blood. I saw his jeans turn red.'

David Robson asked Woodier a leading question that should have been objected to, which was: *'Allison did not go out to terrorise people in the way Duffy did?'* Woodier answered: *'No.'* David Robson: *'Lee Duffy had the town terrified, didn't he?'* Woodier: *'Yes.'* Was the judge awake at this point, because such leading questions are not allowed in court?

I can't understand what the prosecution were doing using Woodier as a witness when he did nothing other than help the defence?

Alongside Allison were Richard Ralph Neil, 20, charged with assisting Allison to get away from the scene and Lee Robert King, 25, charged with attempting to pervert the course of justice by dropping the knife down a drain, both denied the charges.

During the course of the trial various witnesses who were either

175

friends of Duffy or Allison gave evidence. John Fail, Duffy's friend told the court: 'Allison was staggering after Duffy had banged his head on the ground and nutted him several times.'

An acquaintance of Allison's, Adrian Boddy: *'At one stage Duffy picked Allison up in a rugby tackle and smashed him to the floor. Allison just stood there staggering, I never saw anything in his hand. Allison had swung several punches at Duffy but failed to make any contact. It was after one blow which did land under Duffy's armpit that Duffy shouted he was dying.'*

On behalf of the police Dr Alistair Irvine, police surgeon, examined Allison after the fight with Duffy confirmed that the injuries Allison had received were consistent with having spent some time on his back during the fight and that injuries to his head were consistent with having it banged on the ground several times and he testified that there were also indications of blows to his face. Questioned by the judge, Angus Stroyan QC, Dr Irvine confirmed that such blows could have caused a concussional effect and would have caused a significant jarring effect to the head.

With regards Duffy's wounds the Home Office pathologist, Dr John McCarthy, described Duffy's injuries which had included two stab wounds, one to the back which did not nor could not have proved fatal and one to his armpit which severed a main artery (axillary artery) causing Duffy to bleed to death within minutes.

An early morning telephone call, 8am, alerted David James Allison senior to the state of affairs involving his son and Lee Duffy. In a phone call to his father Allison said: *'I think I've killed Lee Duffy.'* When Allison pleaded with his father to get his clothes from a garage rooftop he agreed to do that. Mr Allison senior appeared on behalf of the prosecution and he told the court that his son was crying when he called him and he told his son to give himself up to the police. Allison, a scaffolder, rang back some 3½ hours later at 11.30am saying he'd give himself up at his aunt's house.

The reason Allison gave for having the knuckleduster was because Duffy had threatened him the day before the fatal stabbing and it had previously sat at his mother's for some years.

Q: When is a gun not a gun? **A:** when it's not there. You've read

The Duffer is no more

that Allison claimed someone shouted that Duffy had a gun and that Duffy had held something aloft in his hand and that Allison may have been concussed. A surprise exhibit was produced in court namely a Smith and Wesson .38 revolver said to have been found near the scene of Duffy's fatal stabbing. Blues party DJ, Saidhu Kamara, told the court how a gun (miraculously) 'fell' from a black leather jacket which he found near his DJ box at the Afro-Caribbean centre after the fatal fight. The jacket he said was similar to one that Duffy had been wearing earlier that evening.

On finding the gun Kamara said he'd hidden it in a nearby derelict house and then proceeded to bury it underneath a rosebush at his girlfriend's home. Remarkably, somehow, Joseph Livingstone, a friend of Allison's had found out about this hidden gun buried beneath a rosebush and approached Kamara saying that the solicitor, James Watson representing Allison would like to see the item in order to help with his defence at the trial.

A forensic scientist, Michael Hammond, gave testimony to the court that Duffy had consumed a massive amount of the drug Ecstasy and that blood samples taken from Duffy's body had revealed a high concentration of metabolised cocaine and traces of alcohol. Mr Hammond went on to say that the amount of Ecstasy in Duffy's body was two micrograms per millilitre, which is an extremely high level of the drug and in some cases that concentration could be life threatening. Mr Hammond went on to say that high doses of Ecstasy could produce anxiety, paranoia, symptoms of psychosis together with mood swings and violent irritability. He advised that cocaine could have a similar effect including causing aggressive behaviour. The combination of the two would make each more effective than one on its own.

It would seem that the circus had come to town when a host of witnesses were brought forward to testify to Duffy's gun totting exploits. Witnesses testified that Duffy:

*Often played one-man Russian Roulette in front of Karen Pitelem in her Thornaby home with a loaded revolver loaded with one bullet and that he would say he was 'invincible' before pulling the trigger a number of times as he held the gun to his head.

*He once held a gun to taxi driver Arzur Shan's head in a bizarre game of Russian roulette, he spun the chamber after putting one bullet in to it, fired at the taxi driver's head ordering him to drive 'faster' but the gun never went off and then he pulled the gun away and fired a hole through the taxi roof! This was done to impress someone who was with him.

*Fired a gun off in Middlesbrough's Havana nightclub. Duffy had asked a DJ in a nightclub to dedicate a record to Allison and continuously waived a gun at him while the record played. Fired a gun into the wall of Karen Pitelem's house he was visiting as an unwanted guest in order to frighten her.

*Played three-man Russian Roulette with friends, one man bottled out of it and on the third shot Duffy fired the gun at the wall and the gun went off!

Forensic evidence though showed that Duffy had NOT been in contact with a gun on the night of his death. Which of course dumbfounds any of the testimony given by the DJ Kamara.

Duffy had earlier assaulted a man who tried to save his life. Duffy threw Stephen Pearson backwards and grabbed him by the throat in an unprovoked attack. Later on Mr Pearson saw the fight leading up to the stabbing and ran after the fatally wounded Duffy as he ran in various directions shouting for help. Mr Pearson took his T-shirt off and used it to try to stem the blood spouting out of Duffy's armpit wound. He tied a tourniquet and helped place the mortally wounded Duffy into a car that had been flagged down immediately after a taxi had driven off at speed when it too was flagged down.

When it was Lee King's turn to be represented his defence counsel, Jamie Hill, told the jury that they had to be sure he intended to pervert the course of justice when he disposed of the knife. He said: 'He had just seen his friend Allison having his head pounded on the floor and suffering considerable injuries at the hands of Duffy. It must have been a fairly fraught experience for Lee King. He must have been fairly shocked.'

Earlier Richard Neil had pleaded guilty to unlawful possession of the lock knife but he too denied assisting an offender when his counsel, Ian West, told the jury: 'There is not a shred of evidence that

The Duffer is no more

what Neil was doing was assisting an offender.'

King was found guilty of attempting to pervert the course of justice for dropping the lock knife down a drain but charges of assisting an offender against both Neil and King were dismissed. King received 150 hours community service for hiding the knife and in 1995 was jailed for 18 months for assaulting an off-duty policeman.

Allison was acquitted of murder and walked from the court a free man. Allison punched the air when a not guilty verdict had been returned after two hours of deliberation at the end of an eight-day trial. Allison: '*I'm all right, I'm not sad about the verdict anyway.*'

Quite poignantly Lisa Stockell pointed out that the jury had been swayed by all the violence and she went on to say that too much of Lee's past was brought up in the trial and not enough about Allison.

Duffy's mother, Brenda, and Lisa both burst into tears when they heard the verdict. Brenda Duffy: '*Lee would not have wanted his man to go down, even though I would like his head on a stick in my garden.*'

Some claimed Duffy led a charmed life in being able to avoid so many attempts on his life but in reality it was Duffy's upbringing that helped him avoid this sort of every occurrence due to his lifestyle.

Viv Graham had to be just as diligent as Duffy, but he wasn't and this is what I believe led to his downfall. Someone like Duffy parading around Tyneside would have been a force to be reckoned with and had he of teamed up with Viv as he did with Brian Cockerill for a short period then maybe he'd have had the whole of the north sewn up, as it is now there are factions that keep a low profile and at times they do take the law into their own hands, which results in no less violence then when both Viv and Lee were around. Let's move on to the next chapter.

11

Two Sides of the Moon

The second story I'm going to tell you relating to Lee Duffy's death is based on fact. To every story there are two sides, you've just read the other side and with this side of the story I'm going to tell you it should make the whole of the moon visible to you. (*The Whole of the Moon* was Duffy's favourite song.)

From my own investigations I've been able to determine many flaws in the previous chapter's submission to you. I've interviewed many people in relation to the death of Duffy; many people have spoken to me but only with my guarantee of anonymity for them. That is how I work; if someone comes up to me and confesses something after I've given them my word that'll I'll not drop them in it. I must maintain my credibility otherwise word would spread like wildfire that Richards didn't keep his word and then how far would my investigations get me? I've been let down by certain high profile people, who shall remain nameless in this book, and in particular a man I thought more of than to try a silly stunt of blackmailing me, but I've always kept my word and on that basis I would hope you would bear with me while I try to translate these submissions made to me into a readable format.

For a start I wanted to have it confirmed that Duffy and Allison (nicknamed Buck Weed) did in fact have a conflict going on between them because if I'd found no proof of that then it would have meant all of those people standing up in court and particularly Duffy's killer, Allison, were lying when they told of a running conflict that Allison had with Duffy. But indeed there was a conflict between

Allison (Allo) and Duffy. At a wedding do, John Graham's, Duffy and Allo had a bit of a set to but nothing happened. Years previously they'd had a fight and from other accounts they'd had other run ins with each other.

One night Duffy was out in the Havana pub when he was met up by some friends from Hartlepool from there they got their own taxis from there to the blues in Princes Road where the first attempt on Duffy's life had taken place some eight months earlier. Duffy pulled up in a black cab with some others and he invited some of the lads into his cab saying: 'Jump in here with us.' From there they went on to the Afro-Caribbean centre in Marton Road, which was about 3.15am.

Outside of the centre was a lad called Stephen 'Morph' Reed who was standing there mortal drunk, he was put into a cab and sent home by one of Duffy's party. It seemed that this night was to have a catalystic calamitous effect on many of the people present, as if though something sinister pervaded the place.

That night in the centre a man called Field's had given a letter to someone to pass on to Allo, that person is rumoured to have been Mark Hartley, I was told that Hartley approached Allo, who was up against the back wall, and he was seen to pass this letter to Allo and the next thing Duffy went over and said to Hartley: 'What the fuck are you talking to that rat for?'

Allo at this point looked like a frightened mouse but he still argued with Duffy and he was heard to say to Duffy: 'Do you want it, do you want it, do you want it?' What he was doing at that time was putting the knuckleduster on that was in his back pocket, which falls in line with what Allison admitted under oath in court during the murder trial.

He slipped the knuckleduster on and had obviously given some thought to what he should now do. As Dave Courtney once said, 'You don't run around with weapons and then when it gets to the point of using them bottle out of it because someone is going to have one over on you while you're giving it this with the weapon.'

Duffy replied to Allo, 'Yeah, I do. Get outside and I'll give you it.' Duffy was then heard to say to Allo: 'Don't be getting the fucking knife out, don't be getting the fucking knife out.' He didn't know it was a knuckleduster at that time and during the fight he thought it was a cosh.

They then went outside and the doors were shut, nobody at first seen what happened, they can tell you this, they can tell you that but nobody other than the few present from both sides seen what happened apart from a third party that saw everything and that is the person I pursued to get the following information, which is NOT guesswork on my behalf – it is fact.

Duffy took his top off, note that he was not wearing a leather jacket. That is very important to remember so keep it in readiness for what I'll spring on you later. What he was wearing was a T-shirt, it's a summer's night, he's proud of his body and don't forget he doesn't want anything as cumbersome as a leather jacket on when he's going to a blues party, given that, yes, he did take Ecstasy that night then he would have been far too hot to even consider wearing a leather jacket. At no time did Duffy even have a leather jacket under his arm and at no time did he ever leave this invisible jacket with an invisible gun in the pocket near the DJ box in the centre.

As soon as Duffy' top was off Allo run at him and punched him with the knuckleduster. Duffy grabbed him, threw him on the ground, straddled him and he was nutting him and smashing Allo's head on the ground, bang, bang, bang, bang, bang and then pulling Allo's head towards him to head butt him. Allo was trying to bring his hand over the top to hit Duffy with the knuckleduster. At this point Duffy was heard clearly to shout: 'You can't even beat me with a cosh,' because he thought the duster was a cosh. This is the point where people started coming out of the centre.

Lee King slipped by, come round the back and stabbed Duffy in the back while he was sat on top of Allo. The party that relayed this information to me saw the knife blade catch the light before it entered Duffy's flesh. It was like a torchlight flash, but someone present seen it happen. Now this fits in exactly with what Allison testified to in court: 'Then for some reason he was off me. I was got to my feet by some friends and taken to the wall.' This accounts as to why Duffy was off him in a shot, what other reason would Duffy have had to get off Allo?

The fight was broken up, but at first no one would act to do that. One of Duffy's aid de camps (second in command) got in between Allo and Duffy and pushed Duffy off, he slipped in between them and put his arms around Duffy tight and pulled him up, not unlike the Heimlich maneuver applied when someone's choking on something stuck in their throat.

Remember that Duffy had been shot twice some months before this and he had a bad limp due to the state of his knee and foot, each damaged in different attempts on his life. (Half Duffy's foot was blown away; there was a hole that had to have grafts.)

What happened then was Duffy sat on a wall and he said: 'You can't even fucking beat me with a cosh.' Then Lee King passed Allo the knife. This is in total contradiction to Richard Neil entering a guilty plea to the unlawful possession of the lock knife that inflicted the fatal wound. The reason why King couldn't take the rap for this was because he'd already had convictions for knife attacks and it wouldn't have gone well for him had he been found guilty of having possessed the knife if he was found guilty, which Neil was.

Imagine if it were King on this charge of possessing the knife, the judge would have come down on him like a ton of bricks. You can see now why King didn't want to have anything to do with having possession of the knife.

Duffy hadn't complained about any pains in his back because he was in a fighting mode and the adrenalin rush would have warded off the initial pain. A stab wound doesn't initially give a feeling of pain it's only afterwards. Allo came towards Duffy with the knife in his hand and one of Duffy's men got in between him and Allo.

A clear picture was developing of what was going to happen. Someone was heard to say: 'David, put the knife down. David, put the knife down!' Allo then did a roundhouse move with the knife and shouted at the man in between him and Duffy 'Fuck off!' With that Allo went at the man and it hit him in a similar way that it was to kill Duffy seconds later, but it only nicked the man's skin under his arm and twanged off his shirt whereas in Duffy's case it was to go into an artery.

Allo then went straight for Duffy who picked a little plastic drink bottle up and he was pretending to throw it and Allo did a similar roundhouse move as he'd jut done on a man intervening, the knife entered deep into Duffy's flesh severing a main artery. Duffy immediately put his arm down and said: *'Fucking hell, Allo, you've killed me. This one's serious.'* As Duffy turned to run Allo ran after him and was seen to stab Duffy on the side of his leg, it is thought to have been Duffy's right leg.

Duffy ran a matter of only twenty or so yards from the scene shouting for people to help him. A big fight took place and it is rumoured that Peter Donnelly was amongst them and they ran off leaving Duffy nearby on the ground. I mistakenly advised in a previous Viv book that it was Peter Donnelly who was in the taxi with Duffy when he went to hospital this is not the case.

What had happened was Duffy had brought the Sayers' into town and people were saying they were 'Geordie Gangsters' and it was like a time bomb waiting to go off. But once the kingpin, Duffy, was taken out then they didn't give two hoots about the Geordie Mafia, it didn't matter who they were because they were out of town. So the minute Duffy was taken out of the equation they all steamed into them. Although Duffy was seen regularly with the Sayers' ov Newcastle I have no certain proof that they were there that night. There was a bout twenty people fighting in the street. The Geordie Mafia, without their main piece of artillery (Duffy), got a good kicking from Lee King and the others.

Duffy at this time was sat up in the street shouting for help, his life blood pumping out of him like a fountain and as it hit the floor it made a clapping sound. *'Help me, someone help me,'* was Duffy's words. A taxi, as mentioned in the previous chapter, came and it was flagged down, it promptly did a U-turn and left the scene. I have not been able to trace the driver but had I of done so then you can be assured his name would be up in lights.

A passer by in a car was stopped, the driver's name was John Smith (his real name), and at this point it is clear that the man who stopped the car was Mark Hartley. Whatever he said to the driver it worked and he allowed Hartley to put Duffy in the back of his car. Duffy was now flat out on the ground lying face down and in a state of shock with bright red blood squirting feet high into the air.

As Hartley struggled to get Duffy off the ground a crowd of some few hundred had gathered as if watching some free for all gruesome horror show. One gallant person, Stephen Pearson, stepped forward from the morbid crowd and said he would help. He said he didn't like Duffy but he would help, many are called few are chosen. Hartley took hold of Duffy's top end while Pearson took hold of Duffy's legs and put him into he passenger side back door of the John Smith's Mk111 Ford Escort car. Duffy's head was behind the driver and his feet were bent up across the back seat. Hartley jumped in the front passenger seat, another man run and jumped in the car to get out of the way of a man he'd earlier been fighting with.

Hartley was seen to be on the passenger's obstructive knees in the front of the car and was seen to lean across tending to Duffy who by all accounts was still alive. The driver set off to hospital as fast as he could and as the car went through the hospital gates Duffy took his last gasp and is believed to have died.

The paramedics still applied electric shock to stimulate his heart back to life. An hour or two later it is claimed that Peter Donnelly and another two Geordies turned up at the hospital. Lisa was called on the phone and she says Mark Hartley told her that Lee had been stabbed and when she enquired as to how bad it was Mark Hartley is said to have told her that he didn't know.

Lisa, Duffy's girlfriend, her mother and stepfather, Terry, turned up at the hospital and there they saw the lone figure of Mark Hartley outside of the casualty department. Lisa ran up to Hartley screaming, 'I WANT TO KNOW, I WANT TO KNOW?' 'He's dead, Lisa,' came the reply and with that she became hysterical.

I was very surprised; in fact I was astounded that Mark Hartley was not called as a witness in the subsequent murder trial. The prosecution could have subpoenaed Hartley and I firmly believe his testimony would have altered the outcome as well as the fact that another party was not called. I believe this trial was designed from start to finish and I believe both the prosecution and the defence assisted the end result.

Viv - The Final Chapter

My inside sources tell me that Hartley was arrested at the hospital when he refused to make a statement and had asked to leave the interview until the following day. The police immediately arrested Hartley on the suspicion of murdering Duffy. Of course this was merely a holding method employed by the police in order to keep a material witness in their grasps.

At 3.30am Duffy was killed, at 3.31am the police had a call to say there'd been a road traffic accident (which fits in with the fact that Duffy was lying in the road) and at 3.33am a telephone call was received by the police to say Allison had killed Duffy. The police were already aware of who was responsible they just wanted someone to finger him, in the end Allison fingered himself even though he fancied taking off abroad somewhere.

Again my inside source tells me that Hartley was asked to touch one of three names presented to him while he was banged up in a cell, one of the names was 'Allison'. The person who had called the police told them everything so holding Hartley was just a callous act and by leaving him covered in Duffy's blood whilst in the cell shows the callousness of the police in this inquiry.

The holding cells were to see the arrival of Allison at 2.20pm that afternoon and unbelievably Allison was put some few cells away from Hartley, both men could have spoken to each other, often a ploy used by the police in the hope that if their captives talk to each other then they might learn something.

There is forensic evidence to support that fact that Duffy was NOT armed with a gun and also witness evidence to support the fact that he was not even carrying a knife at the time of the fight or just prior to the fatal fight.

The gun, a Smith and Wesson .38 revolver, was dramatically discovered in a cock and bull story so outlandish that it came close to being a fairy tale. The DJ, Saidhu Kamara, told the court how a gun 'fell' from a black leather jacket which he found near his DJ box at the Afro-Caribbean centre after the fatal fight. Well what a coincidence! Then he says he goes and stores it in a derelict house, yawn, yawn. After that he buries the gun underneath a rose bush in his girlfriend's home. I rest my case on that particular story and Mr

Kamara wants to think himself lucky he wasn't charged with perjury.

My witness evidence is first class and should anyone think of pursuing a civil action against me then you had better remember that in such cases there is much less burden of proof needed to secure convictions resulting from evidence the I would submit and of course any judge presiding over such a civil case would be compelled to refer the matter back to the criminal courts, which would be the case by time I finished off my defence of what I've written here. Believe me I do not write such things lightly.

Yes, King had dumped the knife down a drain, but had the truth come out that he was in possession of the knife and that he was the one to stab Duffy in the back then it would have probably made a bigger story than Duffy's death.

Richard Neil took the wrap for passing Allo the knife when in fact it should have been King who was charged with this as well as the fact that King should have been charged with wounding Duffy with the knife and this would have seen him also being charged with murder in a joint venture charge alongside Allison.

Double jeopardy is a rule whereby once the law courts have acquitted you of a crime then you cannot be tried for that same offence, even if you later confess or if the police discover new evidence. The Criminal Justice Bill, which was announced in the Queen's Speech in June 2001, intends to do away with this 800-year-old rule.

Since the advent of DNA evidence and improved forensic detection it would seem a logical approach in making the court system just as fair for the families of loved ones murdered finding out that the accused goes on to make a confession that they 'did it' after they've been acquitted. Lord Mackenzie of Framwellgate is quoted as saying: 'I have always said that a wrongful acquittal was just as important a miscarriage of justice as a wrongful conviction.'

Killers are getting away with murder and in particular the case of Billy Dunlop who was acquitted of the 1989 killing of single mother Julie Hogg, 22, from Billingham, Teesside after a jury twice failed to agree a verdict. Dunlop strangled and then mutilated pizza delivery girl Julie's body and then hid the body underneath a bath. Three months later the police handed Ann Ming, the keys back to her daughter's property. What the police had missed in the domestic property was soon discovered when Ann Ming made the grim discovery of her daughter's body beneath the bath!

But Dunlop later confessed to a prison officer that he had carried out the murder and as a consequence was charged with two counts of perjury, which he pleaded guilty to and received six years imprisonment. In the meantime Julie's family are campaigning to have the rule changed in order that Dunlop can be tried again for the murder. Mrs Ming, a member of the Teesside branch of Support After Murder and Manslaughter (SAMM) is being assisted by legal advice to find the best way to bring Dunlop back to court.

It has been suggested to Cleveland Police that under the terms of the Criminal Procedure and Investigation Act 1996 it might be possible to retry Dunlop for the murder but the police put the dampeners on that when they said that it would be unlikely that such legislation referred to would apply in the Dunlop case.

The Bill to scrap the double jeopardy ruling is yet to be put before parliament and the Law Commission is recommending that the change, if implemented, be backdated. David Hines of the North-East Victims' Association said: 'People should not be allowed to get away with murder.'

In a macabre twist to the Duffy killing it would seem that the lives of those involved in the killing were fated as if though Duffy reached a hand out from beyond the grave in a gesture of revenge. Lee King the man who stabbed Duffy in the back in that fateful fight with Allison was blasted to death on January 28th 2000. His body was discovered in Penistone Road, Park End, Middlesbrough with shotgun wounds to the head and back. Keith McQuade, 45, was remanded into custody in September 2001 some eight months after the murder investigation had begun.

February 5th 2001 sees the start of the murder trial in which King, 32, is described as a man with a reputation as a womaniser; this is an important fact to remember because I'm going to spring something on you later. McQuade denied the charge.

"McQuade stuck a sawn off shotgun into Mr King's back in a

Two Sides of the Moon

Teesside street in the early hours of the morning and blasted him through the heart at close range. As his rival lay wounded, McQuade reloaded and shot him in the head at close range," said James Spencer, prosecuting.

King had a one-night stand with an ex-lover of McQuade's, Lisa Piercey, 25, after this he called her a 'slut.' Mr Spencer said that McQuade had told a friend that Mr King had made a fool of him over the woman. McQuade said that King told him two nights before he was killed that he had slept with McQuade's former lover. McQuade told the court that King had said to him: 'You are not bothered about it are you, because I was round there that night? She's a slut anyway, isn't she?' McQuade said he replied: 'She's got three kids to three different fellas, it's got nothing to do with me.'

Mr Spencer told the court that McQuade had said: 'He told me about sleeping with Lisa and said she was only a slut. I told him "You don't need to do something like that to me" and I pointed the gun at him. He said "You won't do something like that to me," and he walked away. I shot him once in the back and then in the head.'

It was alleged that McQuade had acted out the killing afterwards to two friends telling them that King had turned his back on the gun saying: 'You wouldn't dare.' McQuade told the court that King had invited him to take part in an armed robbery on a crack house in Kensington Road, Middlesbrough; this was planned for the night King was killed. He went on to say that King had arrived at his lodgings in Kenilworth Avenue, Park End to collect some tools he'd hidden in the back garden. King then produced a sawn-off shotgun, which was wrapped in bin liners at which point McQuade told King that he wanted nothing to do with the robbery.

When King's body was found he was clutching a knife in one of his hands and there was a bag containing two balaclavas. This was McQuade's defence that King had organised the proposed crack house robbery.

They both left the lodgings together and went in opposite directions and the next day he heard that King had been shot dead. When asked why he thought witnesses had evidence against him McQuade told the court that he believed that prosecution witnesses were involved in drugs and had plotted with each other to tell lies. A prosecution witness told the court that McQuade had left a friend's house carrying a holdall in which it is alleged to have had the sawn-off shotgun used to kill King. A mechanic, John Johnson, known as 'Car Jack' told the court that on January 28th 2000 he was working in his garage when neighbour Peter Heeran walked in and he was saying: 'Keith Needs a lift, urgent.' Mr Johnson said he drove McQuade to a nearby mutual friend's home and ten minutes later on his return he heard emergency vehicle sirens. A while later Mr Heeran called in to the garage and told him that Lee King had been shot. Mr Johnson went on to say: 'Heeran said to me, "It served him right, he was trying to get me shot." I told him that I did not want to know anything about it.'

The jury found McQuade not guilty of murdering King. Nearly to the exact day in the same month on the eighth anniversary of David Allison being acquitted of murdering Lee Duffy similarly Keith McQuade was acquitted of murdering Lee King, the man who had stabbed Duffy in the back.

Just as Duffy was stabbed in the back then just as similarly King was injured in his back by being shot in the back and as is claimed, if true, that King was lying on the ground mortally wounded (just as Duffy was) before the next gunshot blasted him in the head then that fits in with how Duffy was stabbed twice. (Although it was also suggested that Duffy was also slashed on the right leg.) For each stab wound Duffy received King had received a gunshot blast as if from invisible hands from beyond the grave. The other twist in the tale is that the woman involved in this was called 'Lisa', the same Christian name as Lee Duffy's girlfriend, Lisa Stockell. As much as Duffy's mother, Brenda, said that her son wouldn't have wanted Allison to go to prison for what had happened then neither did McQuade go to prison and just like Allison he too was acquitted – scary or what?

Just when you think that's the end of the twist to the tale, it isn't. Keith McQuade faced his first murder charge in 1993 and was discharged of that murder when the charge collapsed. Magistrates in Teesside refused to commit him to trial for the shotgun murder of Kevin 'Rico' Richardson. The court ruled that there was insufficient evidence. Remarkably McQuade walked from court a free man in the same year as Allison walked from court a free man when he was acquitted of Duffy's murder. King was murdered on the same estate where Rico Richardson was killed.

After McQuade was acquitted of King's murder Detective Superintendent Adrian Roberts said: 'There is not a shred of evidence to implicate anyone else associated with the investigation, or to suggest a new inquiry. We will not be looking for anyone else.'

In an even bigger macabre twist to this tale from the unexpected you will recall that King was murdered on January 28th 2000. Two days later on 30th January 2000 mother of three Beverly Reynolds, 31, was found hanging by a piece of wire around her neck from a loft hatch – she'd killed herself.

Scaffolder David Allison, 32, found the body of his girlfriend who had returned home on her own earlier after rowing with Allison on a night out in Middlesbrough. It is claimed that she wanted to stay out longer while Allison wanted to return home. It was to be Beverly, though, who had retuned home first by taxi after the row, she had to smash the glass of the door to gain entry because she didn't have a key. Her children were staying overnight at relatives so when she entered the house she was alone.

Dr Jeremiah Murphy spoke at the inquest held in January 2001, he said he was treating Miss Reynolds for depression due to domestic stress and said that she had twice taken overdoses of paracetamol.

On January 31st 1991 three men burst into the home of Lisa Stockell and forced a gun into her mouth in order to find out where her boyfriend Lee Duffy was. Nine years to the day (nearly) **30th January 2000** tragedy strikes again but this time against the man who killed Duffy.

Already Lee King has suffered a horrific gangland slaying and now Allison has been put in the same position as Lisa Stockell and Carol 'Bonnie' Holmstrom when their children lost their father. Duffy's three children are fatherless and now the three children of Allison's girlfriend are motherless!

Just as you think it can get no worse, it does. Beverley was rumoured to be having an affair with Lee King and it was two days after King's death that she committed suicide. You've already heard that she and Allison were arguing earlier in the night and that she was being treated for depression due to domestic stress, it all got too much for Beverley and it is rumoured that she thought that if King was taken away from her and she couldn't have him then Allison wouldn't have her.

The devastation this will bring to Miss Reynolds' children is mind numbing. For a child to lose a parent to death is distressing no one can doubt that and just as Lisa Stockell and Carol Holmstrom had to try to come to terms with the loss of their children's father then it would seem that Duffy is as vengeful in death as he was in life by virtue of the messed up lives in question.

When the police arrived at the tragic scene at Allison's home in the early hours of Sunday it was PC Timothy Lowe, the first officer to enter the house in Ormesby, Teesside, who gave mouth-to-mouth resuscitation to Beverley. PC Lowe told the inquest that he could hear Allison downstairs and he seemed very distressed. 'He became more and more agitated, passing from anger to violence. He went into the kitchen and smashed a chair and threw a radio cassette into the sink. He kept throwing himself about the kitchen. He was saying, "Who will tell the kids? What am I going to do?" He caused damage to numerous items in the house.' The coroner for Central Teesside, Michael Sheffield, recorded a verdict that she killed herself.

If in some way there is a connection to Duffy in all of this tragedy then I feel we're likely to see further tragedies connected with those involved in what happened on the night of Duffy's death. I do not say that because I want it to happen, on the contrary I believe tragedy like this is very rare.

Violence attracts violence and as Duffy once said: 'Those that live by the sword die by the sword.' I base what I say on previous tragedies, look at the Kennedy family from the USA – tragedy after tragedy. A man, Kevin Howard, who had once fought with Duffy also hung himself. Another friend of Duffy's, Docker, was blinded when a car battery exploded in his face and a close friend of Mark Hartley also committed suicide earlier this year.

Two Sides of the Moon

Duffy also used to say: "Treat good people good, treat bad people bad." Many people saw him as a Jeckyl and Hyde character, but I believe he was an adaptable person and has been described as speaking the language of the street and the language of the jet set, someone said, "Duffy spoke fifteen languages," meaning he could communicate in the language of violence or the language of business. You could take him to tea in an old people's home and he'd be most respectful but put him in a blues party and he acted accordingly, he wore his heart on his sleeve.

If those people connected to the death of Duffy and that includes all of those who conspired to pervert the course of justice by telling lies and assisting in some way or another then of course they'll have a propensity to carry on in this way and it's sure to catch up with them. Whether that applies to all concerned is not for me to say but the more involved in such matters people become then it's a bookmaker's dream of giving odds on that something will happen in these people's lives that is out of the ordinary.

My investigations into when Duffy was shot in the first murder attempt at Princes Road showed that this was carried out in a similar fashion to the way Viv was murdered. In Duffy's case the hit men stood in a dark alleyway and shouted him over. (In Viv's case it was a car that was parked in a dark alleyway and from within it they shouted something at Viv to attract his attention so as to get his body square on so he could be a better target.) Duffy though, unlike Viv, had seen the gun that his hopeful assassins carried. This is the difference I was telling you about earlier on between Duffy and Viv.

On seeing the gun Duffy turned and went to run backwards, which given his speed and power would be as fast as some people could run forwards. He jumped behind a car and they opened fire only managing to shoot him in the leg, Duffy had escaped death by the skin of his teeth! They were trying to take him out; they weren't giving him a warning.

The second attempt on Duffy's life as you now know was in an illegal blues party. Three of them walked up to him, Duffy seen them and tried to slip around them in the darkness of the blues. He tried to work his way towards the door but they caught him before he could get out. Duffy instinctively knew they were out to kill him.

One of them pulled a shotgun out of his long coat; Duffy instinctively grabbed the barrel of the shotgun and started fighting with his would be killer. While he was fighting the gun off him one of the other two had a crow bar and started braying Duffy over the head in the hope that he'd let go of the gun. To prove this is true the records would show that Duffy also had quite a few stitches put into the back of his head. There was no time that any of the hired hit men pushed the gun downwards – this was a full blown hit meant to kill Duffy. While Duffy was fighting with the gun one shot went off and missed, which again supports the shoot to kill story I give you.

When Duffy was in hospital he had photos in his possession of the so called 'professional' hit men along with all of their names and addresses written on the back of each photo.

In an update on two of the accused, Marnon Thomas and Leroy Fischer, both now 41, in the second murder attempt on Duffy's life I give you news of when these two made an attempt in 1999 to pursue Cleveland Police Force for compensation for 'malicious prosecution' in a High Court action. Both petitioners claimed damages from Cleveland Chief Constable Barry Shaw following their acquittal in 1991 of involvement in a conspiracy to shoot Lee Duffy.

The Crown prosecutor for Teesside, Keith Simpson, called by lawyers representing Thomas and Fischer, both Birmingham men, to give evidence. Mr Simpson has denied being involved in any deal to grant immunity to Ria Nasir, one of the suspects. The High Court - sitting at Teesside – was told by Mr Simpson that any such deal would need approval at a much higher level than himself.

Ria Nasir had been questioned in connection with the shooting by police treating the case as attempted murder when intelligence reports suggested that some of the men involved in the shooting were seen at or near Nasir's home. Teesside solicitor Keith Leigh, who represented South Bank woman Nasir at the time, had told the High Court that he had been involved in 'striking a bargain' with Detective Supt Len Miller with the aim of having all charges against her dropped if she co-operated with police investigating the shooting, he claimed Mr Simpson was present for part of these discussions. What a pity Nasir hadn't kept her side of the bargain in this alleged deal! It would have meant some sort of justice for Lisa Stockell who, along with another female, was a witness as to the identities of two men involved in this crime.

Nasir's lawyer also claimed he witnessed her - who he said had a drink problem - being interviewed by officers in Middlesbrough police station while under the influence of drink, drinking brandy and with a bottle of brandy close at hand. He told the court: "She was not being interviewed under caution, she was not at risk. I was perfectly happy to let the police conduct the investigation as they saw fit."

Mr Simpson told the court that all he had done was to offer the police advice. He said: "I was there to advise the police about the prosecution rather than the investigation." He had recommended no action against Nasir on the basis that the only evidence against her was an informal unrecorded conversation between her and the then Detective Inspector Ray Mallon and this could not have produced a realistic prospect of convicting Nasir on charges relating to the shooting. Cross-examined by barrister Peter Johnson, for the Chief Constable, he said that on the evidence submitted by the police to the CPS - which included that of Nasir - he was satisfied the charges brought against Thomas, Fischer and others were 'appropriate'.

Both Marnon Thomas and Leroy Fischer lost their case for a frivolous claim when Judge Michael Taylor said: "Whatever shortcomings in the investigation that the case had thrown up - they did not affect the central issue of malice. The claimants had maintained they had been wrongly prosecuted as a result of identification evidence provided in a deal struck between police and South Bank woman Ria Nasir at a time when she was herself a suspect in the case and known to be 'unreliable' as a witness."

Judge Taylor gave judgment in favour of the police and said the decision by Detective Superintendent Len Miller to drop potential charges against Nasir in exchange for information from her was a "totally justifiable" gamble, taken at a time when the investigation was "up against the buffers."

In an outright attack on Thomas and Fischer he said: "It was clear that those directly involved in the shooting were from outside Teesside. With almost all the potential witnesses coming from the criminal community, there was little chance of co-operation in finding out their identities." Judge Taylor added that while it was not his role to decide whether the claimants themselves were involved, it would have served the public better to have convicted several people prepared to use a shotgun in a public place rather than have one woman in the dock.

Fischer, who at that time was serving a five-year sentence for robbery started shouting abuse at the judge and police officers in the court and continued as he was led away to the cells.

Chief Superintendent Miller was delighted with the outcome and said: "I'm pleased the judge supported our decision to take a risk in an effort to catch the people responsible for the shooting."

In another prison letter from Duffy I quote him as writing: *Manny Burgo (boxer) was in the blues last weekend, Allo and some lads were working themselves with Manny, so he knocked 3 or 4 of them out, or so I have been told. (Hope it wasn't Allo)*

A letter dated April 1991 written from HM Prison Durham Duffy writes: *Lee Harrison has been up to see me, well he actually done my head in, teasing me about the Havana, etc. He was at the courts yesterday taking the piss out of the police and generally making a disturbance, you know what he's like, he makes me laugh, he's off his head. I know this is going to sound daft but in a way I have been glad of the break from it all really. Living too fast, too long, it burns you out. But I could think of a better place to take a break like. (Ha Ha) But having said that I've had some brilliant times with you and the lads and I wouldn't change my lifestyle if it meant no more good times like we've had.*

12

What was Duffy all about then

If you'd never met Lee Duffy and he walked into a pub you'd know it was him. One of the stories about Lee Duffy goes like this, one day down the Empire a box van pulls up with about thirty mountain bikes in it, the driver gets out and asks Lee and the man who was with him if they knew where Bobby's Cycles was.

Two other lads were standing around who Duffy knew. Duffy says he doesn't know where the place is but, he says, 'They'll know in there,' as he pointed to The Empire pub. The driver had left the engine running, the driver goes in to the bar and the two lads who had nothing to do with Duffy and his friend jumps in to the van and off they go with it. At that time mountain bikes were fetching £500 apiece so it was a birthday gift to these two lads and it was just before Christmas. The driver comes out and the van's gone!

That very night the man standing with Duffy goes to his mother's house and she says to him, "Have you heard about your mate, a man pulls up from the handicap kids with a load of bikes asking for directions, Lee Duffy knocked him out, broke his cheekbone and took all of the bikes off him for the handicap kids." That's what it was like, it was all added on, it was made to sound evil.

Duffy had such a presence about him that it's been said that he could go into a nightclub with 1,000 people in the place and within ten minutes there'd only be 100 people left in the building, he wouldn't hit anyone but it was just because his presence was there. When Duffy was in prison he was visited by his girlfriend and his friend, when they got in to see him he was walking around in a yard on his own in a big cage. There was eighteen people in that prison trying to murder him, it seemed easier to put him in the block than those eighteen people so he had to stay in the block and this is where his visitors had to go and visit him.

Duffy gets brought out through a door leading into a little tunnel, he's got a joint of blow behind his ear, one in his hand and the prison officers are with him. Duffy was puffing his head off on his joint and the screws never said boo to him. They bring him into this little room and the two guards stand there. Duffy says to them, 'Fuck off!' They say to him, 'Lee, on a visit we've got to stand over you,' his reply was a typical Duffy reply, 'Look you've got me out of the cell but you've got to get me back in the cell, fuck off!' The two screws walked out of the room, that's the type of power this man had.

A lad called Neil Booth went off his head one night, drunk, on top of the Havana roof throwing tiles. Duffy was in a house around the corner and the police come to the house to ask Duffy to get him off the roof.

There has been a lot of talk of Duffy and Viv getting it on in a fight and after having interviewed a lot of people in the know I've put some of those comments together. If the Sayers turned up with this Lee Duffy character Viv's going to be a little bit nicer to the Sayers' than if he was going to be without Lee Duffy there. Rumour had it that a fight was organised between Duffy and Viv in the Havana, but Viv didn't turn up, but this rumour has been proven to be just a rumour and nothing else. The feedback from a second organised fight between the two was that Viv thought he was going to be shot and again didn't turn up.

Someone has suggested that Viv hadn't bottled it but the two actually did meet some time before such a fight was even talked about when a meeting in a Tyneside pub on a very different matter seen Lee Duffy stand on a table and say, If anyone wants to question my credibility then question me.' This was in a matter relating to a man called Craig Howard. Viv was through the bar end and he never opened his mouth. Of course this wasn't a confrontational meeting and Viv wasn't in conflict with Duffy at that time.

An underworld character from Teesside told me: "No doubt about it, Viv was a very hard man but I don't think Viv would have beat Lee. Something the Sayers' might have been worried about was that if Lee and Viv had of got their heads together then they might have blitzed them clean out of the water. But considering it was going to come off Lee was permanently up the Mayfair nightclub (Newcastle) all the time, constantly up Newcastle but Viv wasn't down here. There were two arranged fights and Viv didn't turn up at either of them. Viv had a few doors up there and Lee went around and taxed a few of Viv's men. He wanted to put it on Viv's toes because he hadn't turned up."

"Now then, now then, now then," was Duffy' way of saying 'I'm here.' When it come to being involved in running things on Teesside Duffy couldn't be bothered with things like that, he wasn't business minded, although clever, it wasn't for him. Someone who knew Duffy well described him as a schizophrenic and said, "What you've got to remember with Lee is that he was like a schizophrenic. They're all schizophrenics. They've got to be a schizophrenic.'

Duffy was always discriminated against from being the age of six right up until the day he died, he knew he wasn't going to see the safe side of thirty so what did he have to lose by being himself. As time went on the very name 'Duffy' would bring fear and terror to those around Teesside that had reason to be feared of Duffy. All of the people who suffered at his hands had some connection to the underworld either directly or indirectly. The people who tried to kill Duffy didn't know him; they were contract killers working for others.

When Duffy was shot the second time he was hospitalised for a number of days and to help him overcome the pain he'd smoke dope and of course he was guarded by an armed police office – Duffy was torturing the policeman he'd say to him: 'Come here, do you want a go of this.' During this time in hospital it coincided with his girlfriend Lisa going into hospital to give birth to their daughter. Duffy didn't get to see his daughter being born and had to be content with friends telling him what his new daughter looked like.

Duffy was a sensitive person and in an extract I've taken from a letter he wrote to Lisa Stockell while he was in hospital, and she too was in another hospital having their baby daughter, it shows a compassionate side of Duffy few have seen. The public persona of Duffy was far removed from the private family man those close to him had come to know.

His friends could be counted on one hand but this was through choice. A friend as loyal as Duffy was hard to find but if he fell out with you it could be big trouble if it were to last. One of Duffy's former friends had gone as far as talking to others about killing Duffy, this was one week before he was killed by Allo and rumour had it that he was going to be set up in a nightclub of some 200 people – all were prepared to kill him, he died before this rumour could be proven to be reality. All the people involved in these murder plots were criminals and none of the people were whiter than white but they forgot this minor detail and conspired on regardless.

Duffy is being portrayed in a big screen movie I hope to get off the ground and the person selected out of the many hundreds of applicants is Andrew Hutt. Andrew is a Teesside born actor based in Leicestershire and I know he'll make it big in the acting profession that's why I'm pleased to have discovered his talent. Standing at the same height as Duffy with very similar looks I know he's going to make the part his very own and already he's had coaching in the way of Duffy's mannerisms by those who were close to Duffy.

After a few screen tests with other hopefuls wanting to either play the role of Duffy or Viv it was a difficult decision to pick a Duffy character due to the talent being so good, but I know Andrew will do justice to this role by virtue of his talent, which has to be seen to be believed. The selection for the character of Viv Graham was also very difficult, but more of that later on. Back to the letter Duffy had written to Lisa.

Here was a man who'd had half his foot shot off in an assassination attempt and had his skull beaten with a crow bar and yet all he writes about in this letter, which is written on one side of a card, is the pain and suffering Lisa must have went through, not once does Duffy fall into self pity for his own predicament. He even says he sent flowers to Joanne, Lisa's sister, one of the attack victims.

Notice the neat handwriting, an indication of someone who is

What was Duffy all about then

methodical and artistic. Notice how some of the text slopes down from right to left, an indication he's depressed. The neatness of the handwriting leads me to believe he was a bit of a perfectionist and as we know perfectionists can become frustrated. Maybe this was the key to it all in how Duffy would sometimes fly off the handle, but regardless of that he was also a great thinker.

① Hello Nana, 9a.m.

how you doing then, not too good eh? You sounded really low on the phone earlier. It's doing my head in Lisa. (I just want to see you and my new baby daughter) I know how down you are and I can't be there for you... Now I have to wait, until Monday. Before I can see yous. You were so distant from me on the telephone last night Lisa (you put it across like I'd forgotten you)! I wrote, I sent a couple of little presents, I got Michelle to order flowers and I telephoned twice, to see how you were. plus I give Boothy £20 to send Wendy and Joanne some flowers and I wrote them both a little note saying sorry and thanking them.....

So Lisa, don't think I've forgotten you, Lisa I love the ground you walk on! I'm rock bottom myself Babe, I'm trying hard to keep my chin up. All I want to do, is put my arms round you and see the baby. I know your in pain, jesus you have just had your tummy sliced open and a 8lb baby dragged out, it makes me ill thinking about it. I know exactly what your going through, I'm doing my bro.

Simon Elvin ©

35 SE 4504 - 2
Printed in England
P.T.O

201

Viv - The Final Chapter

At one time Duffy was going to a blues party but he became paranoid and thought the people that shot him were in there. He drives to this house in Stockton somewhere, goes in and the next minute he brings three guns out of the house. He says to a man, who was with him, "Here, get one of them." The man who was with Duffy thought to himself, "Fuck you and get one of them, I don't mind having a fight with someone but if I get caught with this and you shot someone the frame of mind you're in I'm getting 15 years here."

On the way back from Stockton by the suite centre a bobby van goes through the lights. The driver of the transit van was called Martin Shallows; he goes through and misses the car, a Sierra, doing about 60mph. The man who was with Duffy said to Duffy: "Go for it, go for it and lets get out of here, he's got to turn around, he's in a transit van, let's offskys," and Duffy says, "Let's fuck fucking offskys." He pulls up and at that time he's got three loaded guns and ammunition in the car and the man with Duffy is wiping the guns down and the handles of the car down. Duffy jumps out of the car, goes straight over to the bobby van and he says, "What the fucking hell do you think you're doing you?" And Martin Shallows says, "All right, Lee, what's a matter?" Duffy says, "I'll tell you what the fucks a matter with me, you've just nearly crashed into me you daft cunt." The reply was, "Lee, howway, just get yourself out of Stockton mate, no problem, no problem."

Another story I was told goes like this: "Someone had a load of cannabis resin in the car and he got stopped by the coppers for a routing check because it was Duffy. He went off his head like he was a loony and they brought a squad car out to give the car a full check over. They never found the cannabis it was underneath the seat. Instead of him keeping his mouth shut he couldn't."

And another story: "Duffy and his friends, one of them was Lee Harrison, were in a place on Normanby Road and someone went in and tipped Duffy off that there was a load of police outside. An inspector wearing a flat cap and uniform with all the buttons on walks in and he says, 'All right Lee,' and Duffy says, 'Yeah.' 'We want to have a word with Lee Harrison over fines,' said the inspector. Duffy says, 'Fuck off out of here now before I give you it,' the inspector says, 'I can come back...' 'Come back with who you want,' intervenes Duffy.

The man who owns the pub comes in and says, 'There's fucking loads of them outside.' Duffy and his friends know if they go out and drive away that they'll get pulled over so they get a taxi. On their way along Normanby Road all of a sudden an unmarked squad car pulls in front of the taxi and stops and out of the side of the road armed police jump up like in an ambush shouting: 'GET ON THE FLOOR FACE DOWN, GET ON THE FLOOR!'

Everyone but Duffy gets on the floor while he walks around saying, 'Fuck getting on the floor, I'm getting on no floor. Fuck you telling me to get on the floor'. (Obviously Duffy had flashbacks to when he was bullied as a child and wasn't going to be jumped on by armed police. Anyone see any of the CCTV videos of police caught beating innocent people up, maybe Duffy had visions of being kicked or beaten with a truncheon while he was down?) One of the police officers said to the officer in charge that Duffy wouldn't go on the floor and he was told Lee was all right."

Many people have taken what's been said or written about Duffy as gospel, as the definitive guide to what made Duffy tick...bollocks is what I say. I've spoken to the hardest of hard throughout the UK and up to now every single one of these people, with the exception of one, has turned out to be a likable character, why should Duffy have been any different. Usually it is fear of something that brings out the worst in a man. Duffy had a fear of being bullied so he got the first one in, if you weren't a threat to him then fine, if you weren't a low life drug dealer then fine, if you weren't one of those who had bullied him from the age of six then fine, if you weren't someone taking the piss out of one of his few friends then fine – so what gives total strangers who have never met Duffy the right to say he was an evil person. The only ones who had anything to fear from Duffy were the evil ones.

What sort of person sells smack to the children on your estate, what sort of person puts a contract out on someone, what sort of person would stick a shotgun into he mouth of a woman nine months pregnant, what sort of a person do you think Duffy was compared to these? Duffy was not a killer; yes he was a brutality violent man but not a killer. Okay he slapped a few drug dealers around, Billy Murray (actor starred in The Bill) was applauded when he had a drug dealer turned over who was supplying drugs to the kids on his estate and he was applauded for it. Duffy does it and the people are up in arms over it…what gives with people like that?

Tommy Harrison told me some stories about Duffy: "He said to our Lee (Tommy's son), 'I've got something to tell you, something bad is going to happen tonight.' I said to Lee that I said that same thing to myself years ago and it never happened.

Lee once knocked on my door and said, 'I've been shot, I want the bullet taken out,' I said, 'That's not a bullet, it's a shotgun wound, it's lead shot I can't do it you'll have to go to hospital because it'll get poisoned.' It did poison because some of his jeans had gone into his leg. He'd sometimes go missing for days on end up to Newcastle at a pub called the Bay Horse, I used to have to go up and get him.

When the petrol was thrown on him he just whacked the geezer before the geezer had a chance to pull a lighter out. When they had the gun pointed at his belly he just wrestled it to the floor. He was fearless he didn't fear anyone. How many people in Middlesbrough walk around with guns and knives, the people trying to kill him were out of the area and were paid to do him in. I couldn't have seen anybody enticing him into a blues party so he could be killed, they'd have had to do him in. They couldn't have just whacked him because he'd have come back.

When Lee was fighting with Allo that wasn't Lee fighting, he was as high as a kite, he was drunk they were on Champaign, Russian Blacks and he hadn't been to bed for two days. He'd been on Charlie (cocaine) his reflexes were gone. I don't think that would have happened if he weren't under the influence of drink and drugs.

When I lived in North Ormsby he used to go running every day and this day he'd been running and training. He come to my house and said, 'Have you got anything to eat?' Eggs. Sausage, bacon, liver tomato the lot then he'd be off. He gets round the corner and someone wants to have a pop at him, Lee smashed his jaw, clipped his cheekbone with two right-handers. How do you go and train, have a nice meal and go round the corner and see somebody that wants to have a pop at you, I don't know how you can define that. He used to run up the hills pulling a log up with him.

When he got into trouble at the Speakeasy he was in there just having a drink when it was a firm from Leeds causing trouble and he was asked for a hand and they all blamed him, the others never got charged and he did. It wasn't in his nature to be used but it was in his nature to help you. If you were in a bit of bother he'd help you.

I had a bit of bother with someone and he said to me, 'Where are you going?' I said, 'I'm going to go and fight somebody,' I'm coming,' he replied. He was barred from the town while he was on this particular condition of bail. But he'd help you straight away he wouldn't say 'How much are you paying me?'

Lee used to love going out with me, 'Half of them are lovely people,' he said and the people in London, he loved it he didn't swear or anything like that when he was mixing with proper people. He wouldn't swear in front of proper people. Towards the end he started to mix with the wrong people.

That night he went looking for Viv, bang, bang, bang and it cost them nothing. Viv called into my house, as he was passing, but how do you pass. Viv said to me, 'I'm not frightened of nobody me, you know, I'll fight anybody.' I said, 'So will Lee, but why? Who's going to benefit out of it, who's going to benefit out of you and him having it off, why don't you just graft together?'

Viv Graham never came to the Havana club though it was just a rumour. A fight was going to be held in a warehouse outside of Newcastle. He came to see me when it was all getting out of hand; it was like the old cowboy thing wasn't it. I said, 'Use your heads, you've got Newcastle in your hands and Lee's got all of Teesside in his hands. What the hell you want to be running around fighting with other people for I don't know.'

But Lee had this thing about them (Sayers'). They were going to look after him, I think that was the last tango, he didn't need them. He didn't need any money, he could go into a bar or a pub or a club or a restaurant, they'd invite him into the place. I'd say to Lee, 'If you can wine, dine, eat, taxis for nothing what the hell do you want to be going up there for, ham and egg?'

He was going to fight Lenny McLean until he got shot. I went down to London with Norman Jones and I had Mick Jagger and a few other people putting money up for all this. He was fit, he was bouncing then he got shot in the knee. I think Lee would have had the upper hand with Lenny McLean because Lee was young and don't forget he was nearly 18 stone and he could hit hard. I mean I knew McLean and Frank Warren.

I was going to have a go with McLean in '78 in the Empire Rooms, Tottenham Court Road. Lenny come in with young Frank Warren when they done the back street boxing. I've known Frank from being a kid and Ritchie Anderson, I just thought if I were four years younger I'd have just been on the boil because now I'm 59. Lenny wasn't as big as that in the 70s, he was on the gear, he wasn't as big as he was when he died.

I said to Frank if ever you want anything then there's my phone number and I said, 'You'll never spend that,' and I gave it to him on a £10 note. He replied, 'I'm not as bad as you, there's my phone number,' and he gave it to me on a £20 note. And Lenny McLean just sat there and we were eyeing each other up, but I don't think he'd have beaten Lee, I don't think anyone could have beaten him.

Everybody knew Lee because every nick he went to he battered the top man. He'd say, 'Who's the gov'nor in here,' wallop, wallop, wallop and he'd give him it. He just made sure they knew who he was.

Lee did a bit of boxing but it's what's in you that counts, but boxing does help you. You have to train; a Rolls Royce won't run without petrol. He was powerful and he was a big hitter, if he hit you something would break. I said to Lee, 'When you're fighting, surprise them.' He had power and he had speed. It's not how heavy you are, it's the speed.

You could rib him and have a bit of crack with him if he knew you he wasn't a bully. I loaned him and our Lee £5,000 one day and they dodged me with the money. They were upstairs in the Speakeasy and they were saying, 'Oh, the old man's here!' I said, 'Hey, get here, I want you and I want you,' while pointing at the two Lees, 'Where's that money, I want paying you bastards and I want the money now.' They said, 'We'll get you it,' and I replied, 'Well I want it and don't dodge me.' We were laughing, he could have said to me, 'Shut up, you're getting nothing.'

You'd have to get to know him, outsiders couldn't get close to him but if he took to you he took to you and you'd get a million per cent back off him. He was no fool you know, he was very careful who he befriended.

If he was going anywhere he'd make sure it was safe, he'd get dropped off a few streets before or be driven around the place. If he was in a taxi he'd have somebody sitting in front of him. There was a time the police were looking for him, he was out of the back bathroom window and he was off...naked - he ripped all his leg open, but he was off like a shot.

There was a time he got a dodgy passport and flight tickets to go off to Spain to stay out of the road for a bit when he had some trouble, he went to Charrington's garage (Brian Charrington – See Phil Berriman's chapters) and they blocked the garage off. Charrington had obviously got on the phone. Lee would take a car off you, 'I'll borrow that car off you.'

When mobile phones were first around in the early 90s they were the size of building bricks. Lee would drive around in a soft top and have one held to his ear and it wasn't even switched on! I gave our Lee (Tommy's son) a mobile phone, the bill in the first month was £1,100, I said, 'Give me it here,' they thought it was a trend the pair of them.

There was never enough hours in the day for him, cars here and there going all over. They went to the Hacienda and knock the doors open. I said, 'They've got guns, they'll pop you.' They were all running around looking for him in Manchester, he was hid in the boot of a car. He goes to the doormen and BOOM, BOOM he knocked them out. Lee wasn't bothered about doormen, it was like going for the title, you go through the ranks BANG, BANG, BANG just knocking them.

Lee was a good conversationalist but if he was going to be

involved in a fight then he wouldn't talk his way out of it, no, no. There's a story about Lee holding a gun to a taxi driver's head in a game of Russian roulette, he never held it up the man's head it was a lie whoever said it. He just shot a hole in the roof of the taxi before he got out the driver said, 'What have you done to my taxi!'

Lee could drive but he was lethal, straight through traffic lights and we lost count of the amount of wing mirrors he broke. He once said, 'Can I have a drive of your Rolls Royce?' I said, ' You cannot, sit in the back.' He should have had one of those little Daff cars were you put the stick forward to go forward and back to go back.

Lee went to Tenerife with our Lee and they also went to Ibiza, Lee was like a volcano, you could see he was going to erupt so going to these places was a rest for him from going around all the clubs.

When Lee was with Lisa he was a different Lee Duffy altogether, sitting having a beer, watching telly and having a laugh and then say right I'm off to bed now. When Lee was in company though he could take four or five on and when you're young you're buzzing.

I was in Johannesburg and was having a meet a with a princess from Kula Lumpur and there's a big bodyguard about 6ft 5ins, Greco wrestling champ the lot and even he asked me if I knew Lee Duffy!"

Just then Lee Harrison, Tommy's son, arrives and he talks of his trips to other countries and the people he met who either knew or had heard of Lee Duffy: "I flew to Jamaica and one of the people I bumped into said, 'Where are you from?' I replied, 'Middlesbrough,' and he replied in a broad Jamaican accent, 'You know Lee Duffy man?' He knew straight away and he hadn't been brought up in England he was a full Jamaican. He said, ' I was in jail for a week and he came onto my landing and started throwing everyone over the top of the landing.' At that time Lee's name was bigger in the jail then it was outside.

One Saturday night Lee went around the Bigg Market in Newcastle and knocked all the doormen out, first one pub, then the other one, then the other one and so on. I dropped him off while he went and done it (Craig Howard is the man rumoured to have been one of Duffy's main drivers and it is thought that it was Craig who drove Duffy around the nightclub doors when Duffy was in search of Viv.)

and he was on his own, I've even dropped him off in Moss Side on his own when he chinned a doorman in a kitchen. Lee was wearing a white rain hat at that time. When he chinned them he said, 'Go and tell Viv I'm here, get him here, no go and tell your boss I'm here!' They all ran a mile including Dodgy Ray."

Tommy interjects: "People say Viv wouldn't go (to fight Duffy) because the Sayers' would have shot him, the Sayers' wouldn't have shot him, they were just young lads. When Lee went and knocked Graham's doormen out where was Viv? If Viv believed he was going into a death trap in an organised fight with Lee and then Lee goes to Newcastle and knocks his doormen out and tells them to go and tell Viv he was there then he should have come, shouldn't he?

I've worked all the doors, I've fought everybody you want to fight and if a man had of come and knocked my doorman out then I'd have had to go."

With that the interview about Duffy ends and we go on talking about names from the past Johnny Bindon, the Nash brothers and all sorts of other colourful characters who would have handled things differently to the way Duffy performed. Many have suggested that Duffy was a drugs baron and a good for nothing person but after having revealed some of his colourful past and examined his persona I hope I've been able to convey the real Lee Duffy to you and, perhaps, give you a better understanding as to the reasoning behind some of his actions.

No doubt there have been many such characters as Lee Duffy in cities all around the world, but you cannot dispute the fact that there will never be another Lee Duffy in Teesside and I leave the final words to:

Detective chief Inspector Brian Leonard: "There is always someone trying to put their head up and take the place of someone like Lee Duffy because they have seen him get away with it so much. But if there is a lesson to be learned it is this: if you get involved in drugs, violence and bullying you may come to a sticky end."

Detective Sergeant Ray Morton who helped investigate Duffy's death. "It is the end of an era. Many people have tried to emulate Lee Duffy, but they failed."

13

Brian Cockerill – A True Warrior

Lee Duffy. They say you shouldn't start a sentence with someone's name, well I've given Lee Duffy his own sentence because the mere mention of his name in the north of England is a statement in itself. The connection between Lee Duffy and Viv Graham ran deeper than the old disused coalmines in Northumberland and higher than the Transporter bridge in Teesside. Just as Ernie Bewick and Viv had so much in common so did Viv and Duffy but Viv kept Duffy at arms length because Duffy had something quite different about his nature and that was something Viv was wary of, Lee Duffy didn't want to be upstaged by any man, no matter how big and they don't get any bigger than Brian Cockerill.

Brian is as big as a barn door and when the sun shines he has to stand out of the way otherwise the whole of Teesside is in darkness. (See photo on stills pages and web site: www.crimebizz.com.) Brian had a run in with Lee Duffy, known as 'The Duffer', and without any messing about I'll let Brian Cockerill tell us about it.

"Lee was bullied at school the same as me, I was bullied until I was about 13 years old, every day nearly. John Black started training Lee when he was about 14 years old and eventually he started working on the doors for John Black and then Lee got his four stretch but he was doing everything and he was a lot more streetwise than me. I didn't start working the doors until I was twenty, up until about nineteen I trained but I was quiet.

I was about twenty-five and Lee, The Duffer, was going by in a car, I'd just come out of a restaurant and I always remember I had my finger strapped with a metal splint because it was broken. Lee jumps out of the car with his mate and his mate's drinking a bottle of Pills and Duffy says, 'What do they call you then?' I thought he was going to say something like, 'I'm Lee, John's told me all about you.' Anyway I said, 'I'm Brian.' So I'm looking at his mate holding the bottle in his hand and as I spoke Lee hit me on the side of the head with his right hand and I see stars, I fall into a squat position but I grabbed him around the legs and he tried to push me away but he couldn't, he didn't have the strength. I threw him into the wall and I head butted him a few times and hit him with my forearm.

I couldn't punch him because of my finger so I head butted him on the floor and he's shouting, 'John, John get him off me, Failey get him off me.' He's beaten because I'm 23 stone and I'm sitting on him and he hasn't got a chance then so his mate hits me with a bottle so I grabs him and throws him into the car and walks off. My mate's with me and he's a bit scared of them so we walks down the road and I'm trying to get to this other lad's house because he was a fighter and worked on the doors so I thought with the two of us we'd stand a better chance.

I was crossing across a roundabout and pulled one of the metal bollards out of the ground (don't try this at home) and I rammed it at Lee because they were following us and I pushed it at him and he fell back and John Fail, the other kid with Lee, runs off and I was shouting, 'See John Black and we'll fucking fight it out on the field one to one no problem when my hand's better.'

Lee didn't want to get near me and he was just trying to show off because he knew if I got hold of him that he wouldn't be able to get away from me so he's standing off and not getting any closer. As I was walking towards him he was backing away from me.

Afterwards I went down Hintons, a big alley thing, and I went to this Mick Storey's house and Mick come out but they'd gone and then I went to Boothy's house and I said, 'Is Lee in there?' He said, 'No he's not in,' so I replied, 'Tell him I'll fight him.'

So anyway I trained, I went to Eston with Mat Johnson, Mat put Lee on his arse years ago. I'm looking for Lee and he's with this Craig Howard, we come up near the police station in Eston near the garage and they come around in a green 'A'-reg Sierra and I jumps out of my car and they try to drive off so I dives on the car and the weight of me starts bouncing (Brian weighed in at 23 stone) the car up and down and this made Craig stall the car, they got the car going again and drove off and just didn't want to know so I'm buzzing then because I've won the fight without even throwing a punch.

About a month later Lee phoned me in the pub and he said, 'Look can I met you?' I said, 'Yeah, we'll get it on, me and you anytime,' thinking he wanted to fight me. So the next minute he asks me to go to his house the following day. Lisa Stockell (Lee's girlfriend) was there, Boothy and Mark Miller a kid who knocked about with him. Lee walked in, he was putting his boots on and said, 'Look at the size of him, me trying to fight him, I must have been raj,' he shook my hand and he was alright after that.

We then run around with each other after that taxing all the drug dealers for about three months. There were no drug dealers selling drugs then, it all stopped because we just used to take the money off them."

This is the first indication that Lee Duffy knew he'd met his match in someone and that someone was Brian Cockerill so if he couldn't beat him then he'd work with him as collector of taxes. Okay Duffy had a few losses to his name from fights he'd had years earlier but he was still developing his style and had some more developing to do before he would get to be a formidable fighting machine.

Together with Brian Cockerill as a fighting team these pair could have conquered the world but for Duffy's carefree ways and spending money on his friends like there was no tomorrow.

Duffy admitted life was for living and at his young age, early 20s, he was going to enjoy it come what may so any planning for the future was out of the window.

Although Brian was still young, being in his mid 20s, he was to have some run-ins with other hard men in the area. One of the stories told to me by a close associate of Brian's told me of how Brian had a few run-ins with heavyweight boxer David Garside (British title and world title contender).

Cockerill, is said, was to get the better of Garside in two fights.

Brian Cockerill - A True Warrior

The first fight took place at a rave club where Stephen and Michael Sayers were present, the rave had gone on for three days and everyone was full of ecstasy.

Garside had made his way to fight Cockerill and it was suggested that someone in the rave was watching Cockerill's movements in order to report them back to Garside. Cockerill come out of the Rave at nine o'clock in the morning after a heavy three days of raving madness. After coming out from a place that was in total darkness but for the strobe lighting effects the daylight must have been like looking at a million candle power lamp shining into his eyes, but still Cockerill was able to stand up to Garside and it is said bit half of both his ears off in a fight that lasted ten minutes. Cockerill didn't escape injury and he came away with a broken rib and a closed eye and Garside was getting the better of the fight at the end.

The second fight between Cockerill v Garside took place in a tiny room and this time Cockerill managed to even the score and it was suggested that this is what contributed towards Garside retiring from boxing although it has been suggested that Garside was in fact retired from pro boxing already.

Now what I am going to write about next has been gained from information sourced from three very reliable people and given the amount of violence involved I've had to tone it down otherwise I'd have to get the local abattoir to stand by to clear the mess up, in fact the mess afterwards took some cleaning.

Certain names have been withheld, not for legal reasons because if anyone wants to sue me then they're going to be in for a shock because I've got three taped interviews that back up what I am about to write and all corroborate each other yet each was obtained in separate interviews without each party knowing of the other two interviews so please don't go running to the solicitors and wasting all of our time because in a civil court you'd lose because there is less emphasis on the burden of proof and criminal charges could be reinstated for all sorts of nasty things and none of us wants that to happen.

It is not for me to do the jobs of policemen or to turn such interviews over to the authorities, that's why people trust me because they know when I give my word I keep it and I've given my word that I will not use these tapes to incriminate anyone, however if you want to waste your money, about £150,000, in a civil law suit then be my guest.

Here goes. Tommy Harrison was put in a very difficult position when he was facing the twin barrels of a shotgun being poked in his face, Middlesbrough's elder statesman of the underworld pushed the gun away from him and gave the person pointing it at him a few words of friendly advice.

What these people wanted was for Tommy to phone Brian Cockerill up and ask him to call around on some sort of pretext. Tommy wasn't in an immediate position to refuse such a request and some of my sources tell me that in no way did he ever suspect such violence would be used on Brian because if he knew of what was going to happen then he'd not have phoned Brian.

When Brian turned up there was a posse of armed men with handguns, a shotgun and all sorts of other equipment used in butchering animals. At this time Brian was about 18 stones in weight and hadn't trained for some time although he was still a very powerful man he couldn't do anything against such weapons and a fight took place that lasted for some time in which time Brian's legs were so badly hacked and his head smashed to an unsightly mess so much so that Tommy's house was left resembling a house of horrors.

During the sustained butchering a man came in, a man familiar to Brian (not Lee Duffy), and he tried, unsuccessfully, to break Brian's jaw. Not a single bone in Brian's body was broken but his head and legs were a mish mash mess and he should have been dead and if it were anyone lesser than Brian they may well have been morgue material. Some time later one of the attackers paid compensation to Tommy Harrison to cover the clean up bill for his home.

A number of people were arrested and remanded into custody over this totally unforgivable attack but Brian didn't make any statements and as a consequence no one was ever charged with this brutal and savage revenge attack carried out by some of the more familiar underworld characters from Tyneside, Sunderland and Teesside.

A story I was told from a dead underworld character's (Speedy) friend (not part of the three tapes from other sources) indicates that when Speedy was locked up serving time with one of the main players (serving time for a separate offence) in the Cockerill attack he was able to fully explain the side of a story that was withheld and it changed the main attacker's opinion of Cockerill and it made him wish he'd never been involved in the attack.

Some time later when Cockerill was imprisoned for motoring offences of all things ($2^{1/2}$ years) he met up with his main attacker and an apology was made to Cockerill because they were misinformed about the situation.

Others had an interest in Brian Cockerill's fighting power and two in particular wanted to see a match between Brian Cockerill v Viv Graham and hereon Brian recounts what happened.

"Stephen and Michael Sayers were willing to put £50,000 up for me to fight Viv and if it have of come off then they'd have been able to say, 'We've got a better fighter than you now.' I was in a rave club and I was talking to Robbie Armstrong who was Viv's partner and I'd had a fight with a big lad from Stockton the week before, I'd knocked him out and Robbie said, 'Do you know a lad called Cockerill?' Well of course Robbie only knew me as 'Big Bri', he didn't know my second name was 'Cockerill'. Robbie went on to say that the kid I'd knocked out had offered Viv Graham £10,000 to come and fight this 'Cockeril' guy. Robbie said, 'What do you think he'll do?' I said, 'I think he'll beat him,' and he went, 'He's that good!' I laughed and said, 'It's me you daft cunt,' and he said, 'You're joking,' and he couldn't believe it.

About a week later Robbie said, 'Viv doesn't want anything to do with that fight you know,' I said, 'What fight?' 'Stephen and Michael put the £50,000 up,' he replied. I didn't even know anything about it. What they were going to do was put a fight up in a warehouse in Gateshead or wherever it was or Newcastle and they we're going to charge £10 a man to come in and watch it. They'd done all this behind my back without them even knowing. Robbie was saying, 'The fight's supposed to be next month,' and I hadn't a clue what was going on.

Anyway I goes to Newcastle to see Stephen and Michael, I goes in the nightclub and they'd only done it because they knew Viv Graham was coming in that night, but he never come in.

I heard Viv did a lot of bad things with lads up in Newcastle; he invited Stevie Hammer out and then has a punch up with him and punches him in the face. That for me was out of order you know. When I was inside with Geordie kids they used to say that he was a bastard for doing that, he'd get you up, get you pissed, put his arm around you and say, 'Let's have our photograph taken,' and then he'd punch them in the face, he was terrible for it.

I remember how I met Sunderland's Ernie Bewick when Gary Robb had all the rave clubs and Ernie Bewick was brought down by him because I was in Stockton and Gary wanted to open a rave club there. I said, 'You're not opening a rave club down here unless you pay me some money every night to open this club because it's my area so you're not coming down here.

The night come for everyone to go to the rave club and I just told everyone not to go so only about twenty people turned up. So they brought Ernie Bewick down to fight me so I went down to fight this Ernie Bewick. I got there and we ended up shaking hands, he was the nicest person I've ever met, sound as a pound, great.

I used to go and see him every weekend up there in Sunderland. Ernie said, 'I haven't come down for trouble, I'm just getting a few hundred quid on the door, it's your door it's not my door.' They were devastated because they had to pay Ernie a wage and they had to pay me a wage, they used to pay me £1 for everyone that went in. Because there were only twenty people in they thought nothing of it but the next Monday there was over 2,000 people in because I got all the kids to come then and it was a Bank Holiday and Ernie used to come down till about six o'clock. We used to mess about on the door with the pads (boxing pads) and things; he was a nice man Ernie. The night he killed the lad (see Ernie Bewick chapter) he phoned me and I said he should come down.

Ernie had trouble in Sunderland when Garside was brought in but they didn't fight, Ernie fronted him and then another time the Sayers' come and they tried to beat Ernie, but Ernie had about 200 lads waiting in the car park, he had some pull in Sunderland.

Brian Cockerill - A True Warrior

The Sayers' didn't turn up when Garside was there because they were wary of Ernie. I knew Ernie and I knew them so I was trying to sort it out so I was going up and I would go around the clubs with Ernie to meet the lads and that, I even met Gina G.

Paul Ashton from Gateshead come into one of my clubs when I was in jail with his mate Monkey Lyons (Paul Lyons), well it wasn't my club but I was in charge of security and he comes in and says that Paul's putting a wage away for me for when I got out, he was alright with me like that.

Paul had a fight with Viv Graham and he was saying, 'Fucking make him stand still,' because Viv kept jumping around, Viv was only fifteen stone at the time and Paul was over 20 stone. I was inside with Paul and he wasn't strong and I was curling more on the bar than he was benching. Paul could take a good shot on the chin but he wasn't very clever with his hands.

I remember when the armed police come for me because I was accused of having a couple of people shot in the town. About seventeen cars full of armed police pulled up, I was in my car and I just drove off. They got me for dangerous driving but I said I was in fear of my life; they gave me 2½ years!

If I never had another fight in my life I'd be happy. I entered the strongest man competition but three days before I was due to go in for it I pulled my knee out. I often think it's not really worth doing because I'm alright on certain movements but when I run with the ball and pull the tractors it starts hurting. There's not much money to be made from it, look at Glen Ross in Ireland he's still working the doors and runs around in a little Fiat, he weights 35 stone and he's got it wrecked.

When I go out I try to be nice to everyone but when Viv and Lee went out everyone would be frightened of them and they loved that. Lee used to love going into a club and emptying it and I think what's the point of that. I like to talk to people and have a good laugh but when I used to go into a pub with Lee it used to just empty.

He used to give people a punch and I said, 'What will happen is that one day one of those young kids you hit who's 18 or 19 years old now is going to be thirty odd and you're about fifty he's and he's going to give you a good hiding, but obviously he never made that age. The night he died they were spitting on him and saying things like 'Die you bastard', it's true that, the lad up for his murder, Allo, (David Allison) I beat him up after it, he never come out for six months after that.

What happened was he was fighting with a lad in a pub and he was hitting the lad in the face with a stool and I thought he was going to get done for murder if he kept it up so I broke it up, as I broke it up he turned on me so I gave him the biggest hiding he's had in his life, I knocked him out, woke him up and knocked him out again and turned him around and gave him a kick up the arse. How it happened was I'd knocked him out inside the pub and I said there's no room in here and we went outside, he run at me and I caught him with two body shots and a left hook to the head and I knocked him out.

I remember me and Lee went to one dealer's house in Eston and there was about seven locks on the door and he said, 'Big fellah, get this door open,' and I kicked the door and my leg got stuck in it and he said, 'It's on top, it's on top,' and my leg's stuck in this door, that was his favourite saying and he'd wind me up into thinking the police were coming.

He was a get for borrowing cars off people, he borrowed this car off a lad, a convertible and he's going down to Middlesbrough, flying down the road, when he only goes and opens the hood! As we were driving it just blows off and blew away down the street and he just kept on driving.

Another time we were in this car and it stalled at the lights he said, 'Ah fuck it,' and just left the car at the lights, he done it loads of times. He used to take cars off people and just leave them in the middle of the town, it would run out of petrol, he wouldn't put petrol in, he'd just jump on a bus, he was mad.

What I liked about Lee was that after we had the fight in Redcar some months later he come over and he sat and as he talked he gesticulated with his hands and he said, 'You know that day we had the fight was the first time I knew I was beaten and for six weeks I couldn't believe I got beat.' Lee had only been out of jail for a few weeks and he was with this John Fail and as they were driving along he said to Lee, 'Look at the size of this fucker, would you have a go at him, Lee?' So it was Lee being wound up by others and it seemed easy for people to do. John Black used to say he was like a clockwork mouse, wind Lee up and he was away.

So when Lee and me got to be friends Lee said to John Fail, 'I've made it up with the big fellah now so now it's your problem,' and I walked into Fail's house and said, 'And you!' I wasn't going to hit him, I just shouted at him and he went white.

I remember seeing four doormen kicking this young kid on the floor, I went round and knocked two of them out and the police come and grabbed hold of me and the lad punched me in the face, as the police had hold of me they put me in the van and I kicked the van doors off the hinges and I went into a one and I got nicked.

Another time my car got nicked a few years ago when I was in Stockton I was going through Ragworth, Rosewood and Bluehall, all the rough areas, looking for it. I spent a week looking around and every car thief got a good hiding and people were coming up to me in the street and telling me that since I'd been looking for my car there'd never been anything nicked and they went on to say they wished it was me working the streets.

Some time ago a drug dealer was using my name for six months in order to protect him, he was saying that the heroin he was selling was mine, I took offence to how he was using my name because the police were starting to give me bother over it.

The dealer then had the misfortune to be taxed for a lot of money (£21,000) and people suggested it was me that had taxed him.

I then gets a phone call from his supplier and he said he wanted the money back off me and told me I was out of order, I told him to sling his hook so he went to the best fighter in Darlington and he turned around and said, 'What the fuck can I do with the big fellah, I can't fight him!' He then asked who the drug dealer was and when he found out he said, 'I wouldn't do it for him anyway because he's a grass.'

I remember when Peter Donnelly and Joe Hunt (10 year for robbery) tried to get me to team up with them. Joe Hunt's a nice lad, I had a rave club down here and come down and said, 'Are you alright,' I replied, 'No problem,' I'd be in with every firm because everyone liked me and I got on with everyone but some people tried to use me and they'd say, 'You fight him,' and I'd say, 'No, I don't want to do that,'

With Lee though he'd be off doing the fighting for others and that was the difference with him and me. People would get him into Newcastle and fill him full of ecstasy and just have him running about taxing people. He might collect, say, three grand and he'd get one and they'd get the other two and it was him doing the taxing, he was just used really.

I think what it was that with Lee being in the jail for four years he comes out and he was just enjoying himself being in all the clubs and everyone talking about him and he loved to have a fight every night so everyone would talk about it the next day, he loved that.

We used to go on the pads (boxing) with John Black or John Dryden and when you're a big lad you hit the pads hard so the trainer pulls the pads back a bit otherwise it hurts their shoulders over the years. They used to pull the pads back and Lee would say, 'Stop doing that,' because he used to like people being able to hear the big thud of the punch and daft things like that.

When you're young you want to be the best but when you're getting older you can't be bothered with it and if you know you've got it then you'll use it. Now if I'm with anybody and I spill their drink I'll say sorry and buy them another drink but a lot of people take that kindness as a weakness and they think 'He's not that hard, he's not that good.' I'm not being big headed but down here they all want to talk to me, buying me drinks, saying 'My car's been pinched can you sort that out' and things like that.

I was approached by a man whose son, 7, had his motorbike pinched, they'd been to the police, which they're entitled to do and nothing happened. I got it back for them within three hours and I took nothing for it because I was pleased to see the kid on his bike.

At times when I've had trouble though I've had to handle it differently, Stu Watson come down here with Stevie Abadom, Stevie Hammer and all them, about fifty of them come down, a big bus load of them and they come into one of the raves where I was and they all stood in the door and I shouted 'What the fuck are you doing in here,' and Stuey Watson was sitting down, he didn't want to know. I went upstairs come down, it must have been about 200 hundred, we had all the Sunderland crew come down and the lads in the place and I said, 'If you don't go now you won't be able to walk,' they never come back.

And it was some time later when I went to jail and they were all in there, Stevie Hammer, Geoff Brown and others and they were alright, we had a good laugh. Stevie Hammer was a nice lad, we used to sit in the passageway in prison playing dominoes and the screws would walk by when we were playing dominoes looking at us as if though we were mad.

I've had guns pulled on me and you just have to confront people, 'Come on then you wanker,' you know they're not going to do it, you just know when it's certain people, it's all bullshit. There was a lad here, Speedy, if he'd have pulled a gun out he'd have shot you, he used to work with me and he got killed, he got shot. I was working it out the other day there was about ten of us, all top fighters Viv Graham, Lee Duffy Speedy and others they're all dead or in jail.

When I was in jail I was moved around all the time and the police would contact the prison saying I should be in the block because they knew if I was in the block it would stop me getting my cat 'D' (open prison status), which I should have got because I was only in for dangerous driving.

(When sentences like this are handed for such offences it make you wonder if the police are actually telling the judges to put such men as Brian behind bars for long terms of imprisonment because they want them removed from the community. Compared to a man, a banned driver, that nearly killed a young girl in a hit and run incident who only gets six months behind bars it makes you wonder how judges reach such decisions and that makes me think there's some sort of back door from the office of the CPS right into the judge's chambers! Worth thinking about when I examine this later.)

I was being shipped to different jails all over and I remember when I was in Walton jail I had a fight with one of the best fighters in there, he was bullying all the screws and they were frightened of him. He took a copper's eye out and got ten years, Duckdale they call him about 24 years old, a tall kid, I knocked him out in there and I got cat 'D' after that."

There ends the interview, Brian has so many interesting things to say you could fill a book on him and I believe my good friend from Merthyr Tydfil, in south Wales, Julian Davies, who runs the unlicensed fighting website: www.geocities.com/unlicensed2000 is going to write Brian's life story, yes I know you're all going to say 'Why isn't Steve Richards doing it?' Well I think since Brian's a true warrior then it should be Julian writing it, although Julian courteously asked me if I was writing anything else on Brian before he decided to do it. Julian's got a book coming out soon called '*Real Fighting Men*' and that also features Brian Cockerill within it and if that wasn't enough Brian is also featured on the underworld hire a Crimebiz star web site of www.crimebizz.com you can hire your favourite underworld character for that special event or promotion or a hard man actor or film extra. (www.crimebiz.co.uk, www.crimebiz.org, www.crimebiz.net)

As much as Viv Graham was sought after to solve people's headaches when they were up against it then equally so it must be said of Brian and after having met him I came away knowing I'd met a true warrior.

I leave the final word in this chapter to Richard Horsley from Hartlepool. Rich is also to feature in the book '*Real Fighting Men*'. Rich told me a story relating to Viv: "Years ago about '92 I fought this big guy in a nightclub in Hartlepool, he was well known from a family of known people, and he used to run the doors in Hartlepool, anyway after he disrespected me for the second time I called him on and done him. I broke his jaw, broke both his legs and also stitched him up, I hear rumours that VIV GRAHAM is coming after me as the guy had paid him, anyway they told Viv that I was a bad guy and that I jumped him for no reason with a couple of lads and broke his legs with an iron bar, pure fucking lies. Anyway Viv phoned someone in the town, and asked what I was like, and the lad told Viv I was a straight guy and would never take a liberty with anyone, Viv said he had a feeling they weren't telling the truth and dropped it. There are always two sides to every story."

14

Gary Ward

This is a follow up to the chapter about Gary's case, which you'll find in Viv 2. I'd like to start off by saying a thank you to the governor of Frankland prison, Ivor Woods, for allowing special visits in order for me to sit and go through evidence with Gary. People forget one thing about prisons and that is they are not there to impede justice but are in fact there to allow justice to happen by assisting those with claims of injustice and if that is to allow a prisoner access to those helping them secure justice then that in itself is the first step in the right direction.

Prisons are also there to act on behalf of the public's safety and if that is by virtue of keeping convicted people locked up then that's all good and well but when they act as judge and jury and decide all within are guilty as sin regardless of any claim to injustice then that is not a judicial act but an act of perverting the course of justice and I accuse the governors of certain prisons in the UK of acting as judge and jury. Therefore when the governor of Frankland prison allowed me access to Gary for specific interviews relating to his claims of injustice then that is assisting justice to be done, thank you Mr Woods.

Just to recap on Gary's situation, May 1994 he was convicted of the murder of Mark White whilst Ward's co-accused, James John Docherty, was convicted of the manslaughter, both eventually entered guilty pleas. The murder of Mark White took place on Blackpool beach and the cause of death was asphyxiation by drowning. See a fuller account of this in Viv 2.

Viv - The Final Chapter

To save space I will not recap too much other than to say that at the time of Mark White's unfortunate death Gary Ward claims he was fighting with Viv Graham some 1/4 of a mile away from where Mark White was savagely beaten before being left naked to drown in the sea.

Why then did Gary Ward enter a guilty plea to the charge of murdering Mr White, well at first Gary entered a not guilty plea and was prepared to accept an alternative charge of manslaughter, but the court refused to accept this. Dramatically Gary changed his plea to that of guilty and his co-accused, Docherty, changed his plea from one of not guilty to a one of guilty to manslaughter in the full knowledge that his co-accused would have to do the longer term of life imprisonment for his plea. Ward and Docherty had each gone up a notch and were sentenced accordingly – Ward received a life sentence whilst Docherty received seven years imprisonment.

I became involved with Gary's case in 1998 and still argue his innocence although that seems to have fallen on the deaf ears of the Criminal Case Review Commission (CCRC). How can a man who makes a plea of guilty suddenly decide that he wants to appeal against his conviction, simple really...he thought he was responsible for the death of another man he was fighting with at the same time Mr White was being murdered 1/4 of a mile away. Anyone heard of the case involving Keith Twitchell who was jailed for 20 years back in 1982 on charges of manslaughter and robbery.

Keith won an appeal to have his conviction overturned due to the fact that the West Midlands Serious Crime Squad had extracted a confession out of him by dubious means. Now I'm not saying that was the case with Gary but what is important is the comparison of a man who confessed for various reasons to something he didn't do. The police tied Keith to a chair and threatened him with violence and told him he'd leave the room feet first and on that basis he was left with little alternative but to sign a confession.

Now look at this scenario, you're on remand in prison awaiting trial and you're pregnant girlfriend is a regular visitor (Obviously if you're a woman reading this then you're going to have to pretend it's the other way around.) Your co-accused tells you to take the charges on your back otherwise something might happen to your girlfriend and given your co-accused's propensity for violence it doesn't seem like an idle threat. This is what happened to Gary. (See Viv 2)

It was only when Gary was some weeks into his prison sentence that he discovered a photograph of Mark White in a newspaper he was reading that covered the murder story and to his shock he realised that this was not the man he had been fighting with who he thought he had killed. What had happened was that Gary was convinced that he had, somehow, been responsible for Mark White's death and to some extent accepted that he must have had a hand in the death of a man who drowned some 1/4 of a mile away from where the fight between Gary and some other men took place outside of the Time Gap pub. (Again I would ask you to read Viv 2 in order to secure a more detailed account.)

During the course of events the police conducted a number of interviews with the two accused men and each interview, not surprisingly, conflicted with the others. You see, Gary had succumbed to pressure from his co-accused and was under duress to take the blame for his part in what was thought to have been a murder and no doubt Gary was shiting a brick as to the consequences. I mean he'd had this fight with a man he'd previously been taunted by one week earlier and given the set of circumstances surrounding the murder investigation he didn't seem to have much choice but to go along with it all and confess. After all no one told Gary that the fight he was involved in was a different fight to the one Mark White was on the other side of.

Unwittingly Gary had confessed to the Mark White murder when in fact his victim had no doubt picked himself up and dusted himself down and limped home in a state of nakedness. Think about it, if the same happened to you, say, you become involved in a fight and the next thing you hear the news that a man has been murdered nearby to where you had the fight then obviously you would think that you've had some sort of involvement in that death...accordingly Gary thought the same.

You may say that the possibility of two fights happening simultaneously is just about impossible. Well what if I was to tell you that two murders took place just about simultaneously would that convince you? Arthur Leak, 49, from Sunderland Road, Gateshead was set on fire after he was doused in petrol in late September 2001. (A matter of a few days after this another man was set on fire in the toilets of a pub, in Sunderland. To date no witnesses have come forward.) Some 1/2 of a mile away in Camborne Grove, Gateshead a dismembered woman's body was found in an outhouse in a backyard all in the space of a few days from when Arthur Leak died. Can you now maybe accept that such coincidences do happen?

All along Gary has made representation that he fought with a man outside the Time Gap pub and he's never wavered from that statement right from start to finish. He's been accused by the CCRC of changing his statements and what he told police and solicitors but in this he has never wavered.

I appreciate something about life and that is everyone tries to please the rest of the people around them and it is always at a cost to themselves. Gary is no different in that he does genuinely try to please you by being cordial and polite and I believe this is how his wording has differed to the solicitors who have dealt with his case over the years. What has not changed though is Gary's basic story that he had a fight with a man other than Mark White and it does fit in with his original police statements. Gary is not a liar.

Gary has continuously appealed against his conviction and when his appeal was mishandled by the Royal Courts of Appeal he applied to the CCRC for a review of his case for consideration that they should refer it back to the court of appeal. When you read further on you'll find that the appeal court handled Gary's case with a great deal of misadministration and I believe his case should be re-heard by the appeal court on the basic principle of Article 6 of the Human Rights Act – Everyone is entitled to a fair trial.

I can tell you that there is not one shred of evidence against Gary and yet the CCRC do nothing but latch on to worthless forensic testimony that isn't worth the paper it's written on. I have already discredited the forensic evidence against Gary in Viv 2 and I have further submissions to make herein about the quality of forensic evidence against Gary.

Gary Ward

The CCRC claims that the forensic evidence suggests that Gary's boot prints correspond with the pattern, configuration, size and extent of wear of foot marks found on the sand near the body and in addition to that, they claim, the sole of one of his boots corresponded in terms of pattern component with a mark found on the deceased's back. Remember that the tide had come in and gone out – the sea covering and then uncovering Mark White's body. It is hard to explain then how the body of the deceased lay perfectly still under the flow of the tide while the sea washed over him, then covered him before going back out and leaving everything as it was before this happened?

In a statement from a forensic scientist, Mark Andrew Daly, who worked out of the Chorley Forensic Science Services dated 6th December 1993 he says:

'There is no conclusive association between the footwear taken from WARD and any of these marks and as such I cannot totally rule out the possibility that these marks have been made by another pair of boots or shoes of the same pattern, size and general wear as the boots taken from WARD.' Yet the CCRC are acting as the prosecution or so it would seem!

I would like to bring in an expert witness but not on behalf of Gary Ward...not on behalf of the police but on behalf of you my reader. Let's say you were in the unfortunate position of facing a murder charge and based on the expertise of expert witnesses you are found guilty it may well be the end of the story because, say, based on expert testimony you were locked away then you would have a hell of a job in knocking such expert witnesses, but in this case there is not one piece of expert testimony that goes against Gary! The CCRC though use the expert testimony as though it was some sort of magic wand capable of making something out of nothing!

Who questions the testimony of such expert witnesses, who questions the validity of forensic reports, who cares at the end of the day because you've been found guilty you may face little prospect of discrediting forensic evidence. In fact that reminds me of a book my dear friend Jan Lamb the Angel of the Underworld was working on, *'Guilty or not – Who Cares'*. The book covered many incidents of women that had been convicted of crimes they were all innocent of. Jan can be booked from the web site: www.crimebizz.com.

Well now there is one very creditable expert who has come clean about such forensic evidence being tainted. I thank Tom Wilkinson of the Press Association for helping me track down Dr Zakaria Erzinçlioglu, I have sought his permission to call him Dr Zak.

Dr Zak the former head of a forensic research center told me: "Many forensic scientists lie and cheat because their livelihood depends on it and without a doubt many innocent people are in prison because of it. Many so called expert witnesses are called upon by solicitors to give a particular answer and if that answer doesn't fit in with what they want then you are dismissed as being unhelpful.

Emotional blackmail is used to urge the forensic team to come up with the right answer. All the greater, then, is the pressure upon them to produce answers to questions, solutions to problems. In over 50% of the cases I've been involved in I've found something not quite right."

Dr Zak also claims that police have asked him to destroy evidence before a trial and he went on to say that for a fee you could get forensic scientists to say what you want them to say in a criminal trial.

After reading Dr Zak's book *'Every Contact Leaves a Trace'* I was very concerned to find out how rogue forensic scientists work and I would like to thank Dr Zak for his help and guidance. Without a doubt I know that Dr Zak's particular book I mention should be read by every policeman in the world and if you want to really dig into forensic science then I can recommend another book by Dr Zak which I've also read and found very helpful, *'Maggots, Murder and Men'*. Given then what Dr Zak is able to reveal I am somewhat skeptical of certain forensic reports based on how Dr Zak has revealed such goings on behind the scenes.

After I re-read the forensic reports relating to Gary Ward's case I could see what Dr Zak meant when he told me about how emotional blackmail is used. In all of the reports relating to Gary's case the forensic scientists start off by saying what the police have told them in relation to the death of Mark White. What the fuck has that got to do with the work they carry out, I don't know. I mean if a forensic scientist is cross referencing blood samples or checking to see if hair samples match those from a controlled group or determining if the blood on a garment is the same as the blood in a test tube that's been handed to them to compare then why does he or she need to know all the grisly details that cannot help them in their tests?

In a matter relating to feathering tests done on Gary's boots the scientist rattles on about how the naked body of Mark White was found on the beach approximately 500 yards south of Manchester Square. What this has to do with his conclusion I do not know but it is clear that the police have told him of the emotional details and perhaps this has swayed the scientist to come to the conclusion that the prints do match because earlier on in his report Mark Andrew Daly states that in his opinion in relation to a mark on the deceased's back and the left boot taken from Gary Ward it '**would support the view that this mark was made by this shoe.**' Now compare this to what the same forensic scientist states at the end of his report which I have already pointed out to you: '**There is no conclusive association between the footwear taken from WARD and any of these marks and as such I cannot totally rule out the possibility that these marks have been made by another pair of boots or shoes of the same pattern, size and general wear as the boots taken from WARD.**' Maybe now I am starting to see how valueless these reports are.

The CCRC say in their report '**The left knee of Mr Ward's jeans provided a weak positive reaction to a test indicating the probable presence of blood** (Notice the use of the word 'probable', it might as well say 'the probable presence of peanut butter' for what use it is.) **although no obvious bloodstains were present. The jeans had been hand-washed by Miss Lambert.** (Gary's girlfriend.) **The forensic scientist's report does not make it clear whether this blood** (hold on didn't it say the 'probable' presence of 'blood' and yet here the CCRC have now decided it IS blood?) **is said to be of the deceased.**' You can bet your last penny that if it were the same blood group as that of the deceased then it would have been stated as being just that, but it wasn't. I would consider the

CCRC to be working for the police given the negative way they have reported their findings on Gary's case in their Provisional Statement of Reasons.

Another forensic scientist from the Chorley Forensic Science Services, Michael William Scarborough, states: '**An area on the left knee of the jeans SH1 provides a weak positive reaction to a test which indicates the probable presence of blood, no obvious bloodstains are present in this area. These jeans are clean and have <u>probably</u> been recently washed. No blood was found on the boots AP1, 2 or T-shirt SH2.**' Notice Mr Scarborough's talents at detecting the <u>probability</u> that the jeans may have been recently washed. Considering that Miss Gail Lambert had made a statement to the police saying that she had washed Gary's jeans it's obvious that the police had passed this information on. How can you tell if jeans have been recently washed without doing specific scientific tests? When you put on a clean pair of trousers taken from your wardrobe you expect them to be clean and they will look as if they were recently washed otherwise you wouldn't wear them and in fact they wouldn't be hanging in the wardrobe, BUT they could have been hanging there for weeks so how do you know when they were washed? Last week, last month, yesterday?????????

Gail Lambert was the girlfriend of Gary and in her home the police found a stolen video recorder, which she wasn't charged with and when you consider that Gary's co-accused's mother was charged with offences relating to washing her son's clothing then it beggars belief how Gail Lambert escaped similar charges, suddenly though Miss Lambert becomes a prosecution witness and she's bending over backwards to help the police. In Miss Lambert's statement she says:

'**At 4.45am on Tuesday 7 September 1993 I heard the key in the door and Gary came home alone. I was sat on the sofa and the living room door opened.**

I saw Gary standing there. He was <u>covered in blood</u>. He was wearing a white T-shirt with a small motif on the left breast. I think it is an eagle in a circle. Blue 'Joe Cool' jeans and black twelve hole dock martin boots. The T-shirt was <u>splattered with blood</u>, which had run. His jeans were <u>covered in blood</u> and were

wet through. He was wearing a black leather jacket covered in blood. His dock martin boots were absolutely <u>caked with blood</u> and sand congealed together.

He said, "IT'S OK IT'S NOT MINE". I asked him what had happened and put my arms around him. I was so relieved that he was home. He said "IT'S OK I'M NOT HURT." He sat down on the sofa and told me that he and Jim had been fighting with three lads outside The FOXHALL PUB and the fight had gone on to the beach.'

Miss Lambert describes Gary's jeans as being 'covered in blood' and yet nothing was found on them in the forensics apart from a <u>probability</u> that there was blood on the left knee. And she goes on to say '**His doc martin boots were absolutely caked with blood and sand congealed together'.** For so much blood to be present then you would think that cross contamination is on the cards, but later on you'll be surprised at my findings.

When the police are interviewing Gary it is claimed that someone has bitten the body of the deceased around the bicep area of each arm and on the penis. One of the interviewing police officers asks Gary:

DI T: '**Right now, would you be prepared, and you can consult your solicitor if you want, to give to establish who did or did not bite this body. From the teeth impressions. Do you want to consult about it privately or can we take it.'**

Gary Replies: '**I'll do that.'**

When a forensic odontologist is brought in to identify bite marks as, perhaps, belonging to Gary the results revealed exonerated Gary from having bitten the deceased but interestingly enough two other suspects separate to Ward and Docherty are named as GARY PRITCHARD and BRIAN RUSSELL FAWCETT.

Witness Statement

MR GORDON W.J. COPLEY FORENSIC ODONTOLOGIST

I am a Forensic Odontologist trained **by the London Medical** College in Forensic Odontology. My qualifications are L.D.S. H.G.D.S. R.C.S. (Eng.) and the Diploma of Forensic Odontology (L.H.M.C.)

At the request of Det Supt. G.G. Gooch, Blackpool C.I.D. I

attended on Wednesday 8th September 1993 the Blackpool Mortuary with the Police Photographer to examine and photograph a male victim found on the Blackpool beach. (Authors comment: What difference does it make where he was found? Here again we've got emotional use so as to soft soap the jury if it went as far as that.)

I also was called out on Friday 10th September 1993 by Det Insp Turner to collect alginate impressions of suspects GARY PRITCHARD and BRIAN RUSSELL FAWCETT. At the request of Det Insp Turner, Blackpool C.I.D. I attended Blackpool Police Station on Sunday 12th September 1993 to examine suspects GARY WARD and JAMES Docherty and to take the necessary dental alginate impressions. From my clinical examination of the victim I found suspected bite marks on the upper right arm, the upper left arm and on the upper and dorsal surfaces of the victim's penis.

The suspect bite mark of the right arm

After a detailed comparison with the photographs provided by the Police Photographer of the right arm injury of the deceased with the upper and lower study models of the four suspects I found there were no similarities with the dentitions of these individuals and the separate marks of the Injury. It is therefore impossible to assess the origin of this injury.

The suspect bite mark of the left arm

When studying the injury to the left arm of the deceased, in my opinion, there was no consistency with the bite mark injury therefore I can find no points. END OF QUOTE

So there you have it in black ands white, even the bite marks did not match up with Gary's teeth impressions. Notice the two other mentioned suspects, what more do we hear of them…nothing!

The CCRC has taken a whole jumble of forensic reports and twisted them to their own advantage; I mean look how the following forensic report starts:

CHORLEY LABORATORY

JWI -Knuckle Duster, from Michael Ball, Solicitors
GJJL - Pillow from 61 Lytham Road (Supposed to have Viv Graham's blood on it)

Gary Ward

Background Information

I have received the following information regarding this case from Lancashire Constabulary.

At about 4.20 am on 7th September 1993 the naked body of Mark WHITE was found on the beach approximately 500 yards south of Manchester Square. Blackpool. The body was lying face down in the sand just below the tide line nearby were clothes which also had been covered by the tide. Several feet away from the body were areas of bloodstained sand. It appeared that the deceased had suffered an assault; he had lacerations to his face and scalp together with numerous abrasions and bruises to his trunk. A post mortem examination established the cause of death as drowning. End of quote. So you can see once again the emotive side of things enters into it all. The report goes on to say:

A crowbar and a T-shirt were recovered near to the scene but these are not thought to have been used or worn during this incident. End of quote. Two pieces of evidence are totally ignored, who did the T-shirt belong to, who handled the crowbar and why, did someone stumble on the body of Mark White and commit a probable sex act before leaving him to die, the probability is that in fact NO sex act took place because the police may have just wanted to discredit the credibility of Docherty and Gary whilst they were on remand making people believe they were sex attackers!

What follows is my own submission to the CCRC on behalf of Gary Ward made in 2001:

I am somewhat concerned in relation to the Provisional Statement or Reasons (This is a reply from the CCRC setting out their findings for or against the case being referred to the court of appeal.), which I feel has fatal flaws within it. I enclose two copy pages from Miss Gail Lambert's statement as my first submission, although I feel you will be given a similar submission from Mr Ward's solicitor, Miss Jill Ghedia, of Lloyd & Co, as I have advised of the same.

I feel we need more time, I understand you have granted an extension to 6th August but I feel we need longer and that request will also be made from Mr Ward's solicitor. In order to submit a full and proper case we need to review all of the undisclosed evidence, based on fact.

I would ask you spare a few minutes in reading the enclosed copy of book containing a chapter relating to Gary, I initially sent a copy of the book to yourselves when it was first published.

On the surface you may well feel that this is a way of sensationalising Gary's case...I can assure you, though, it has been an applied effort on my behalf to make people see sense. I fear the CCRC have not seen anything other than Gary's guilt and have overlooked some simple basic facts and that is the forensic evidence actually works for Gary and not against him as has been implied in the CCRC's Statement of Reasons. There is not a shred of forensic evidence against Gary, yet there is strong evidence to support Gary's case.

I feel there is, perhaps, a need that we should obtain DNA samples from the pathological remains of Mr Viv Graham and have them cross-referenced with the blood samples on the pillowcase. (Details in book.)

Circumstantial evidence such as the pillowcase and lack of comparable blood and the way the forensic tests support (because there was no cross reference of blood samples) Mr Ward's argument that he didn't hit or touch Mark White would make it likely that in fact what Mr Ward says is true. Removing blood is notoriously difficult and even after many years of weathering ultra violet light testing can help discover blood.

Which makes it even more absurd that emphasis should be placed on any of the blood samples relating to Mr Ward, as the forensic testing actually exonerates Mr Ward as opposed to helping convict him.

The court of appeal INCORRECTLY stated that Mark White's blood was found on the knee of Mr Ward's jeans and I feel that the learned judges at the Criminal Appeal Court were subconsciously swayed by this incorrect assumption, which is in itself an indication of how sloppy the appeal was handled and had representation been made at the Royal Courts of Appeal, which it wasn't, on Mr Ward's behalf then this matter would have been handled quite differently and the incorrect assumption made by the learned judges could have been corrected there and then…not now some many years later. An appeal should not be allowed to fail when judges make incorrect assumptions that are allowed to sway their judgement in such a serious matter and that is why I feel Mr Ward deserves another chance.

The CCRC place no real stock in this mistake and in fact they say that the decision of the Appeal Court would not have been any different if they were aware of their grave mistaken assumption. If that is to be the case then why the great battle to get Hanratty's DNA samples???????????????? If the police can hold evidence such as clothing in the case of Hanratty for 40 years how is it then that the police have destroyed evidence relating to Gary's case after only a few years? Great stock was placed in the fact that Hanratty's DNA proved he had committed his foul deed, yet when it comes to Mr Ward wanting such similar mistakes reversed the CCRC place little emphasis on the weight of such a monumental mistake.

Such mistakes have been made in the past and have gone by without correction…here we have the chance to have such a mistake placed before the court so as it can be put right. What might the court's decision have been without such INCORRECT assertions?

Whether the blood on the pillowcase is proven to be that of the late Mr Graham's is of no real consequence to the mistake which the Criminal Appeal Court has made, it would make no real difference to neutralising such a mistake – but it would substantiate that a fight took place between Mr Ward and Mr Graham as opposed to a fight having took place between Mr Ward and an 'unknown' opponent.

What is certain though is that Mr Ward did NOT have a fight with Mark White by virtue of the FACT that the forensic tests prove there to be no correlation of blood samples. What is certain though is that Mr Ward's co-accused, Docherty, might have had, if we are to believe the forensic testing report, some contact with Mark White, even though his clothes were laundered it didn't wash away the traces of possible co-related samples. Yet no such 'possible' blood matches were found on Mr Ward's clothing, which made the job of the police more difficult so how lucky for them that a set of pyjama's were obtained from Mr Ward's girlfriend. (See further on.)

Viv - The Final Chapter

Mr Ward's 'blood stained' clothes were hand washed by his girlfriend (Gail Lambert), which would not be as significantly efficient as machine washing away any blood, yet the 'pillowcase' taken for forensic tests from Gary's home of 61 Lytham Road, Blackpool, is intact and hasn't been washed, the very item bearing blood samples is considered worthless by the CCRC when in fact it should be waived around like a Union Jack flag and flouted in the face of the Criminal Appeal Court. The pillowcase is claimed to be the item Gary cleaned himself up with after the fight outside of the Time Gap pub and this would have been of significant value in proving that Gary had not attacked Mr White. Blood was in fact found on this pillowcase yet because it doesn't match Mark White's blood group it is deemed worthless when in fact it should be hailed as a piece of defence evidence that supports an appeal.

Not a single spec of Mark White's blood was found on Mr Ward's clothes or in the home of Miss Lambert, the very home that Mr Ward entered with his boots supposedly caked with a cocktail of congealed blood and sand, very strange when you consider that recently the police found one speck of cordite (which could have been cross contaminated by police or even have come from a firework) in the coat pocket of the alleged killer, Barry George, of 'Crime Watch' presenter Gill Dando and it was this one speck that helped convict an alleged innocent man. Yet in Mr Ward's case there is not one speck of blood that belongs to Mark White to be found in the very place that Mr Ward decamped with congealed blood on his boots, surely the carpet deserved some examining and even removal by the police forensic team, after all this was a murder inquiry?

There is a STARTLING piece of evidence in Gail Lambert's statement that has been totally overlooked by ALL and that is an addendum she makes to her statement on page 5 of her statement sheet. Miss Lambert states on page 5 that Gary was '...**standing there. He was covered in blood. He was wearing a white T-shirt... The T-shirt was splattered with blood** (sic no comma) **which had run. His jeans were covered in blood and were wet through. His dock** (sic) **martin boots were absolutely caked with blood and sand congealed together.'**

Gary Ward

Surely such a forensic team on a murder investigation would locate a single speck, at the very least, of Mark White's blood from the area Mr Ward was sitting or standing in from Miss Lambert's home. Mr Ward is a large gentleman, well over six feet tall and powerfully built, surely the poundage per square inch pressure would allow for some seepage from his boots into a soft carpet

Miss Lambert goes on to say: **'He said "It's okay it's not mine (blood)."....asked him what had happened and put my arms around him.... There was <u>congealed blood on his forearms</u>... He took all his clothes off and I soaked his T-shirt and jeans in the sink at my flat because I know he only had one pair of jeans and would have needed them. Gary went to bed... I took a bowl of water from the sink and cleaned his boots outside at the back. There was a lot of congealed blood on them.'**

Mr Ward has not ever denied being involved in a fight and he has not ever denied having blood on his clothing, but what has been denied and has been supported by the forensic tests is the fact that none of the blood was that of Mark White! Had a speck of that blood been matched to Mark White then the case would have been a closed case and Mr Ward would not be able to support his argument, yet here we have the forensic laboratory and technicians on hand to support Mr Ward in what he claims and all the CCRC can go on about is the feathering tests of a footprint that '<u>probably</u>' wasn't Mr Ward's print.

Miss Lambert states she carried out her duties of cleaning the blood from Mr Ward's clothing and boots, in a matter of fact way, as if an everyday occurrence, but she wouldn't possess the expertise of removing every speck of blood nor have the necessary cleaning fluids to mask such an appalling mess as she described and then proceed to do the same to her home and her own clothing that she was wearing during this alleged clean up operation?

I had overlooked this piece of VITAL evidence in all of my past efforts and only now does it strike me squarely in the face. Where are the pyjamas Miss Lambert refers to in her statement and why does she make a point of adding this to her statement, there is no record of them having been examined in the forensic report? I believe the pyjamas were taken by the police for forensic testing, I believe traces of blood would have cross-contaminated from Mr Ward to Miss Lambert during the hug they shared on discovering Mr Ward wasn't injured in any way.

When washing Mr Ward's clothes by hand residue would have splashed on her pyjamas, when she washed the Doc Marten boots why wasn't the cleaning area examined, why didn't the police take (or did they) the cleaning materials, the bowl, the duvet cover, the couch, the carpet, etc. Where did Mr Ward wash himself, where is the towel he dried himself with, where is the sponge? (Update: In reality the police didn't take these but they did take the drainage U-bends from underneath her sink and they revealed nothing.)

Undisclosed evidence held should now be looked at very closely and I feel this should happen without further delay in order to corroborate what I suggest and that suggestion is that evidence which could have helped acquit Mr Ward was purposely withheld. Viz the clothing Miss Lambert was wearing was of no use to the prosecution since it would only confirm what Mr Ward would state in court and that would have been that he didn't have any such fight with Mark White although unwittingly Mr Ward believed Mr White to be the 'other' man he fought some one quarter of a mile away from where Mark White met his death. Given that, yes, Mr Ward did have a fight he had no reason to disbelieve it to be any other person than the deceased, Mark White, until he saw a photograph of Mr White in a newspaper some months after he'd been sentenced to life imprisonment and he realised this wasn't the man he had fought with and therefore the man he thought he was convicted of murdering was in actual fact more than likely in all probability still living.

Mr Ward was in genuine belief that the deceased was in actual fact the man he had battled with and was NOT applying the defence of 'Duress' to the charge of murder he faced but he applies the defence of duress as to the explanation of why he changed his plea to a one of guilty on the second day of his trial.

The argument of duress is not being applied to this case in the way the CCRC are looking at it and the definition of duress is gone into in great detail by the CCRC, all good and well if the defence for the murder was a one of duress but that has not ever been claimed by Mr Ward therefore it seems academic and an exercise in shovelling smoke to pad out the Provisional Statement of Reasons.

The CCRC incorrectly state that change of plea by Mr Ward was brought on by the presence of Miss Lambert in court. Miss Lambert was in fear of James Docherty yet she appeared for the prosecution and was prepared to give evidence against her boyfriend regardless of the consequences her potential perjury would cause.

Gail Lambert was in possession of a stolen video recorder, yet she didn't face charges of handling stolen property, a small price to pay for having Miss Lambert as a prosecution witness especially when you consider her admittance that she put Mr Ward's leather jacket in a bin bag after reading the Gazette newspaper carrying the Mark White story on its' front page. This in itself was an admission of being an accessory after the fact and as you read her statement it's amazing what addendums she adds as her memory is jogged by the police. I feel Miss Lambert was coerced by the police into making such a statement that contradicts the forensic evidence on display.

We have Miss Lambert pulling a blood stained newspaper from a bin liner, the newspaper is paced on the carpet and yet no thought by the police is given to testing the carpet area in question for cross contaminated blood samples, strange especially since Miss Lambert states Gary's Doc Martens were caked with congealed blood and sand?

I believe that Miss Lambert has been liable to some sort of prosecution due to items being found in her home and for this reason the police gave her a way out and she wasn't prosecuted for washing Mr Ward's clothes (unlike Docherty's mother who was prosecuted for washing her son's clothes.) Miss Lambert does go on to say that had she of known Mr Ward was responsible for something like that then she wouldn't have washed his clothes.

Altogether a very negative statement in that she is in belief that Mr Ward has perpetrated the murder of Mark White, yet it is only in response to her own dubious situation that she makes these remarks. She goes on to say that feels sickened that she had any involvement with anybody responsible for taking another's life. Yet she freely washed the 'congealed' blood she claims was on Mr Ward's clothes and boots without a second thought. This act may well have repulsed the average female of her age, but not Miss Lambert and yet later she shows remorse at her actions in cleaning the clothing of Mr Ward.

I would now ask that those pyjamas Miss Lambert was wearing are found and I would also ask that ALL undisclosed evidence now be looked at thoroughly, as this is a very sinister situation and I feel that this is new evidence in the waiting. (Author's note: Sadly we recently learned from Blackpool police that the pyjamas had been destroyed, see copy letter later on.)

The blood on the pillowcase was NOT that of the deceased, Mark White, therefore it ties in and in my opinion corroborates Mr Ward's assertions he was fighting with someone other than Mark White. Gail Lambert, Gary Ward's girlfriend, further states: **'Jim (Docherty) would change his voice and swear at Gary. Gary used to tell me he was frightened of Jim (Docherty) and thought that if he didn't go along with something Jim was capable of harming him.'**

This, if it is true, supports Mr Ward's assertions that duress was applied to him by Docherty and that threats were made and suggestions that Miss Lambert's safety would be in jeopardy if Mr Ward didn't enter a plea of guilty when told to do so. Docherty used to store weapons including a hand gun at Miss Lambert's home via Mr Ward and if what Miss Lambert states is true then we are to believe there was a threat of some sorts applied to Mr Ward for his sudden turnaround in court from a 'not guilty' plea to one of 'guilty' rather than being persuaded to do so by the presence of Miss Lambert at the trial as the CCRC suggest. Indeed Miss Lambert's presence at court compounded the threat that Docherty had made to her safety.

I will be working towards a successful ending in this case and to date I feel the CCRC have been more of a hurdle than the actual appeal process, which I know we can have a good chance of winning and given that we do overcome the CCRC obstacle I have high hopes of success when all would be submitted to a full court hearing by a full legal team as opposed to a paper submission as what happened in Mr Ward's last appeal where he had no legal representation to argue his case and correct the learned judges in their fatal mistaken belief that Mr Ward had the blood of Mark White on the knee area of his jeans. They could do nothing other than what they did when armed with this incorrect knowledge, I would therefore ask the CCRC to correct this travesty of justice. END OF MY SUBMISSION ON BEHALF OF GARY WARD TO THE CCRC.

What follows is an extract taken from the CCRC's Provisional Statement of Reasons under reference number 01062/97. I quote this because Mr Keith Cartmell has threatened to take me to court for defamation. Well all what I can say then is he should also take the CCRC to court because I quote word for word from their published work which has been seen by many people. (See copy of Cartmell's letter later on.) It must be pointed out that what is quoted is from legal papers and is the representations of Gary Ward to the CCRC and their interpretation of what he has submitted in support of his claim of duress as to why he entered a plea of guilty and therefore the following extract is included. It is not my opinion, it is not my work but it is from the CCRC.

Quote: **Representations to CCRC**

Mr. Ward made the following representations to the Commission:

6.1. Duress

• From the outset Mr. Ward was subject to threats as, after the murder and upon leaving Ms. Lambert's flat, he said to her *'Don't say anything please Gail or you will get hurt'* (see statement of Ms. Lambert dated 11.09.93).

• Admissions at the police station were made as a result of threats made by Mr. Docherty, the co-accused, via Mr. Ward's solicitor, Mr. Keith Cartmell. (This claim is made in a CCRC document, it is not my wording or a substantiated claim but a word for word extraction from an official documents based on Mr Ward's unfounded claims.

• Whilst Mr. Ward was at Blackpool Police Station, Mr. Docherty's solicitor, Mr. Michael Ball, Cameron & Ball Solicitors, came to see him in the police cells. Then on 20 September, the solicitor produced a knuckle-duster to the police. On that day Mr. Docherty was interviewed by the police a fourth time and identified the knuckle-duster as one which Mr. Ward had had possession of and used on the night in question. At a later court appearance Mr. Docherty removed from Mr. Ward's bundle of papers, the copy of the contemporaneous note of his fourth interview. Mr. Ward also cites this as a breach of Article 6 as he was unable to properly prepare his case without all of the relevant paperwork. UNQUOTE

Here is Mr Cartmell's letter of intent QUOTE:

Dear Mr Richards.

Re: <u>Gary Ward</u>

I am in receipt of your letter of the 6th August, which I read with some astonishment. Firstly I should comment that I find the contents of your letter offensive and clearly defamatory. Should you choose to publish any such comments let it be assured that proceedings for defamation will be commenced.

I note you make reference to a previous publication, which I am now obtaining and will comment again further in due course.

I would also say that I am at a loss to understand how criticism appears to be being pointed solely at myself in relation to this case. I am at a loss to understand how Mr Ward and yourself appear to have overlooked the fact that during the course of the case both Junior and Leading Counsel represented him. Indeed, Mr Ward had the benefit of advice from two Queen's Counsel. The first he had a meeting with when I was not present and as a consequence of what Mr Ward told Counsel, that particular Counsel had to withdraw from the case. As I understood from that particular Barrister's Clerk. Mr Ward had made damaging confessions. Notwithstanding, a further Queen's Counsel was appointed and Mr Ward had the benefit of very experienced advice throughout. He has of course subsequently had advice from other Solicitors and presumably other Barristers, who have conducted appeals on his behalf. If, as you say. Mr Ward was not represented at an appeal, then that is the first I have known of that and obviously cannot comment further. UNQUOTE

I'll tell you what prompted me to write to Keith Cartmell, it was an unsigned letter from Cartmells Solicitors to the CCRC dated 10th

Gary Ward

April 2001. The final paragraph of that letter stated:
'We have to say, in conclusion, that we are aggrieved at the later criticism that Mr Ward now seems to make against the Practice. He was fully and comprehensively represented throughout the proceedings and was content at the outcome, realising his fate. As we say, to our knowledge, he has instructed two other firms of Solicitors to endeavor to appeal this matter, we presume unsuccessfully. Obviously the case has now reached yourselves. Given the consistency of Mr Ward's story throughout the proceedings we do fear for his state of mind in pursuing this matter in the way he now does and obviously fear for the damage that he must be doing to his parole prospects. We trust this now fully details our position. However, if we can render any further assistance please let us know.

Yours faithfully,   **Cartmells'**
UNQUOTE

What prompted me to reply to Keith Cartmell was the fact that I was incensed to read the writer's opinion on the state of Mr Ward's mental health, which has never been in question, and I believe this gives rise for an action from Gary Ward against Cartmells Solicitors and not as Mr Cartmell says in his letter to me for an action against me for defamation. I have been dealing with Gary over a three year period and never once have I questioned his state of mind and in essence it all brings in to question my state of mind because I'm just as keen as Gary in fighting his case therefore shouldn't I fall into the same category as Gary in having my state of mind questioned. What about the Birmingham six, the Guildford four and the likes should they have thrown away the chance to fight their cases just because they might have had a question mark against their state of mind because they fought on to clear their names?

The assertion Cartmells make that Gary must be damaging his parole chances also incensed me because parole is only offered to those who admit to their crimes, how many innocent lifers must have admitted to a crime simply so as to obtain parole? The mind boggles at how unfair the system is. A man successfully overturned the way

243

parole is considered for those who only admit to their crimes.

Mr Oyston, chairman of a football league club, was convicted of sexual offences and continuously denied the offences and he successfully obtained parole after challenging the system in the courts, sadly this does not apply to those serving life sentences – I believe it should. Why should justice be denied to anyone simply so that those sitting on parole boards can justify their fat ass positions?

Can you see why I became angry at Cartmells dangerous claims which he made to the CCRC and I believe may had some influence on their decision. All what I can say is that for Cartmells to slag off their former client could be construed as defamation and it might well be that it is Gary Ward who pursues a civil action over this clear case of defamation.

I now add a letter from Gordon Marsden in which he asks the CCRC to help obtain handwriting samples from Docherty. The CCRC did not authorize Mr Marsden's request, which is typical of the one sided way in which the CCRC work.

****

GORDON MARSDEN MP
Labour Member of Parliament For Blackpool South

Westminster Office
House of Commons
London SW IA OAA 2HH

Constituency Office
132 Highfield Road
Blackpool FY4

Sir Frederick Crawford
Chairman
Criminal Cases Review Commission
Alpha Tower
Suffolk Street
Queensway
Birmingham B 11 TT

Gary Ward

17 March 1999

Dear Sir Frederick Crawford

Mr Gary Ward

I understand that you have received a submission in September 1998 from Gabb & Co Solicitors (Author's note: Not the firm acting for Gary at this present time of writing.) on the case of Mr Gary Ward, who is one of my constituents. Along with others I have become increasingly uneasy as I have looked further into the trial account and other documents relating to this case as to the circumstances of the trial and sentencing. Gary Ward has always maintained that he confessed to killing Mark White only under duress and threats from James Doherty against his then girlfriend and brother - and I have seen copies of letters alleged to have been sent by Docherty to him after their conviction in which these threats and intimidation appear to have been continued.

I am told by Mr Ward's solicitors that crucial to any re-opening of the case is evidence that these letters were written by Mr Docherty. It appears however that they do not have access to sufficient authentic examples of his handwriting for conclusive analysis of the letters to take place. I would be grateful for your advice on whether it is possible for the CCRC to request such samples as part of your re-examination of the case. While being aware of the backlog of cases that the CCRC has to consider, Mr Ward's solicitors are conscious of the fact that Mr Docherty is currently being considered for parole and that it may prove more difficult to obtain the samples after his release.

I look forward to your response.
Yours sincerely,   Gordon Marsden
****

Viv - The Final Chapter

Below is a letter that I cannot believe. Since day one of Gary's appeal and subsequently from then on it has always been pointed out that the forensic evidence obtained from items seized by the police should be kept safe. Now the whole framework of what I've been working on seems to have been kicked into touch by the actions of one police officer authorising evidence to be destroyed.

****

Lancashire Constabulary
County Police Office
Bonny Street
Black-pool
Lancashire
FYI SRL
Your Ref JG1MRB/Ward

11th September 2001

Dear Sir/Madam
In the absence of Detective Superintendent Turner, I have been asked to reply to your letter of 21st August 2001, regarding your client Gary Stuart Ward and his application to the Criminal Cases Review Commission, following his conviction for murdering Mark White in Blackpool in 1993.

1 have had the enquiries made to which you refer in your letter, with the following results:
Seized from 313 Lytham Road Blackpool
1. A video recorder
2. Sink 'U' bend (Exhibit reference PMB 13)
3. Bedroom sink 'U' bend (Exhibit reference PMB 12)
4: Kitchen sink 'U' bend contents (Exhibit reference P1MB 11)
5.Kitchen sink 'U' bend (Exhibit reference PMB 10)
6.Prison letter (Exhibit reference PMB 9)
7.Evening Gazette 9.9.93 (Exhibit reference PMB 7)
8.Miscellaneous papers (Exhibit reference PMB 8)
9.Entertainment licence Ward (Exhibit reference PMB 6)
Seized from 61 Lytham Road Blackpool
1.A bloodstained pillow

Gary Ward

This item was sent for forensic examination, albeit I am not aware of any result. Similarly, I am informed that a pair of pyjamas was seized during the course of the investigation but it is believed that they were not sent for examination.

Furthermore, I am able to state that no white carpet was seized during the course of the enquiry and as a consequence no such item was submitted for forensic examination.

I also have to inform you that all the exhibits in this case were destroyed in the mid 1990's on the authority of the then Detective Chief Inspector on the pretext that they posed a health hazard

I hope this information is of assistance.

Yours sincerely

Detective Inspector PW Broome

****

Well that certainly has caused some consternation and I feel that Gary's lawyer must now proceed in a heavy handed way to get this conviction overturned in view of the loss of valuable evidence and in particular the pyjamas of Gail Lambert which would have given certain evidence one way or the other as to the blood transference from Gary's T-shirt. The other matter is that the original appeal to the Criminal Appeal Court was mishandled by the judges in what they suggested about Gary's jeans bearing the blood of the deceased!!!!!!!!!!!!!!!!!

As we know this is not the case and forensic evidence supports this in favour of Gary yet the judges got it totally arse about face and the CCRC say this bad judgment would not have changed the outcome of Gary's appeal...bollocks is what I say to that. The judges thought, incorrectly, that blood from the deceased was on Gary's jeans...well of course the judges would see this as a certain connection and to be honest if I'd heard that then I wouldn't have been working on Gary's case for the last three years.

I quote the following case Condron v UK in which it was instrumental in bringing about certain changes to European law and a European ruling prohibits judges from second guessing what juries may or may not have done in dealing with evidence. In Gary's case the CCRC are second guessing what the judges in Gary's appeal would have come to the conclusion of if they didn't incorrectly assume that the blood of the deceased was on Gary's jeans...the CCRC are breaching this ruling and therefore I know that this case should be back in the appeal court just on that basis but my fear is that the CCRC do not know this!

The CCRC live in an unreal world full of magical solutions and wizardry that can overcome all – I've news for them and that is the real world only works on facts.

On a final note: The Home Secretary, at that time in 1999, (my old sparring partner Jack Straw) upped Gary's tariff from ten years to twelve years. This was immediately after I'd included Gary's plight in the Viv 2 book, now doesn't that seem like a coincidence or what? Maybe Mr Blunkett, the present Home Secretary, will add another two years on after this book is launched. It's a gathering of judicial masons. Also the CCRC wrote to me and told me not to contact them directly over issues concerning Gary. I'm the only independent investigator in the UK working on such matters free of charge and they start to break out in spots at my involvement, doesn't that tell you something?

Gary doesn't' want sympathy he wants your support. All letters of support for Gary sent via the publisher will be passed on to him. At the present time of writing Gary's stepfather, Trevor, is in the process of setting up a website in support of him, no web address is available at present but if it happens then you will be assured that it will be listed on the following website on the underworld links page:
http://www.bronsonmania.com

GARY WARD IS INNOCENT

15

T

UK PHONE 07050 800499

This is T a man for all seasons. I rate him as the best there is when it comes to BIG criminal cases. Forget your driving whilst banned, forget your domestic burglars if it's a case where you need brains then this man runs his brains on the most difficult cases there is.

He doesn't work for anyone at the time of writing because lawyers are feared of his portfolio of names he's done work for. You mess them around and word spreads fast and since most firms of lawyers in the UK work on bread and butter magistrates' court stuff then you can understand why they just want to trundle on along that road.

If you're up to your neck in REAL trouble and you can pay for his services then this is the man for you and that's a personal recommendation from me, Steve Richards. You'll see later on near the end of this book that I give two other firms of lawyers as recommendations, they'll handle anything and offer legal aid, but if you can pay then this is the man for you.

T is a man of principle and a great thinker, he's worked for various law firms but most have let him down particularly Nicholas Green & Co solicitors of Manchester who accused him of slipping paperwork to the police, now had T of been a coke head then maybe the police could have held him to ransom and blackmailed him into showing them his clients' defence papers so when Nicholas Green visited certain high risk prisoners advising them of T's double crossing tactics all stood firmly by T and told Green to piss off. That is the strength of T and shows the regard held for him by high-risk prisoners including Charles Bronson now called Ali Charles Ahmed.

Nicholas Green was looking for a way to ditch T because many of the clients served by Green were starting to consider T to be just a little bit special. But one thing got in the way of ditching T and that was the fact that T had been specifically asked to handle the case of Popinder 'Pops' Singh Kandola of Handsworth, Birmingham who was facing charges of supplying class 'A' drugs.

Pops made it clear that he wanted T on his case and of course this scuppered Green's plans of ditching T, well at least until Pops' case was over. Pops case started in September 2000 and T was pulling out all the stops to win the case and when it looked like T had done his job Pops was happy for Green to dump T.

So when T was abroad on business Nicholas Green went around to T's home, after Pops was practically acquitted, and retrieved the paperwork T had in his possession relating to all of the cases T was working on. Backing Green in all of this was Pops Kandola because he knew he didn't need T anymore. To show what T overcame for a case involving Pops' brother I enclose some of the surveillance notes. Which were freely given by the Kandolas for publication in order to highlight how they claim to have been fitted up

Statement made against Bakhtawar Singh Kandola
(Pops' brother)

For the purposes of this statement I wish to be known as Charlie. This is not my true name it is my pseudonym. Dated 28th September 2000

'I first met Mr CAMPBELL in Wolverhampton about three to three and a half years ago. I knew him as Sammy. I was introduced by a person I knew and he knew. I don't wish to name that person. I don't think it's relevant. It was not a policeman. It was a meeting in relation to cigarettes. They were interested in cigarettes. I had a way of getting them in the country almost undetected. They said they would get in touch. They being Sammy and some of his colleagues.

They gave me a phone number and I rang them a couple of days later. We met in a pub in Wolverhampton. They weren't interested in the cigarettes but they were interested in the route to bring in other stuff. The people present were myself, Sammy, my friend which name I do not wish to give, Terry (Author's note: This person called Terry was Bakhtawar Singh Kandola – better known as Tarri Kandola) who I think was Asian and Gearbox who was Sikh. These were the people who were present on the first occasion.

I asked them what sort of stuff they were talking about and it turned out they were talking about hard class A drugs. They said heroin. They wanted me to be a courier, I said I would think about it but had not the slightest intention of doing it because I do not like heroin.

They were all talking. Terry (Tarri Kandola) was doing more of the talking than the others. We were all openly talking about heroin we were not talking about cigarettes on this occasion. I then left and said I would be in touch. I didn't get in touch.

Some months later I was stopped at a British airport in possession of a small amount of cannabis, it was a kilo and a bit. It wasn't for my own use or for selling. I was doing someone a favour. My own feelings are that I don't think cannabis is dangerous. I know what heroin does to people and that is the big difference between that and cannabis.

During the time I was in prison, I believe that was 1998, 1 spoke with a Police Officer, I know as Eran. He wanted to speak to someone in relation to drugs. Eran came to the prison with a chap called Paul who was also a Police Officer. I mentioned what had happened in Wolverhampton when I met with Sammy, Terry and Gearbox. Paul said he would be very interested to meet me after my release from prison. At a later stage during my sentence Paul came to see me with another Police Officer whose name I cannot remember. Paul said he was very interested in the people I had mentioned, Sammy, Terry and Gearbox. He said he would contact me shortly after my release. This was towards the end of my sentence.

My reason for wanting to talk to the officers is that a friend of mine died from heroin. He left four boys and one of those is now an addict as well. I've seen his family destroyed and I've seen his wife on the verge of suicide. I really hate what that stuff does to people. The reason I went to the police was that I don't like heroin. I do not speak to them for payment.'

Viv - The Final Chapter

Charlie the informant was released from prison in January 1999 and was approached by police to become an informant so as to infiltrate the drugs gang, which included Tarri Kandola. Further on in Charlie's statement he talks of meeting up with Sammy who asks him if he can get him a gun:

'The only people in the house were Sammy and me. The television was on and it was showing the passageway and outside the front door. He had a Morris Minor in his driveway. I could see this on the screen. It was his own security system.

Sammy made a cup of tea. I told him I had been in prison over cannabis. I wish to add that it was Sammy who mentioned heroin first without a doubt. He said he was doing quite well since I had last seen him. I said what are you at, and he said he was at the brown stuff I understand that to be heroin. I said I needed some money and he said he could let me have some. I declined that. It was at that time that I started to talk about the price of heroin in Ireland. I told him I could get £35,000 to £40,000 a kilo for it. I told him I had made enquiries and I had. He sounded interested I said 1 had no finances as I just come out of prison. He said he would contact his own people and recommend me to them and maybe I could have half a kilo to take over to Ireland myself and then bring back the money. The money left after the initial outlay for the half kilo would be split between us.

Sammy said he would contact me in a few days. He had my mobile phone number. Sammy also asked if I could get him a handgun. He said he had a grievance with a few people. He also said it would be helpful in the business he deals in. He didn't need to repeat what that business was. I took it to be drugs.

It was only the third time that I had met him and he seemed to trust me. I found his offer to speak with his colleagues and recommend I could have half a kilo of heroin as unbelievable.'

Charlie met with the police and they put in a police officer that was Irish and he would be called 'Joe'. Joe was to act as an interested party who would be introduced to the Kandola outfit by Charlie the informant.

'This person would be Irish; I was to introduce them to each other. Sammy agreed to meet with me and this man. He said he would bring someone with him as well. I was then taken to a hotel in Birmingham by the Police where I stayed the night. I was paid £125.00 expenses for the hotel and travel, as I had had to pay for it myself. Simon, Paul and Adrian were at the hotel.

The next morning I was taken to another hotel where I met an Irishman who was a police officer by the name of Joe.

T

The officers asked me if I would take Joe to meet Sammy I agreed to this I signed another paper about what I could and could not do I could discuss heroin but we were not allowed to receive heroin. I cannot remember what else was on the sheet.

Joe and I went by taxi to a hotel on the Hagley Road, Birmingham around the time of the Cheltenham meeting. Joe and I sat in the hotel we had coffee and waited for Sammy and his friend. After about ten to fifteen minutes Sammy and his friend came. I introduced Sammy to Joe and Joe to Sammy's friend. Sammy introduced his friend to me as Pops. He was a small Asian man.

I felt at the time of being introduced to Pops very strange as Pops put his arms around me and said he was glad to see me. Joe said to Sammy that I had got the prices in Ireland wrong. It was nowhere near what I had said however, you could get a better price than in England. Joe also said to Sammy that he was part of a group of people and that he would deal directly with Sammy. He didn't say what group of people. Joe said to Sammy that I would get my cut from any deals alone. Sammy asked if I was agreeable to that and I said I was.

Pops was introduced as Sammy's boss or the main man. Pops knew Ireland and asked about Dublin. He said that he had airline stewardesses who worked for him on runs into Dublin and used them as couriers. He didn't say which airline. I also have to admit I cannot remember him saying which drug they were carrying. He said he had businesses in Belgium and Asia and that he dealt in large quantities of heroin. I was quite surprised as he didn't look that sort of person. He also said he had business in Dublin which we could get into later but he didn't expand on that.

Sammy was saying what he could do in relation to providing Joe with heroin. Joe said that on the first occasion he would like to deal with a small amount just so we could get to know each other and if that was okay then we could progress. We all agreed Joe and Sammy swapped phone numbers. They said they would be in touch. This meeting was totally relaxed and everybody appeared to get on well with each other.'

Everything seems to be going hunky dory for the informant until!

'I believed that the arrest of these people would take place in a few months time. By then I would have distanced myself vastly from what had taken place. Therefore Sammy and his associates wouldn't have linked me to their arrest.

A police officer called me a short time later and told me that Sammy had been arrested. I asked who had been there and I was told it was Joe and he

Viv - The Final Chapter

had identified himself as a police officer. I went berserk on the phone because they would know that I had talked to the police. I was worried for the safety of my family and myself in that order.'

The police did nothing to help protect the identity of the informant by virtue of the Irishman breaking his cover and revealing himself to the Kandola gang as a policeman.

We continue with Charlie's statement: 'The police said that I could be moved from my address to a safe location. Then I asked for money to help me to move home and family. The safety of my family was first and foremost in my mind. The police gave me £10,000 in total. (Author's note: £10,000 was pulled out just like that.) As I said I didn't do what I did for money. However, because of the way things turned out I didn't have any choice but to take the money.

That is about it. I now know I have to give evidence in court. If I was a single man I would stand up and say what had occurred and not hide behind anything because of what I believe in. However, 1 have to take into consideration other people and for these reasons I am wary and frightened but I will still do it. I will attend if required. I have been asked if I understand that I am a registered informant and I agree that I am.'

The case against Bakhtawar (Tarri) Singh Kandola looked to be overwhelming and a firm of lawyers, Salhan & Co had let him down and now T was needed more than ever. Kandola agreed to take T on a private basis and after a two week trial Kandola was acquitted and the bill came to £25,000. Now T is the type of man who would keep his word and work on a case regardless of such a promise, but it would be a bonus if Kandola were acquitted. T tells us what happened:

"Basically he (Tarri) agreed to hire me as part of his legal team to pay £25,000 if I succeeded in getting him off. I agreed to do the case on the basis that his own solicitor Messrs Salhan & Co had let him down.

He was charged with conspiracy to supply others a class A drug and the CPS considered him to be the main person in the conspiracy. After a two-week trial he was found not guilty and his relief was overwhelming. People throughout the country from Newcastle to London to whom he confirmed he would pay the said amount congratulated him. These people promise anything but once they're free they forget the very person who got them off.

If I hadn't of got both Kandola brothers off then they'd be doing 30 years minimum between them. I would give a word of advice to those seeking to do business with these villains; they are the Accrington Stanley of the villain world pretending to be Premiership villains."

T

There you have it, in a nutshell it really is sad that T was let down by these two jokers and it shows that there isn't honour amongst thieves and the reason for putting this particular chapter in the book is to show how the underworld can turn against their legal team and maybe this is why so many in the legal profession do stay with the bread and butter jobs. So if you want T it looks like you're going to have to put some of the money up front thanks to the crooked Kandolas.

I have personally taken the time out to speak with the Kandolas over the telephone so as to ascertain for myself that this really was the case and sure enough Tarri Kandola confirmed to me that he would be paying T the money he owed, which was lodged as his bail surety. Even further to that I have spoken with some underworld figures of importance throughout the UK and they have also been able to confirm that the Kandola brothers broke their word to T. Those underworld figures that confirmed this story are Premiership league players and have no reason to lie to me over such matters and they regularly blow £25,000 on parties and get togethers.

Dealing in any sort of controlled drug can carry penalties but class A drugs bring certain prison sentences if proven against those charged with such offences, I believe any less of a man than T being involved in such a defence team would have resulted in certain convictions and lengthy prison sentences for the Kandola brothers.

Bakhtawar Singh Kandola

16

Murderers, Muggers, Thugs & Buggers

I don't know about you but I've always been intrigued by women involved in violence. What makes them do it; I mean women have a totally different system of thinking than us men. What about the murder committed by nursing home worker Alison Firth dubbed the 'Angel of Death', she took the life of an old lady, Alice Grant, by poisoning her with an overdose of Chlormthiazole, a sedative. Firth was found guilty of this mindless murder carried out in May 2000 and only days before when a care assistant went to adjust the pillows on Mrs Grant's bed Firth was reported to have said to her, "Why bother, she's going to die anyway."

I covered the case of Maxine Robinson in a previous Viv book. Maxine from Birtley, Gateshead was branded a child killer in 1995 when she was convicted of the murder of her five-month-old son and 19-month-old daughter when she was accused of smothering them and was jailed for life. Experts have claimed that new evidence will cast doubt on her conviction. Her defence claimed the deaths were cot death syndromes, but when you consider that under an equation known as Meadows Law comes up with a one in 73 million chance of two babies in the same family dying of cot death it looks like an uphill struggle to prove her innocence. However a scientist, Dr David Drucker says his research has put doubt on the way Meadows Law works. This has put doubt on the 100 or so convictions of women jailed for such cot deaths, but to date Maxine remains behind bars.

January 2001: An appeal is lodged against the six-month sentence, which attracted national publicity after Denise Carr, 32, bit off the testicle of Neil Hutchinson, 29, when he attacked his new wife Shelley and Denise from Gateshead intervened. A drunken Hutchinson pinned Denise down on the floor and started to hit her and in the struggle to get free she worked her way out squeezing beneath his legs, when her mouth got to his testicle area she just wildly bit him in order to get him off her and it certainly made Hutchinson's eyes water when he realised he was one testicle short of a full set.

Women's groups were up in arms over the sentence imposed on Denise and I agree with them, but the judge was a man and any man who's been kicked in the balls will tell you that it fucking hurts…does it not!!! By virtue of the judge being a man it was obvious that Denise would go to prison. Hutchinson had only been married for a few weeks when the incident happened and rumour has it that he and his wife have split up as a consequence of this fight.

Surprisingly enough Hutchinson was not charged with assaulting Denise, but of course it would probably have been male police officers doing the investigating and like I said it doesn't narf hurt when you're kicked in the balls so no surprises there.

July 2001: A 20-year-old mother of one, Kimberley Brazell was given a 30-month prison sentence for three mugging attacks on teenagers in Hartlepool. The first attack was on a 14-year-old girl when Brazell snatched necklaces worth £200 from her neck. The next attack saw Brazell go up to two teenage girls and ask them if they wanted to buy any gear, they of course refused and Brazell proceeded to grab two necklaces worn by a 16-year-old girl, pulling them tight until the y snapped. The final mugging involved Brazell and a male walking towards a 14-year-old girl and her friend and similarly as Brazell had previously done she reached out and pulled two necklaces from the girl's neck. Are women becoming more violent?

August 2001: Teesside Crown Court jailed Pamela Downey, 34, of Redcar for 18 months after she pleaded guilty to attempted robbery. Downey wore a black stocking over her head when she attempted to rob the Coatham Fish Bar in Redcar. Standing in the Fish Bar was an elderly gentlemen customer who Downey grabbed and she said, "If you don't give me the money I'll stab you." A brave shop assistant tackled Downey and as she ran away her stocking mask was pulled off revealing that she was a female. After newspaper reports of the crime Downey decided to hand herself in. Now that does set women apart from most men, here was a woman who was facing up to her mad half hour escapade but she had 18 months ahead of her to think it over,

Viv - The Final Chapter

thanks to Judge George Moorehouse.

August 2001: A three-girl gang terrorised a 15-year-old girl next to a disused pub, The Five Wands, in Bensham Road, Gateshead. The ringleader of the girl gang was 17-year-old Delia Smith who burnt the face and chest of the gang's terrified victim and then held broken glass next to her neck. Another gang member 17 year old Gemma Francis joined the third gang member, Kelly Stobbart, 18, in punching and kicking the girl. Threats to make the girl jump off Tyneside's Redheugh Bridge caused her to break away and flag a passing taxi down and make good her escape. All three gang members admitted grievous bodily harm and Smith was sentenced to 18 months detention and training order, Francis was detained for 12 months and Stobbart was sent to a young offender institute (YOI) for 10 months. You might think that the sentences were too little, well so did the Judge William Crawford but his hands were tied due to their ages.

September 2001: Mother of two, Karen Bilton, 37, received a 2$^{1}/_{2}$ year prison sentence for an attack on Melanie Archbold who was celebrating her 21st birthday party in The Brewer's Arms pub in Houghton. Bilton used her platform shoes to cause head injuries in the attack which resulted in her being found guilty of wounding with intent. On the whole women do receive longer custodial sentences than men but in the next case it seems to fly in the face of justice compared to this one.

September 2001: The equestrian jet set fell foul of trouble when Gina Sassetti, 33, had just finished modelling in a fashion show organised by her boss's lover Christine Tate, 41, when in a totally unprovoked attack Tate punched, scratched and then kicked Miss Sassetti down a flight of stairs in the Bowes Manor Equestrian Centre, in Birtley, Gateshead which is run by Stephen Gair, Tate's lover. The court gave Tate a 12-month conditional discharge after she admitted the assault. It was rumoured that Miss Sassetti had been flirting with Mr Gair and this is suggested as the reason for the attack. The family of Miss Sassetti denied the flirting accusation and complained at the lenient sentence given to Tate.

September 2001: Court number 4 at Newcastle Crown Court was the scene for tears when Shelly Thompson, 19, of Johnson Street, Teams, Gateshead was given four years detention in a YOI for savagely wounding Tracey Bourne, 20, in a Newcastle nightclub, Powerhouse 2. Thompson, a lesbian, smashed a glass or bottle over

258

Miss Bourne's head, also a lesbian, before slicing her face open causing a 10 centimetre long wound needing 45 stitches leaving her permanently and horrifically disfigured.

Miss Bourne was in the toilets of the Powerhouse when Thompson barged in calling her a "slut"; this was because her earlier sexual advances were spurned. After the attack she left the club hoping not to be tracked down but a diligent club doorman obtained her mobile telephone number. Thompson was told that she had better hand herself into the police because she was caught on CCTV video coming out of the toilet covered in blood. This call prompted Thompson to hand herself into the police. (This is good doormanship - remember the murder of Penny Laing in a previous Viv book. Miss Laing died after being slashed across her neck and that attack left a lot to be desired from club doormen that evening.)

Thompson denied having caused Miss Bourne's horrendous injury that happened in March 2001 and elected for trial by jury, inevitably with all of the evidence stacked against her she was found guilty. In the pre-sentence probation report she foolishly insisted she was innocent, which does not bode well with judges. Some sort of repentance is sought in cases like this and my own investigation into this attack brought me to the conclusion that Thompson was 100% guilty, but she was in a state of denial.

A poor mitigation did not help when Thompson's defence barrister Richard Bloomfield said: "There was no sensible or rational motive it was momentary madness where alcohol has been consumed. Miss Thompson is upset and sorry such serious injuries were caused. I have here two references submitted by a family friend and a solicitor. Her sexuality could cause problems in prison given her offence is one of violence." Judge Tony Lancaster said: "Miss Bourne is permanently scarred from a 10cm disfiguring wound leaving her with a daily reminder. Thompson is still unable to accept guilt. The least sentence of imprisonment I can give you is four years detention, take her away." Thompson broke out in tears, tears of self-pity. She made Miss Bourne go through the ordeal of a trial and after being found guilty is, what I believe, got her the four years although the judge could have given her seven years. Even so

Viv - The Final Chapter

Thompson had conveniently secured employment during her period on bail and it was said by her defence counsel that she was in a steady (lesbian) relationship it didn't fool his honour Judge Lancaster.

Such an attack in a Newcastle nightclub can only add to the concern some revellers have expressed to me about such crimes taking place in the city centre, maybe this will be a warning to others that this sort of attack will not go away quietly like Thompson sneaking out of the club door hoping to escape into the dark of night.

June 2001: Okay this one isn't in date order as the previous ones; I've left one of the stupidest crimes I've just about heard of until last. A teenager was caught on CCTV video performing a sex act with a horse! Drunken Stephen Spalding, 18, got behind the horse before performing the sick sex act. The attack happened at 1am while the horse was grazing on grass at William Street, Felling, Gateshead, yards from Spalding's home. A security guard tipped off police and it led to Spalding being charged with buggery with an animal and attempted buggery with an animal. Both offences were transferred to Crown Court because of the seriousness of the charges.

The horse was tethered and that explains why it didn't run off. Later on when police examined the CCTV footage and they identified Spalding. The court heard that the black and white horse, described as piebald pony, was bought by its owner as a pet for his children. The horse described as a placid animal before the attack underwent a character transformation.

When Spalding was questioned about the attack he at first denied it and then admitted to only stroking the horse and when he was shown the CCTV footage of the attack said it was "disgusting" and denied it was him.

Spalding gave a guilty plea to outraging public decency, which was accepted by the prosecution and his defence barrister, Glen Gatland (A colourful character who warrants a book being written about him.), told the court that his client was too ashamed and afraid of reprisals to start a new job. A 12-month conditional discharge was given to Spalding.

17

Murderers Square Mile

I could have written a whole book on this subject matter because there is just so much murder and death in this square mile that there has to be something going on that can be explained in a scientific way that will make sense of it all. My answer to it is that the area is riddled with some sort of evil atmosphere that grips people with a madness…what other explanation can there be for the amount of murders and violence committed in such a compact area?

The area in question is in Gateshead and is about one square mile in size and a lot of the avenues are full of run down flats that go for sale for as little as £8,000 and if derelict can go for as little as £5,000.

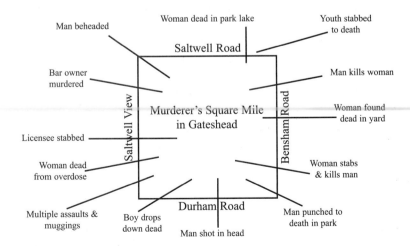

Man beheaded · Woman dead in park lake · Youth stabbed to death

Bar owner murdered · Saltwell Road · Man kills woman

Murderer's Square Mile in Gateshead · Saltwell View · Bensham Road · Woman found dead in yard

Licensee stabbed

Woman dead from overdose · Woman stabs & kills man

Multiple assaults & muggings · Boy drops down dead · Durham Road · Man shot in head · Man punched to death in park

Viv - The Final Chapter

The area is marked out on the previous page, I would like to be able to write something about each murder but lack of space as we reach the end of this book does not allow you or me that privilege and one again we've filled the book before I can get it all crammed in, it's like trying to put a quart into a pint pot. Originally I had planned a book called *Murderers Square Mile* but given my involvement with that many projects it looked like it was not ever going to be written so I've put this very condensed version together, maybe some one will write such a book in the future. So it is with that reason I can only give you a smattering of the goings on.

The body in the boot murder happened in July 1997 and was a pretty grisly murder. Rectory Road is named after the rectory of a church being located on it and maybe this is some sort of clue as to the cause of the problem in the area. Munir Ahmed owned many properties and one of them he had just rented out to former nurse Christopher Larsen. Larsen, 31, struck up a good relationship with his new landlord, Mr Ahmed, 56, so there was just no reasonable explanation as to why Larsen snapped and smashed his victim's head into pulp with a hammer and then was rumoured to have decapitated his victim with a spade and then went on to hide Mr Ahmed's body in the very car that belonged to his landlord which was parked less than a mile from Larsen's flat. No one seen him do this?

Of course Mr Ahmed was missed and a search was underway and Larsen had even become concerned as to the whereabouts of Mr Ahmed. In court Larsen gave no evidence and there was just no explanation given as to the reason for the murder, of course the blood stains on Larsen's jeans matched up with Mr Ahmed's and the case was solved, even so the trial lasted for two weeks. Judge David Hodson said the reason for the murder of the 'gentle' man was a mystery. What had possessed Larsen, a former nurse, to commit such an evil crime?

That leads us on to another murder on Coatsworth Road when Kathleen Milroy, 34, was found strangled to death in a backyard in January 1994.

One of the most tragic cases in the square mile was that of the manslaughter of 16-year-old Simon Clarke who was stabbed to death by Mark Yusaf, 19, in an Easter Monday robbery. Yusaf as far as I can find out was intent on taxing Simon of his sports coat, Simon refused to hand it over and Yusaf then stabbed him fatally in the heart. Yusaf claimed self-defence and was given eight years for manslaughter. At the time of the stabbing Yusaf was on bail from Liverpool magistrates' court for kidnapping, blackmail, robbery and assault charges. When Yusaf failed to turn up at Liverpool magistrates' court bail was extended even though he was of no fixed abode at that time. This led to both Northumbria and Merseyside Police Forces coming under investigation from the Police Complaints Authority for their handling of the case.

A fatal stabbing took place in Northbourne Street when George Flynn, 36, was stabbed in the chest by his lover Linda Savage, 29, mother of two, in May 1999. Although Mr Flynn lived for five days after the fatal knife attack it was shock and loss of blood that led to his death. Charges were adjusted against Savage from wounding to murder. The row that led to the murder was over who fathered their seven-month-old daughter, Charlie. It was claimed that Mr Flynn attacked Savage for the first time in their relationship. At her trial Savage admitted manslaughter based on the fact that she never meant to cause Mr Flynn serious harm and later on forensic tests actually proved Mr Flynn was the father of the child in question. Savage was branded 'pure evil' by Mr Flynn's mother, Flora Milne, after Savage was given three years probation.

A bloody body lay in a back alley of Whitehall Road near to the victim's home in Windsor Avenue. John Hall, 33, was shot in the back of the head in execution style after leaving a late party at 1am on 4th August 1999, his body was later found at 2am. As they left the Bensham Arms pub an argument broke out between John Hall and another man, this argument continued during the next hour and as a consequence it is believed that a female pulled the trigger of the gun on the instructions of her boyfriend, who had been arguing with Hall, so as to confirm her love for him.

Hall, a minor criminal was shot with his own gun - 1/3 of the gun was his. The gun was shared between three small time drug dealers; Hall was said by the people in the area to be a one. Each would have the gun for one day and then pass it on to the next whose turn it was; this wasn't John's day to have the gun.

Word soon spread of who the killer was but police were having a difficult time in getting people to come forward with information but since the people John Hall was mixing with were from the drug world it didn't lend itself to dialogue that would help catch Hall's killer.

Viv - The Final Chapter

Eventually John Hall's friend, Martin Cavanagh, was charged with his murder but mysteriously a key witness, Susan Black, died from a drugs overdose, which altered the balance of the evidence and Cavanagh was acquitted of murdering John Hall. The police are not looking for anyone else in connection with Mr Hall's murder.

Cavanagh has carried out attacks on other people and in one incident he went looking for one of Gateshead's hardest men and as result he had the end of his nose bitten off by someone he had antagonised. At present time of writing Cavanagh, 32, faces further charges of threats to kill Kelly Ellison, 26. He has had attempts made on his life by those involved in the murky world of drugs.

In a twist to the tale Sandra Black, 39, the auntie of Susan Black, mentioned above, was murdered and her dismembered remains were found in a coalbunker in Camborne Grove, Gateshead, in September 2001. William Francis Johnston, 22, has been charged with her murder. A post-mortem examination revealed Ms Black of St Mary's Court, in Gateshead, died of serious head injuries. A woman, who was detained with the man, was released without charge.

Amazingly the square mile supports a large Jewish population of some 300 families as well as many hundreds of Jewish students from around the world. A brief history of how they settled in Tyneside: In 1887 a Lithuanian Jew arrived in Newcastle, which already had a small Jewish population. Not being able to stand the enthusiastic Christians trying to convert him he went to live in Gateshead, others followed and they settled in Derwentwater Road/Corbett Street. By 1912 they had built a small synagogue, which was replaced by a one in 1938 on Bewick Road. The area is now a centre of learning.

The murderers square mile seemed to follow a young Jewish student when David Myers, 20, made a trip from Gateshead to London to see his parents in Finchley. He was attacked and stabbed more than 20 times by Nabil Ouldeddine, 27. David required six hours of surgery to save his life, Ouldeddine faces attempted murder charges. The anti-Zionist Al Muhajiroun group warned all Jews that if they support Israel in the Middle Eastern conflict then they would become targets. Sadly that is all I could squeeze in to this chapter, but if you knew the whole story you would be as concerned as I am.

18

Murder & Bits 'n' Bobs

Just before I start this chapter I'd like to thank the many thousands of people who have written to me, even the ones who told me my grammar was shite because without you there wouldn't be the drive in me to push on. Hopefully you'll follow my puritanical writing style in the next four books I'll be publishing, thank you.

Paul Logan unsolved murder: Two men murdered Paul **Logan**, 25, the pizza delivery driver from Shotley Bridge two nights before Christmas 1993, seven days before Viv was murdered? It is claimed that the same two men responsible for this murder could also be responsible for Viv's murder.

My own inquiry has revealed some interesting pointers, Joe Marshall a convicted gunman gave evidence to the police naming the alleged killers of Paul and I have been able to unearth a piece of information which might be true or might not be, it is claimed that £5,000 was paid to the two men in question in order that Paul would be given a good turning over - the men went too far and as a consequence they accidentally killed Paul. The Geordie Mafia underworld has it that one of two killers is definitely a heavyweight informant who gets away with selling drugs under the watchful eye of the police while it is claimed that the second man is said to be in prison serving time for offences of violence.

In a twist to the tale PC Jeff **Hunt**, 33, was given a three-month prison sentence for misconduct as a public official following an arson attack on a van belonging to Hugh Logan, father of Paul. The man responsible for the petrol bomb attack, Keith Suddick, 36, was jailed for carrying out the attack in Shotley Bridge. Information on this murder or any other murder: **Crimestoppers, run by civilians, Freephone: 0800 555111**

Viv - The Final Chapter

Julie Smailes unsolved murder: The murder of Julie Smailes, 27, is claimed to have been carried out by John Thompson, 27, who took his own life. Julie from Leadgate, in Consett, County Durham was murdered on 30th October 1996. Julie was found strangled and with 45 stab wounds to her body and her killers set fire to her house. Rumours in the underworld suggest that one of the killers still lives in the Consett area and another, a man, is working or has worked in Scotland. Police claims (DNA evidence links him to being in Julie's home) that Thompson had an involvement cannot be discounted, but others were involved. Thompson's widow, Michelle, 32, said that his nine-page suicide note handed to her by police some two years after his death exonerates him from the Julie Smailes murder.

Peter Beaumont Gowling unsolved murder: On Valentine's Day 2001 Peter Beaumont Gowling, 52, was assassinated by two men (if CCTV footage from a nearby hotel is correct) who entered his downstairs flat in Osborne Road, Jesmond, Newcastle. Mr Gowling had been shot gangland style with multiple bullet shots to the head, chest and back with a small calibre handgun. (Probably a .22, which is favoured to cause the maximum internal damage as it bounces around inside the skull. A heavier calibre bullet would pass through giving the victim a chance to live.) Mr Gowling was a flamboyant character living the jet set lifestyle while associating with Premiership league criminals - straddling both worlds until in 1996 he was caught with two suitcases of drug money containing £540,000, which he was taking to Ireland. He was given an 11-year prison sentence and £1m of his assets was confiscated.

The drug syndicate Mr Gowling was working for raked in £500,000 every two weeks…it was a big operation and rumours of an IRA connection were rife. After his release from prison in January 2001 he said: "I believe that my debts to society have now been paid in full." I believe this was a veiled way of his saying to the drug syndicate he once worked for that he had served time and any money he owed them should be written off. Rumours started to drift around the underworld that Mr Gowling had some 38 offshore bank accounts stashed with some of the drug money he'd been creaming off from the syndicate.

Although the estimate of 38 bank accounts may have been a little exaggerated there were other rumours saying he'd sold 22kg of uncut cocaine that belonged to the syndicate and along with the missing money it so incensed the syndicate that they had to send a message out to others that they wouldn't get away with it and the way of doing that was to have Mr Gowling murdered.

Analysing the hit - it was a semi professional multi-tap hit. The SAS manner of killing Mr Gowling with multiple shots (double, treble or quadruple tap) to the head and heart was classical even to the point of a low calibre gun being used, BUT there were a few mistakes made which makes me believe that the people responsible have not killed before. My sources tell me that a pro hit man would have made sure the body was not found and the killers would not have run from the scene, as did the two men caught on CCTV. Running always attracts people's attention and if the two men caught on CCTV footage were the killers then this proves they were not pro. If this is the case then anyone knowing but not connected with the murder plot will reveal all to the police if they are ever pulled in for other charges…time will tell.

Kevin Nightingale murder: Back in 2000 four people had been arrested and charged with Mr Nightingale's murder but within months the CPS withdrew the charges against one of the four men, Dean Barrow, who was serving time because of his involvement with the *Boss Gang* from South Tyneside. Twelve months after being charged the other three suspects Joanne Morgan, (Her husband) Ian Morgan and Shaun Doyle all from Hebburn, South Tyneside had charges discontinued against them.

During the early hours in February 1996 Mr Nightingale, 33, was shot at outside of the front door of his home in Lytton Park Estate, South Shields, South Tyneside after returning from work at the Oz nightclub in South Shields. It was Mr Nightingale's wife who found him bleeding to death. Previous to this Mr Nightingale's home had been the subject of an arson attack, he was peppered with shotgun pellets and he was shot at with a crossbow. I've had to alter the write-up after three people were arrested in July 2001 for the murder of club doorman Kevin Nightingale and await trial.

Stephen Sweeney unsolved murder: Upholstery factory boss Stephen Sweeney, 45, was shot at close range with a handgun whilst he sat at the desk of his Gateshead factory on the night of 8th July 1998. His lover, Carol Taylor, found his body after 9pm when she went to check on his whereabouts. Police set up an incident room at Northumbria Police Headquarters, in Ponteland, Northumberland and are using the Holmes 11 Home Office serious crime-recording log to sift

Viv - The Final Chapter

through information. Inquiries into the murder have taken the police to Spain and Amsterdam, but my own inquiries in the criminal underworld reveal a possible Manchester connection possibly in connection with a bad debt or even closer to home but for legal reasons I cannot divulge that information. Mr Sweeney, even though conviction free, had links to the criminal underworld and this may be the saving grace that helps catch his killers.

Sara Cameron unsolved murder: Good Friday, 21st April 2000 was to be the last day in the life of pretty blonde student Sara Cameron, 23, when she was murdered after getting off the Tyneside Metro and walking to her home in Earsdon Village. Sara's body was found in a field near to her home. I believe the murder was an opportune attack on her and that her killer will kill or strike again. Given the cycle that these attackers work in I would be looking for various attacks on females set at monthly intervals or between 100/113 days apart. On the Thursday night at 11.30pm a witness said they heard screaming, which may have been those of Sara in distress? **Crimestoppers, civilian run, Freephone: 0800 555111**

I do not intend to list the endless stream of unsolved murders in the north because they have already been covered in thousands of column inches by press. But it shows a marked increase in violence and the lengths killers are prepared to go to. Murders connected to the underworld have more chance of being solved due to informants and police intelligence methods but non-underworld murders stand the least chance of being solved as time goes on.

Gary Thompson: An appeal bid in July 2000 by the drug-crazed killer of a 90-year-old war veteran failed. Murderer Gary Thompson, 43, had his appeal turned down for the callous killing of Thomas Hall in November 1997 when during a robbery he beat up, gagged and tied Mr Hall to a chair and turned the heating off leaving Mr Hall to spend the night in a freezing temperature. Eleven days later Mr Hall died in hospital of pneumonia.

Stephen Abadom: An attempted murder on Heather Honey, 27, for a debt of £200 she owed Stephen Abadom, 47, resulted in Abadom being given a life sentence at Leeds Crown Court for the July 13th 1999 9mm gun attack. Under the 'three strikes' rule he must serve at least four years before he can be considered for parole. Abadom, formerly of Wallsend, Newcastle appeared in court alongside Johnny Howe, 39, in

Murder & Bits 'n' Bobs

May 2000 jointly charged with attempted murder. Howe of Newcastle had driven with Abadom to the home of Ms Honey in Perkinsville, Chester-le-Street, County Durham. For some unknown reason the entrance to Ms Honey's home had an exterior security gate to the entrance door, which meant that even if the inner door was open that the exterior gate would not allow access, but the caller could be seen and spoken to through the grill. (Drugs dealers so as to give them time to get rid of any drugs during a police raid or for them to serve their drugs through the security gate usually use this set up. So other than this gate being for security I cannot make such a claim in this case.)

Abadom fired a shot into the back of Ms Honey as she ran away from the sight of Abadom with a gun pointed at her and it is claimed that during the course of her being attended to by paramedics that Abadom called her mobile telephone and said: "Am I going to get my £200 now?" Howe was given 18 months imprisonment when he entered a plea of guilty to a blackmail charge.

In a twist to the tale Ms Honey, with a new identity, was interviewed in her new hideaway home by the press some two years after the gun attack and her photograph was plastered in a Tyneside newspaper. Given her claims that she feels there is a gangland 'hit' on her life it seems rather odd that she should allow this and if a journalist could track her down with her new identity it should start alarm bells ringing for Ms Honey although to be fair Ms Honey did say that she would be moving abroad to live with friends to escape although she said she would always be looking over her shoulder.

Stephen and Michael Sayers, two well known underworld figures from Newcastle, are serving lengthy sentences behind bars for demanding money with menaces...I don't really wish to go into that because the victim cannot be named because a court order protects him and there are certain factors involved in the case that tie the victim into having friendships and business associations with underworld characters from the north. I think it only fair that if I were to criticise the Sayers' brothers then I should also be able to tell the FULL story warts and all about how they were convicted and the people involved but that is not possible due to the court order.

What I can tell you though is that letters shot back and forth between the Sayers' lawyer and the Joe Hunt's lawyer. I want to show you something that is hypocritical. Clive M Hindle of Hindle Campbell

Solicitors, North Shields wrote a letter to Tony Weldon on 21st June 1996. At that time Mr Weldon was on remand facing serious charges for robbery. And I quote from Mr Hindle's letter that has become public domain due to so many copies being distributed throughout the prison system and within the community:

Quote: *My own view is that they* (Sayers') *had a great deal to do with him (Joe Hunt) being off the scene and my information is that they are responsible for both of you being in high risk Category A security at the present time. The Sayers brothers are controlled by D.C. Henderson of N.C.I.S.* (National Criminal Intelligence Squad) *They inform to him regularly and through him they had your security categorisation changed. It was not aimed at you, but you were caught in the crossfire.* (Author's note: All gained from an unnamed source, which is dangerous conjecture in such circumstances. DC Henderson didn't even exist!)

I am sure that if the police want you to cooperate, they will at some stage want you to give evidence against Joe because their case is not that strong against him. It is far from a certain acquittal, as you seem to think in your letter, because of the forensic evidence, which, on the face of it, looks as if it has been manufactured. **End of quote**

A solicitor is making remarks about something that we all know is dangerous to do and certainly for such claims to be made there must be some sort of proof. A policeman would have had to divulge such information or a statement with a name on would have had to be seen yet none of that was forthcoming from Mr Hindle and not a shred of evidence existed for him to make such outlandish and dangerous claims. In a letter fired off by the Sayers' lawyer, Richard Haswell from Smith & Haswell Solicitors (Now Haswell & Cornberg), Chillingham Road, Newcastle dated 28th August 1996 to Clive M Hindle it points out the **dangers** of making such outlandish claims:

Quote: *We have been handed a copy of your letter of the 21st of June 1996, which was being sent to Mr Tony Weldon.   This letter was sent to our clients from Mr Weldon....*

If it is a genuine letter, could you please advise us in relation to the first paragraph on page four, how you can state that our clients are informants and are being run by DC Henderson of NCIS. Our clients are clearly upset at what has been written in this letter, as they are not police informants. You have placed their lives in danger. Further more the contents of your letter concerning the Sayers brothers is clearly defama-

tory in that you are stating categorically that they have blackmailed Mr
XXXXXX. *You were also stating that they were informants. We would*
like a reply letter to this letter as soon as possible please. **End of quote.**

Heavy stuff, eh? In a defensive reply from Clive M Hindle to Richard
Haswell he says that the only thing he would alter would be the identity
of the officer concerned and that he got his information from a 'credible
source'. Well believe you me I've had information relating to many
underworld figures from credible sources but it doesn't mean it's gospel
and I can tell you that as a fact such information is not easily obtained.
I would not like to go about saying I had information from a *credible*
source naming this one and that one as a police informant just on the
basis of a 'credible source' yet Hindle did this in a letter to another party.

I have had letters from many prisoners claiming that half the
underworld in the north are informants and if I passed copies on to those
concerned it could start World War Three, but I am responsible in my
handling of such matters, without positive proof such matters should not
be bandied about. Lawyers are not gangsters and should stick to
practising law.

The only solid proof of someone being a heavyweight informant is
to get a copy of their statement made against others. Glasgow hard man
Paul Ferris undeservedly praised up a fellow countryman of his, Grant
Turnbull, in his book, *The Ferris Conspiracy*, and when a statement
Turnbull had made to the police was sent to Ferris it seemed to quell the
exuberance of Turnbull who was in the same prison as Ferris. The only
other way to prove an informant's status as being registered is to get it
directly from the police as was allegedly done by a computer hacker but
a man paid dearly for this when he went to the Copthorne Hotel, on
Newcastle's quayside to secure such information from the alleged
hacker and he was shot in the jaw in an attempted murder plot. The man
(the alleged hacker), said "Sorry, John, I've got to do this." He had the
gun pointing at the man's forehead at the time and when he pulled the
trigger the gun jammed, which gave the injured party time to fight the
man's arm. A shot was fired and went into the victim's jaw, but he
managed to drive away and drove himself to hospital. The gunman
handed himself into a police station and when eventually convicted was
given a four year prison sentence? (As mentioned in another Viv book.)
The man who was shot...John Sayers senior. He was trying to secure
evidence to show that one of his sons was 'fitted up'.

Viv - The Final Chapter

So you see there are dangers involved in calling people 'informants' and when I received a letter out of the blue from Clive M Hindle and I read the contents I was somewhat surprised at his claims that I would be putting the life of his client, Joe Hunt, at risk if I were to claim Hunt was an informant especially as Mr Hindle had written a letter to Mr Tony Weldon suggesting that the Sayers' brothers (Stephen and Michael) were police informants. (As already shown in Mr Hindle's correspondence previously covered in this chapter.) Hindle Campbell Solicitors letter to me – 7th June 2000.

Quote: *Dear Mr. Richards,   RE: Joseph Trevor Hunt*

We act for the above. Mr. Hunt, is, as you will probably appreciate, familiar with your books. It has come to his notice that you have been requested to include some derogatory material in relation to him in a forthcoming book which we understand is likely to be published in the course of the next few weeks. **Temporarily end quote.** (Mr Hindle's assertions against me all but claim that I work for the underworld, which I take GREAT exception to, you will have read the contents of this and other books I've written and on that basis you will see that I act without fear or favour. No one had asked me to include any details relating to Joe Hunt in this or any other book. My own research had tied Hunt in with a security firm being run in Newcastle and partnered by Peter Donnelly. Information's do get passed on to me and that is it. I do not make any promises to make anyone famous or more infamous than they are.) Let's continue with Mr Hindle's letter:

Quote continues: *This material has a tendency to suggest that Mr. Hunt is a police informer. The suggestion arises from certain actions which were taken in connection with the sentence which Mr. Hunt is now serving. As those actions were taken by the writer and not by Mr. Hunt himself, we know the allegations to be wholly unfounded and untrue.* **Temporarily end quote.** (Mr Hindle refers to a weapons cache that was reported to the police. In the underworld Hunt was known as the armourer, which I cannot do anything about. On behalf of Joe Hunt his Solicitors advised the police of a weapons cache, which in my opinion doesn't make Hunt an informer given that others could have secured the gun/s and carried out all sorts of carnage with the weapon/s.)

Quote continues: *The effect of such allegations, particularly on a serving prisoner, is of course quite devastating. The effect is far worse if they appear in print in a respectable published work where the author appears to be lending credence to those remarks.*

Allegations of this nature can be so dangerous to life and limb that we have no doubt that, if they are to be made, Mr. Hunt will have the right to seek an injunction to restrain publication on the basis that (a) they are untrue and (b) they are malicious and intended to put him in jeopardy. **Temporarily end quote.** (Now this has me a little baffled, it's okay for Hindle to claim that the Sayers' brothers are informants and put their lives at risk and yet he can act on scurrilous information and send me a letter saying I would be putting the life of his client at risk if I were to call Joe Hunt an informant, does Hindle think me altogether so mad as to put anyone's life at risk. Yet he is prepared to put the life of the Sayers' brothers at risk without a second thought. What about the killers of Paul Logan being classed as informants, are any of those two killers going to come forward and say, "Hey, although I killed Paul Logan I want it to be known that I'm not an informant," or Peter Sutcliffe the Yorkshire Ripper saying, "Look I admit to killing all those prostitutes but I didn't alter a car registration plate." If Hindle can claim such acts to be malicious then of course his act of alleging the Sayers' brothers to be informants was tantamount to putting an Osama Bin Laden fatwah on their heads. There cannot be a *get out of jail* card for lawyers when they claim such things and any proof that the Sayers' brothers were informers should have been given to support a wildly inaccurate statement that I believe could lead to a complaint being made against Hindle to the Law Society, but that is not for me to pursue and if Mr Hindle wants to sue me then he can get his ass in the queue already forming or behind Jack Straw's legal team (Treasury Solicitors). **Quote continues:** *We have advised Mr. Hunt that we suspect that you will not lend your reputation to the furtherance of the malicious acts of others and in those circumstances, there should be no matters which would unduly concern out client. However, if there is truth in these rumours and you do propose to publish some material derogatory to our client, would you be kind enough to let us know immediately.* **Temporarily end quote.** (Oh yeah, just like Hindle to say that, did he give the Sayers' brothers a chance to respond to his allegations before he sent his damning remarks to Tony Weldon, did he hell.) **Quote continues: You may telephone and speak to the writer at any stage if there is any aspect of the matter you wish to discuss, but you will probably appreciate that we are limited by privilege as to anything we can say. End of quote** (Meaning, sorry we can say fuck all.)

In May of 1999 David Glover wrote to me and expressed concern at

Viv - The Final Chapter

certain things I'd written in the Viv 2 book. I went to seek out his father who at that time worked at a car lot in Dunston, Gateshead and left a message asking him to call me. I also wrote back to Glover at Swaleside Prison, in Kent with my phone number but to date he hasn't responded therefore I am not able to put fully his side of events in the Billy Collier kidnap and torture trial. Glover alleges that the trial transcripts tell a very different story to the one I wrote of in the Viv 2 book and he promised to send me copies, but again like the expected telephone call they failed to turn up. Should Glover ever wish to send me further details that he claims he has relating to the matters he mentioned in his letters I will be only too pleased to consider them for inclusion in a book I'm working on that doesn't relate to Viv and will be published next year called '**Sex, Drugs & the Stamp Scam.**' I would include anything worthy in a chapter called 'Headaches' and that relates to all the pain in the arse things that have happened to me whilst being a book publisher including being criminally blackmailed for more money per title, really!

What follows has already been discussed in the Viv 2 book on page 229 where Paddy Conroy says Glover told him he is to go QE (Queen's Evidence) in the Viv murder case and that he was going to get a reward and he even went as far as telling his co-accused in the Collier torture trial what he would spend his money on. Back in 1998 when I spoke with Superintendent Keith Felton at North Shields police station he told me that Glover had said things in relation to the Viv murder but he was not fully right in the head and he couldn't be believed. Therefore what follows, on that basis, cannot be relied upon at all as being accurate and in fact I believe it to be an invention by Glover in order to help him get off with the Collier torture trial. Bear in mind that Glover had the conversation that follows in February of 1995 some ten months before the Collier torture trial in Dec 1995. He'd hoped to get off with the Collier thing and when he did he would be going witness against the Sayers brothers of Stephen and Michael.

Boy did that plan go down like a lead balloon!!!! Even though Detective Chief Inspector Felton put in a statement to the court on Glover's behalf the jury found Glover guilty...that really fucked Glover's plans up for a big payday at the expense of the Sayers'. To date, at time of writing and at time of printing, no one has been charged with Viv Graham's murder therefore I reproduce a précis of what Glover told two visiting police officers, DC J Bower and DC A Trotter, at HM

Murder & Bits 'n' Bobs

Prison Birmingham on Wednesday 22nd February 1995 at 1.30pm:

Glover was shown by DC's Trotter and Bower a video recording of Sackville Road, Newcastle upon Tyne. Glover indicated an area of bungalows in the street stating that the murderers of Viv Graham had gone to one of them after the killing. When asked how he knew this Glover said, "I drove the getaway car."

When asked what exactly he meant Glover said, "I drove the getaway car after the shooting." When asked who did the shooting he said, "Michael Sayers."

Glover was asked to tell the story of his involvement from the beginning and gave the following story: -

He stole an old, blue Escort from Birtley from a car park near the baths. He took it by jiggling the locks. He was with Michael Sayers at the time and they drove to Heaton, in Newcastle parking the car somewhere in Sackville Road.

They arranged that Glover should collect Michael Sayers later that day. In the middle of the afternoon Glover collected Sayers in the stolen car and was directed to various places looking for Viv Graham. Sayers said he was going to shoot Graham in the legs in retaliation for some ongoing dispute. They went to Graham's house but his car was not there. They then drove around Wallsend and discovered Graham's car parked in a street off the High Street next to a flowerbed.

Glover parked the stolen car in a back lane with a view of the back of Graham's car and Sayers walked over to Graham's car and smashed the driver's window. Glover stated that he saw the hazard warning lights flashing and assumed the alarm had been set off. He could see that Sayers was walking up and down the street where the car was parked. Then he heard three shots fired, looked and saw Graham on all fours beside the car. Sayers ran back to the stolen Escort, got in and Glover drove off.

Glover stated he was directed which way to drive eventually arriving at a back lane some where in Heaton. He torched the car and both he and Michael Sayers were picked up by Stephen Sayers and Tony Leach in a burgundy Shogun vehicle.

Glover stated that Sayers had used a .357 Magnum, which was grey in colour, which he kept in a shoulder holster and always carried. He stated he believed Sayers was high on cocaine at the time and that they both believed Graham was only wounded.

It was pointed out to Glover that all of the details of the murder had been well publicised and that he had not told us anything about the way the shooting was carried out that could not have been read in a newspaper. He

Viv - The Final Chapter

was asked if he could give any details which would add credence to his story. He said that during the getaway drive he hit something damaging the front of the car and that he believed the car was a woman's because it had a box of tissues and some furry toys in it.

He also said that he had a tape recording of Michael Sayers bragging about the shooting. This had been recorded without Sayers' knowledge at a Karaoke night in a Newcastle pub. Glover claimed to have the tape in safekeeping but would not disclose where. He also said that there were other things he could say that would convince us his story was true, but that he'd save these until a later time.

At the time Glover gave this account he was in a restraining body belt having previously self inflicted injuries on his wrists and damaging his cell. We pointed out to Glover that in the circumstances any further conversation held on the subject would be with his legal representative. He stated he would be happy to repeat his account and give further details of the incident in an interview in the presence of his solicitor Mr Harrison. He was informed that we would arrange to interview him at the earliest opportunity convenient with his legal representative. At 2.20 pm that day the visit with Glover was concluded.

Next page, if you can read it clearly, is a witness statement from the then Detective Chief Inspector Keith Felton (now Superintendent) confirming David Glover (junior) is a registered police informant. This was used to help Glover in his kidnap and torture trial for which he was given a ten-year prison sentence. (Mentioned in past Viv book.) Now if Mr Hindle is reading this then this is the sort of proof we need, not guesswork or information from a 'credible source'.

What you have to consider is this, Glover had a lot to gain and the nearest Stephen and Michael Sayers had got to shooting anyone on the night of 31st December 1993 was shooting a game of pool. They may well have bragged of shooting Viv but it served their purpose in having people believe they could have carried out such an attack. I do believe though that the person who shot Viv might have intended to give him a warning by shooting him in the legs but it went wrong.

In a letter to me that is claimed to be from a serving police officer, who wishes to remain anonymous, that was involved in one of the murder investigations relating to Paul Logan and Viv. He or she does claim that whoever killed Paul Logan also murdered Viv due to the same MO (modus operandi) being used. *Both Logan and Viv were lured away from their locations they were at just prior to the murders by

Murder & Bits 'n' Bobs

NORTHUMBRIA POLICE

Form MG 11

Witness Statement

(CJ Act 1967, s.9 MC Act 1980, s.102, MC Rules 1981, r.70)

Statement of ..... Keith FELTON

Age if under 21 O'21 (if over 21 insert 'over 21'). Occupation DETECTIVE CHIEF INSP

This statement (consisting of 1 pages each signed by me) is true to the best of my knowledge and belief and I make it knowing that, if it is tendered in evidence, I shall be liable to prosecution if I have wilfully stated in it anything which I know to be false or do not believe to be true.

Dated the 20 day of OCTOBER 19 95.

Signature K Felton

I am a Detective Chief Inspector with the Northumb. Police currently stationed at Wallsend as Crime Manager.

Throughout 1992 I was a Detective Inspector attached to the Northumbria Police Drug Squad.

In September of 1992 I was contacted by Detective Sergeant Sam SMITH of South Shields C.I.D. in relation to drug related information into the activities of the CONROY family. As a result I was introduced by Sgt SMITH to David GLOVER at South Shields Police Station.

Subsequent to this meeting David GLOVER was registered by me as a police informant under the pseudonym "Adrian SCOTT".

On 21st September 1992 in agreement with "Adrian SCOTT" I obtained authority for this informant to participate in an operation in which controlled drugs where to be delivered to an address on Tyneside. The operation was codenamed "CHESTNUT MARE".

K Felton

Signature K Felton   Signature witnessed by

August 1993

means of a telephone call. *Their assailants were in vehicles in which they made their escapes from both murder scenes. *Probability that both victims knew their assailants. *Each murder was for revenge and because of this Northumbria Police are aware that the same assailants killed both men some few days apart. *The assailants' propensity for violence is well known to Northumbria Police. AND my view is that the closeness of the murders links the killings to having been carried out by the same two men.

The letter certainly has information in it that only an investigating officer could really know and because of that I want to protect the identity of the source in case I write anything else that could expose them so I will not quote from the letter any further. I can tell you that the Stephen and Michael Sayers, in my opinion, did not murder Paul Logan or Viv and certainly Glover was not involved either. Police informants are like a dog's tail and the police are the dog's body – the tail is starting to wag the body for their own gains!

Raggalds Pub Murder – Queensbury, Bradford: Morgan Duffy, 34, and John Spalding, 44, were convicted in 1996 for the murder of Michael Briggs, 40 – both men were given life sentences. Further to this they were also given 15 years in prison for the attempted murder of David Baines the publican of the Raggalds pub in Queensbury, Bradford and upholsterer John Paisley. I raise this case because it was to have been featured in a full chapter in this book but thanks to HM Prison Service breaching Mr Duffy's Human Rights by denying him a 'Media Visit', which he is entitled to under English Law proclaimed by the House of Lords under the Symms & O'Brien Ruling (1999). I also accuse the Governor of HMP Full Sutton of acting unlawfully and breaching this Law Lords ruling as well as Lindsey French, Head of Media Relations for the Prison Service by breaching Mr Duffy's basic human rights as laid down by law. Mr Blunkett, sir, I hope you get to hear of this! Jack Straw did and he did nothing!!

The Law Lords ruled in 1999: *A Home Office ban on convicted prisoners talking to journalist investigating possible miscarriages of justice was unlawful.* Are you reading this Mr Sutcliffe?

Gerry Sutcliffe, MP, was as much use as a chocolate fireguard. I sent him a copy of the 'Symms O'Brien' ruling and he then had the audacity to tell Mr Morgan's mother, Pat, that I (Steve Richards) was a "bit of a character." A member of Her Majesty's Government is doing nothing in this unlawful matter!!!! I have seen all of the paperwork in this case and I have also seen a transcript of a back room deal done between the police and a Crown Court judge in order to get one of the prosecution witnesses, David Baines, off with gun charges, sue me if it's not true Mr Blunkett!

I advised Morgan to contact the police and report the governor and Lindsey French to the police for what I believe was perverting the course of justice, he did and guess what, yeah you've guessed…the prison said it was not a police matter – I say it is! I needed to see Morgan directly before doing my undercover work in Bradford and there were questions I needed to put to Morgan that could not be asked over the telephone because I believe the Prison Service might have passed such taped phone calls on to the police. Since my investigation would involve me poking my nose into a bent copper's dealings in Bradford I couldn't afford the police finding out certain things. (Now we find that the bent copper concerned is suspended therefore my element of surprise has gone.) Also a valuable piece of evidence that would have had finger-prints on it was conveniently 'lost' by police. Therefore I give my apologies to Mr Duffy's mother, Pat, for the total lack of regard that all of the people mentioned have for the 'Symms O'Brien' ruling. That is my sole reason of not pursuing a winnable case for her son. Since I have visited a number of prisoners in the UK under this ruling I find it hard to believe that the Government can deny Morgan this visit, but when you consider it was only after Jack Straw pursued me via the High Court for an earlier mentioned incident that my visit as an Investigative Author was denied to Morgan. British Justice…really? Mr Duffy has ONLY been denied justice so what does it really matter and of course this chap Richards is on his case and we all know about him…don't we. Gerry Sutcliffe can have the pleasure of saying these things take months from where he sits; every minute that Mr Duffy is locked up is a minute too long, Mr Sutcliffe.

Finally. As always I try to seek out answers to certain questions, I put a lot of questions to Stephen Sayers, one of the Sayers brothers, but because of certain unforeseen circumstances that Stephen says has risen he can't comment on the matters I wished to air in this chapter. However, Stephen has been able to comment on other matters and word for word I reproduce what he wishes you to see.

I have been asked to comment on what Ernie Bewick had to say about

Viv - The Final Chapter

a certain incident (Chapter 7), which took place in a rave club in Sunderland one night. Let's put the record straight once and for all.

Firstly if I was going anywhere for trouble I would not be taking my wife and her two friends with me who happened to be out with me that night. We arrived at the club. I knew of Ernie Bewick by reputation and asked for him at the door out of courtesy because I hear he was approachable although I had never met this man before.

Whilst waiting in the foyer my brother, Michael, turned up with Paul Ashton. Ashy sets eyes on the Hammer (Stevie the Hammer – Chapter 2) who also happened to be in the club at that time and they made an immediate B-line for each other...and that's how the scenario that Ernie Bewick mentions all started.

Stevie the Hammer is a man who my brothers and me have known personally for a number of years and we regard him as a friend. When Ashy and the Hammer set eyes on each other basically it was between the two of them, knocking everybody to one side. Remember these two men are 18 and 20 stone apiece. This was a rick between two Geordies and nothing to do with the club or anybody else.

Well all hell broke loose with these two in the thick of it then up pops Ernie Bewick making a lot of unnecessary noise. I am a strong believer that if you're going to do something there's no need to talk or make a show of things. Well the club was packed and I noticed there were four or five groups of Geordies. One stood out in particular and that was a group mainly from the West End of Newcastle. If the Devil could cast his net he'd have had a right result that night! These men have a reputation for extreme violence and rightly so.

So in the middle of all this there's Ernie Bewick storming from one end of the club to the other shouting Sunderland people this and Sunderland people that. As I said I had my wife with me and the last thing I wanted was trouble. Mind you all the Geordie lads were now getting the hump with this little man. At one stage I had to plead with the West End lads not to do him, as they were all tooled to the hilt.

I told him, "Ernie, calm yourself down because these people are tooled up and are going to do you!" His reply was, "We have guns as well," I says, "Maybe so, but these people use them for a living not for flash. There's one hell of a difference!" I came to the conclusion that this man has obviously taken too many blows to the head in his boxing career. To understand what sort of a predicament he was in, believe me when I tell you it would have resembled Custer's last stand! If he lived another hundred years he will never come as close to getting it as he did that night. The West End lads would have attacked this man at once if I had not defused the situation. What thanks do I get, well I will tell you...he gives himself a gee at my family's expense by saying he not only challenged me and my brother but he chased us from Sunderland.

This man, the likes of him are not capable of chasing me and my brothers in a schoolyard game of tuggy never mind anything else. Yes Ernie is a man who can fight and I respect him for that, but as no doubt he will be reading this with interest...don't judge my brothers or me by the people you also associate with in Sunderland because you have no one to compare us with. It would be right to say, 'Don't get your ambitions mixed up with your capabilities.'

People in the know will tell you there are different levels of violence, fighting men and violent men, a fighting man will fight you and his object will be to knock you out and put you to sleep for a couple of minutes, whereas a violent man will put you to sleep permanently.

If this challenge, what he describes, had of taken place in my brother's presence and mine it would certainly have been accepted, but not there and not then and certainly not in the presence of my wife. Let me tell you we would not have tolerated it in any shape or form. As for the Bewicks, the Cockerills and the Garsides of the North East all I can say is that it's fortunate for them that they are not from Tyneside, as believe me their antics would not be tolerated.

Well there you have it...or just about. I want to finish on the note of John Henry Sayers, the brother of Stephen and Michael, John was released from prison after serving a long sentence for robbery. He wanted to set up a taxi company because he'd finished with crime and he knew if he so much as farted in the wrong direction then the police would lift him. When representation is made to Newcastle City Council for a licence to run a mini cab company the police attend, the council have a war cabinet and reject it. So what I want to know is this, how come a convicted fraudster can run a security company and be paid from North One and Newcastle City Council and continue to draw money from a publicly and European funded project? Peter Donnelly appeared before Newcastle Crown court in a long firm fraud case that involved a Welsh slate company being ripped off for £23,000. Donnelly with past convictions for dishonesty, burglary & resisting arrest, Section 18 assault (18 months imprisonment), theft, Road Traffic, Driving Convictions, Drink Drive, and Fraud.

Glen Gatland defending in the fraud case said: "Mr Donnelly is employing over 40 people, his VAT, Tax and National Insurance are being paid. In a VAT check the VAT man came up with nothing in the company. He arranges contracts. The offence was committed 22 months ago and his business is very successful and Mr Donnelly makes an offer of full compensation to the slate company and to pay prosecution costs if given a suspended sentence." Mr Gatland then suggested to the judge, Judge Crawford; QC, that the sentence on Donnelly be deferred for three months. Judge Crawford said, "People can't buy their way out of prison."

Councillor Tony Flynn, head of Newcastle City Council, was asked what he thought of such a company (D.H.Security) being run by a convicted felon and his reply made for interesting reading: 'The **company...would be unlikely to meet the Authority's criteria for inclusion in our standing list of contractors which the authority would allow business to be conducted with. However the development on which the company has been employed is a complex one, being managed by a consortium of partners in the form of a joint venture agreement between the City Council...'** I cannot comment any further due to lack of space.

Acknowledgements and thanks to the following

Northumbria Police Force, Tom Wilkinson (Press Association), Mr Cartier, George Oxberry, T, Rod Jones, Dave Ford (Has a book coming out called 'Who's the Thief), Dr Zak, Ms Arrani and all the others who helped.

Websites of interest:

www.crimebiz.co.uk   www.bronsonmania.com
www.johnsayers.com   www.miragepublishing.com
www.totalcrime.com   www.crimethroughtime.com
www.robertmaudsley.com   www.dave-courtney.com
www.blake.co.uk.   www.amazon.co.uk

Special thanks to Waterstones Bookstores
www.waterstones.co.uk

My Personal Unsolicited Recommendations

283

Other titles from Mirage Publishing

Viv (Graham) – 'Simply the Best Vol.1 True Crime
*True Crime paperback 242 pages *Foreword by Gazza *£7.99
*ISBN No: 1–902578-00–7 *Mono Stills

New Year's Eve 1993, hard man and notorious underworld figure Viv Graham's life climaxes in a violent end. The Geordie Mafia is unfolded. Gripping catalogue of Murders, Kneecappings, Shootings, Stabbings, Glassings, Drug Dealing, Protection Rackets, Blackmailing, Robberies, Torturing and more. Feared gangland reprisals abruptly end academic views. Hitman based in Manchester - his professional opinion on the gangland assassination of Viv. Manchester v Newcastle - Super City comparisons. Riots across the North East of England, eventually dominoes throughout the UK. Graphic details of Viv's murder. The funeral visited by some of Tenerife's underworld. Viv's involvement with celebrities Tim Healy and Gazza. Gazza – "My comments on Viv." Viv - Tyneside's own 4th Emergency Service.

Viv – and the Geordie Mafia (Vol. 2) True Crime
*340 pages *World-wide Best Seller   *Mono stills *RRP £9.99
*ISBN No: 1-902578-01-5

Police arrest the author and two researchers, seizing computer & disks in the hope of catching the killers. Blackpool's Candy Rock Resort underworld revealed & explored - Drug Dealing, Kidnapping, a beach murder and the club doorman scene. Convicted Beach murderer alleges Viv was his alibi. Murders, Kneecappings, Shootings, Drug Dealing, Protection Rackets, Torturing and Scams. Liverpool's club doormen scene compared to Newcastle's. Viv's three lovers fight over insurance payouts. Insurers describe his death as 'self inflicted'. Viv's three lovers reveal intimate details, love 'em and leave 'em, not likely they became his possessions! The truth! When Reg Kray visited Newcastle, was he kicked out like they say – original 'Geordie Mafia' member reveals all? Plier's torturer Paddy Conroy claims jury-rigging helped convict him. Exclusive. Viv's mother and father interviewed. Viv's murder suspect gives an exclusive interview! Tyneside's Pubs 'n' Clubs guide.

Ramraiders True Crime by Stephen Richards
*Paperback *16 Pages mono-stills UK RRP £7.99 * Foreword by
Freddie Foreman ISBN: 1-902578-10-4

The 'Yellow Pages' ramraid gang. £l00m ramraid gang escape totally undetected into Europe, the biggest and cleverest ramraid ever! Bizarre ramraids as well as the wacky and weird. Top ramraiders reveal all about the business. The ramraid phenomenon was a crime exported worldwide. Spectacular ram-raids in the UK, Australia and New Zealand. Police were rendered impotent by the gang's ability to defeat them. £3.5m ramraid gang given a total of 33-years behind bars. Counter surveillance techniques, getaway routes explored, attempted murder— and more! Prison life uncovered with never before published photos smuggled out of UK prisons showing the true extent of this gang's power right under the noses of prison authorities — drink and drug parties within prison. Prison violence becomes a way of life for the gang that started a crime wave of ramraiding throughout the world — their own story.

The Charles Bronson Book of Poems: 'Birdman Opens His Mind'
*ISBN No: 1-902578-03-1. *RRP£7.99 *Full of Bronson's colour hand drawn illustrations
*Some Surprises & More

Colour illustrated adult humour - hardback cover. Bronson's laughing all the way to the crematorium written and colour illustrated by the Poet from Hell. Get one if you can. In Charlie's own inimitable style and in his own words he will make you laugh. Don't get hooked up on the word 'poetry', 'humour' is the word - don't miss it! In short supply, sure to become a collector's item.

Charles Bronson – 'Sincerely Yours' – Video Documentary *Directed by Stephen Richards
*£15.99 *2½ hours ISBN: 1902578198 VHS Format

The one the UK government tried to ban. The one that Jack Straw took Steve Richards to court for. The one that got Richards a three-week prison sentence for. Exclusive footage and audio action never

Other titles from Mirage Publishing

ever before seen or heard. Features: Joe Pyle; Snr., Lord Longford, Kenneth 'Panda' Anderson (the original Geordie Mafia), Andy Jones (owner of 'Crime Through Time Museum'), Tony Lambrianou, Charlie's mother; Eira first time filmed interview, Loraine; Charlie's cousin, Ray Williams; long time civilian friend of 30+ years, Jan Lamb; 'The Sport' newspaper celebrity pinup, James Crosbie; Scotland's most prolific bank robber, John 'Alf' Lodge; Wales' answer to James Crosbie and that flash showbiz character Dave Courtney and 'Harley', Charlie's gangster dog. Audio of an actual prison hostage-taking situation involving Charlie! 'The Swellbellys' a contemporary punk band from Scotland perform a song for Bronson('Caged'). Jim Dawkins, formerly 'Prison Officer Dawkins', used to guard Charlie in HM Prison Belmarsh!

See Bronson boxing in an unlicensed fight, watch a gun fall to the floor of the boxing ring out of someone's coat pocket, as one hell of a fight breaks out. A highly controversial documentary, worryingly, for the authorities. Can be ordered from any bookshop if you give them the ISBN number of 1902578198.

'Silent Scream' – The Charles Bronson Story
His own story in his own words – 'Autobiography'
*Serialised in national UK newspaper for five days. *16 pages of stills.
*ISBN: 1-902578-08-2. *RRP £15.99.

The silence has been broken with this best seller. The truth about Bronson's life and his ill treatment by the authorities in penal and mental establishments. He's had more porridge than Goldilocks and the three bears. He's taken more hostages inside of prison than any other UK prisoner. Holds many awards for his art and writing. Banned from the *Guinness Book of Records* - holds six world records for feats of strength and fitness. More prison rooftop protests than anyone living or dead. Violence, violence and more violence, inflicted on him by the prison service! In Bronson's own words find out what makes him tick and explode. Hannibal Lecter is kids stuff compared to this real life action, full of sex and violence. Given a top review in UK's 'Front Magazine'. Bronson's story in his own words.

'PUBLIC *consumer* ENEMY' Investigative Consumer
Amazing little A-Z Handbook of how to complain and Win!' *You, the
consumer, are being ripped off *Paperback pocketbook *ISBN 1-902578-02-3 *RRP £5.99
Police arrest author and his researchers for alleged deception after national food and drinks companies complain to the police about the amount of complaints they're receiving! Simply put it's THE *complainer's bible*. Don't join Internet companies who claim to complain for you, this book does it all for you, includes legal advice. Repays its RRP time and time again. A must-have for anyone whoever complains.

'LEGENDS' – By best selling authors: Charles Bronson & Stephen Richards True Crime *ISBN
1902578-11-2
*Hardback *100's of photographs *RRP £14.99 *300+ pages
Serialised in a national newspaper for four days. Banned by a national chain of bookshops but can be ordered from any Watersone's bookshop or Amazon.co.uk. The **OFFICIAL** Charles Bronson guide to who's who in the underworld and beyond. Legends that Charlie feels deserve space in this A-Z guide of Criminals and those connected in some way to them. Includes a chapter from Manchester's Paul Massey. Short succinct write-ups. Bronson goes overboard in this book with a universal appeal. Nicknames leave little to the imagination: The Mummy, The Wolf Man, The Human Slug, Semtex Man, The Pie Man, The Wizard, Cannon Ball, Quasimodo, Voodoo Man, The Promoter and hundreds more – all real people. Legendary Scottish Bank Robber, James Crosbie - guest contributor for Scotland's chapter. Foreword by Joe Pyle Snr. Ireland isn't forgotten either. Icons are few Legends are many.

Looking at Life by Joe Pyle 'The Hood with a Heart'
*ISBN: 1-902578-09-0 *RRP £8.99 *Full colour photographs & Illustrations *Foreword by
actor Ray Winstone
Take a moment to read this, please, and in doing so you'll help some terminally ill babies at the only

Other titles from Mirage Publishing

hospice for babies in the UK. Some of the hardest men in the UK helped contribute towards this book - some of the softest hearted people you could ever wish to meet. Features inclusions by Gerry Adams the President of Sinn Fein, Sir Elton John, Sir Trevor McDonald, Richard Branson, Mohamed Al Fayed, Lulu, Roger Daltrey, Roy Shaw, Freddie Foreman, Dave Courtney, Tony Lambrianou, Charlie Richardson, Charlie Bronson, Johnny Nash, Frank Maloney and many, many more. Joe Pyle as featured on TV's 'Hard Bastards' and in Blake Publishing's 'Hard Bastards'.

'A Sting in the Tale' (Hardback)
*Only Biography authorised by STING *RRP £14.99 *ISBN: 1902578-13-9 *Mono Stills
*Foreword by Sting

An eye-wateringly funny book will guarantee to have you laughing and in stitches regardless of whether you're a Sting fan or not. Short succinct chapters show the bizarreness of what it's like to have such a world famous rock star as a friend. Written by Sting's closest friend for the past 38 years, the only book to be given Sting's blessing covering his life with the author from their schooldays right up to Sting's marriage to Trudy Styler. Serialised in News of the World, Sunday Mail's Night & Day mag book of the week, Top Review in the Independent on Sunday's Review mag, featured on Richard & Judy show, TV, Radio, Sunday Life (Belfast) - top review, Sunday Sun, Outlandos Web Site (Sting's fan club on the Web)

'The Machine' (Hardback) Autobiography
*ISBN: 190257818X *RRP £14.99

Ian Freeman tells his story of his rise from club doorman to World Vale Tudo Champ. Full of the ups and downs of his life's journey and his fight to become the champ of the UFC in the USA fighting cage, in fact the only Briton to go there and win them at their own game.

FUTURE TITLES
'Crime Through Time'
*Hardback *ISBN 1902578–17-1 *Multiple stills (some colour)
£14.99 *Crime/Celebrity/Taboo Subjects March 2002

The Black Museum of Gloucester's book will reveal a carnival of horror within. Taboo subjects. Each chapter has a foreword dedicated to it by someone of importance. A private collection of astonishing exhibits from the extreme to the bizarre has attracted a worldwide attendance to this very unique museum. Museums are for softies – not this one. This book will make your hair stand on end. Forget about Crippen or the London Ripper, this stuff is eerie, ghoulish and sinister. First time ever such a book has been put together from Andy Jones' private collection, many items up until now have been kept under lock and key - dare you look at what is within! Nazi Holocaust covered – photographs too harrowing to talk of. The criminal underworld explored, fetishes of the sex world exposed, Oswald Mosley's Black Shirts, Ku Klux Klan, an explicit look at law and order beyond comprehension and some revelations that should rock the government. Features a cover police considered prosecuting over.

'Sex, Drugs & the Stamp Scam' True Crime Autobiography
*Due for release in November 2002 ISBN: 1-902578-15-5
*Mono Stills (Not for those with a weak heart) £14.99

"Nazi, Nazi, Nazi," was the ongoing chant that became louder and louder with each 'Nazi' that the children in the schoolyard were directing at a frightened looking boy seeking refuge by the locked door to the school building – England 1960's. "I'll kill you, you little bastard," the balding man said to the eight-year-old boy as he had his hands grasped around the boy's throat lifting him clear of the floor. As the boy's face turned blue and he made choking sounds he was dropped like piece of hot coal. One man's story of overcoming racial hatred, a turbulent and violent upbringing, the trauma of prison life, plots to blackmail him and his rise from the ashes of a wrecked and plundered life. A story too unbelievable to believe. A very, very special true crime story from the man with the Golden Pen – acclaimed best selling investigative author and Underworld Expert Stephen Richards. Every word carrying part of Richards' soul, every comma and full stop bearing testament to his efforts. Full to overflowing with violence, sadness, nymphomaniacal romps, sexual fetishes so bizarre they

Other titles from Mirage Publishing

nearly kill those taking part, lesbian romps, wife swapping, underworld drug deals and ultimately the subject matter in question - 'Stamps'. A story of oppression, racism, hatred, neo-Nazis, love, deceit, crime and a soul-destroying end that will see you cry for those that could not. Hard hitting yet sensitive enough to have you share the pain of the characters within. Richards will not fail to light up your passions, fuel your anger and leave his mark in the depths of your mind for the rest of your life with this creation.

Solitary Fitness by Charles Bronson & Stephen Richards
Paperback with photographic illustrations due March 2002

The secrets of Charles Bronson's phenomenal strength and fitness. All book titles can be ordered from any good bookstore, worldwide, by quoting the ISBN number. Don't take "NO" for an answer because they can order any of the current stock of titles in. (Not those listed under 'Future Titles' until the release date.) In the unusual case of difficulty you can order books by post directly from Book Traders (Address at the end.) or from the merchandise section of the following website **www.miragepublishing.com** (where credit cards are accepted) OR Send cheque or Postal Order (P+P free in the UK) Europe send payment drawn against UK bank or Euro Cheque or International Money order + 10% for P+P. Rest of the world send + 20%. British Forces using BFPO address is postage free. Always try your localbookstore as we have accounts with all of the major bookstores (Waterstone's, Ottakers, HMV, Thins/Volumes, WH Smith, etc.) in the UK and our book wholesalers' export to 106 different countries. All prices are in £ Sterling.

Price List - Reminder

Viv (Graham) – 'Simply the Best (Vol.1)	£7.99
Viv – and the Geordie Mafia (Vol. 2)	£9.99
Ramraiders	£7.99
Birdman Opens His Mind - Charles Bronson	£7.99
Sincerely Yours (Video) Charles Bronson	15.99 P & P add £2.00
Silent Scream (Bronson's own words)	£15.99
PUBLIC *consumer* ENEMY	£5.99
Legends	£14.99
Looking at Life Joe Pyle.	£8.99
A Sting in the Tale	£14.99
The Machine	£14.99
Viv Graham Poster (A3 size – not shown in this book)	£1.99
'Bronson' Metal Pen	£1.00
'Bronson Bizarre Artwork Poster	£1.99

UK PRISONERS 50% off Books only

Make Cheques or PO Payable to BOOK TRADERS Total £......

P+P for books/posters/pens is free in the UK. Europe add 10% rest add 20%. We <u>do not accept credit cards</u> when ordering direct.

Send your payment with order, delivery name and address to:

BOOK TRADERS, PO Box 161, Gateshead, NE8 4WW, England

Pay by credit card on website **www.miragepublishing.com**

Hire your favourite underworld celebrity, film extra or hard man actor

www.crimebiz.co.uk